Muslims and Jews in America

Commonalities, Contentions, and Complexities

Edited by
Reza Aslan
and
Aaron J. Hahn Tapper

MUSLIMS AND JEWS IN AMERICA

First published in 2011 by
PALGRAVE MACMILLAN®
in the United States—a division of St. Martin's Press LLC,
175 Fifth Avenue, New York, NY 10010.

Where this book is distributed in the UK, Europe and the rest of the world,
this is by Palgrave Macmillan, a division of Macmillan Publishers Limited,
registered in England, company number 785998, of Houndmills,
Basingstoke, Hampshire RG21 6XS.

Palgrave Macmillan is the global academic imprint of the above companies
and has companies and representatives throughout the world.

Palgrave® and Macmillan® are registered trademarks in the United States,
the United Kingdom, Europe and other countries.

ISBN: 978–0–230–10860–8 Hardcover
ISBN: 978–0–230–10861–5 Paperback

Library of Congress Cataloging-in-Publication Data

Muslims and Jews in America : commonalities, contentions, and
complexities / edited by Reza Aslan and Aaron J. Hahn Tapper.
p. cm.
Includes bibliographical references.
ISBN 978–0–230–10860–8
1. Jews—United States—Social conditions—21st century. 2. Muslims—
United States—Social conditions—21st century. 3. Judaism—Relations—
Islam. 4. Islam—Relations—Judaism. 5. United States—Ethnic relations.
6. United States—Religion. 7. Religious tolerance—United States.
8. Intercultural communication—United States. I. Aslan, Reza. II. Tapper,
Aaron J. Hahn.

E184.36.S65M87 2010
305.800973—dc22   2010036747

A catalogue record of the book is available from the British Library.

Design by Newgen Imaging Systems (P) Ltd., Chennai, India.

First edition: May 2011

10 9 8 7 6 5 4 3 2 1

Printed in the United States of America.

To Isaiah Everett and Delilah Yareyach,

May you gain strength and meaning from your namesakes in working to
build our world into its potential.
—AHT

To Roger, Zoha, and Selah,

May you grow up in a world free from prejudice and bigotry.
—RA

For the Muslim, Jewish, Palestinian, and Israeli participants and
alumni of Abraham's Vision,

May we all see a day when AV and its programs are no longer needed.
—AHT and RA

ABRAHAM'S VISION

Proceeds from this volume are going to Abraham's Vision (AV), an educational organization founded and codirected by Aaron J. Hahn Tapper, and upon whose board of directors Reza Aslan has served, as a founding member, since 2006.

Abraham's Vision is a conflict transformation organization that explores group and individual identities through experiential and political education. Examining social relations within and between the Jewish, Muslim, Israeli, and Palestinian communities, AV empowers participants to practice just alternatives to the status quo.

One of AV's flagship programs, the Unity Program, educates Muslim and Jewish fifteen- to eighteen-year-olds about Muslim-Jewish relations, Islam, and Judaism, while strengthening the relationships students have to their own communities and religious traditions. It is our hope that this volume will assist future generations of these communities in creating new paradigms of intercommunal commitments to justice and peace.

More information about AV's innovative and revolutionary programs can be found at www.abrahamsvision.org.

CONTENTS

Foreword by Congressman Keith Ellison (D-MN)   vii

List of Contributors   xi

Introduction   1
Reza Aslan

Part I   Case Examples: Lessons Learned?

One   You Can't Handle the Truth...or Maybe You Can   9
         Rabbi Brad Hirschfield

Two   Who Put Hate in My Sunday Paper?: Uncovering the
         Israeli-Republican-Evangelical Networks behind the
         "Obsession" DVD   21
         Omid Safi

Three   Children of Abraham in Dialogue   33
         Rabbi Amy Eilberg

Four   The Khalil Gibran International
         Academy—Lessons Learned?   45
         Debbie Almontaser

Part II   Identity Formation: Muslims, Jews, and the American Experience

Five   Evolving from Muslims in America to American
         Muslims: A Shared Trajectory with the American
         Jewish Community   57
         Imam Feisal Abdul Rauf

Six   The War of Words: Jews, Muslims, and the
         Israeli-Palestinian Conflict on American University
         Campuses   71
         Aaron J. Hahn Tapper

Seven   Muslims, Jews, and Religious Visibility on
         American College Campuses   93
         Taymiya R. Zaman

Eight   J Street and Current Directions in American
Muslim-Jewish Dialogue   107
Hannah Ellenson and Rabbi David Ellenson

Part III Challenges and Opportunities in Reaching across the Divide

Introduction to Speeches by Rabbi Eric Yoffie and
Dr. Ingrid Mattson   117
Sayyid M. Syeed

Nine   Inaugural Address at the Forty-fourth Annual
Convention of the Islamic Society of North America   121
Rabbi Eric H. Yoffie

Ten   Address at the Sixty-ninth Conference of the
General Assembly of the Union for Reform Judaism   127
Ingrid Mattson

Eleven   Integration or Separation: The Relationship between
Iranian Jewish and Iranian Muslim Communities in
Los Angeles   133
Saba Soomekh

Twelve   Challenges and Opportunities for Muslim-Jewish
Peacemaking in America   145
Salam Al-Marayati

Part IV Toward the Future: New Models in Jewish-Muslim Relations

Thirteen   Beyond Sarah and Hagar: Jewish and Muslim
Reflections on Feminist Theology   159
Aysha Hidayatullah and Judith Plaskow

Fourteen   Status Quo versus Solution: A New Middle
East Playbook   173
Eboo Patel

Fifteen   Sacred Text Study as Dialogue between
Muslims and Jews   177
Rabbi Reuven Firestone and Hebah H. Farrag

Sixteen   American Jews and American Muslims of Love   191
Rabbi Michael Lerner

Afterword   201
Peter A. Geffen

Acknowledgments   203
Index   205

FOREWORD

CONGRESSMAN KEITH ELLISON (D-MN)

The thing to understand about Muslim-Jewish relations in the United States is that they are just fine. It is easy to see how someone might not believe it. After I was sworn into office in January 2007, becoming the first Muslim elected to the U.S. Congress, someone dropped an article on my desk entitled "Jews, Muslims, and the Democrats" by Gabriel Schoenfeld. The point of the piece was that my election signaled the rise of an American Muslim political voice that would ally with Democrats and undermine Jewish political interests.

The author was wrong, and he is not alone. Too many people misunderstand the meaning of Muslim participation in American politics, and so fear it. But the overwhelming number of Jews and Muslims in the United States, by the example of their lives, remind all Americans of our deeply rooted heritage of religious tolerance.

I am reminded of an event that took place at my own mosque in Minneapolis during Ramadan 2007. Imam Makram El-Amin, leader of Masjid An Nur, and Rabbi Marcia Zimmerman of Temple Israel, leader of the Twin Cities' largest Jewish congregation, decided to bring their congregations together to break the fasts of Ramadan and Yom Kippur. The Jewish and Muslim fasts coincided on the calendar in 2007, and these two leaders saw the break-fasts as an opportunity to demonstrate the unity and commonality of the two faith traditions.

The imam and the rabbi received RSVPs for only 100 people, but 120 showed up. People just made room. When evening fell, Muslims offered dates and water to guests, and then prayed, as Jews, and a number of Christians, looked on. The rabbi then called her congregation to the center of the *musalah* (the mosque's prayer room) and observed the end of Yom Kippur with prayers, song, and ritual, as Muslims looked on. The rabbi was careful to explain the symbols associated with the sacred Jewish "Day of Atonement." Then came time for the meal, only there wasn't quite enough food for everyone because not everyone had RSVPd. The imam and rabbi called this a "good problem." Everyone simply shared, and went home full.

One nice evening does not prove universal harmony and bliss. But it does demonstrate that Jews and Muslims can interact positively with one another if they want to. Indeed, this happens all over the country, all of the time. Muslims and Jews are not bound together in a zero sum game. As religious minorities their interests often run parallel. What is good for American Muslims (e.g., religious tolerance, equal opportunity, anti-hate crimes legislation) is good for American Jews as well. Muslims and Jews both have an interest in keeping public spaces open and free for all faiths. In 2009, over 1,200 anti-Semitic incidents of violence, defacement, or desecration were reported. There has also been a recent sharp rise in anti-Muslim incidents—by some accounts an increase of over 1,000 percent after 9/11. Studies show that so often the same people who hold biases against Muslims hold biases against Jews as well.

As religious minorities in the United States, Jews and Muslims share a common experience. When I was sworn into the U.S. Congress with my hand on the Qur'an owned by Thomas Jefferson, Jewish colleagues (and many others) offered words of support. Congresswoman Debbie Wasserman Schultz and I commiserated about the trials of breaking new ground. She chose to swear in on a *Tanakh* (Hebrew Bible), not a Christian Bible. Her 2005 swearing-in ceremony ruffled a few feathers, too.

Interestingly enough, my detractors were a multireligious bunch, including talk show host Dennis Prager, who is Jewish, and Judge Roy Moore, who is Christian. Prager objected to my use of the Qur'an because he believed that it broke an American tradition. Judge Moore, who famously demanded that an iconic representation of the Ten Commandments be on display in the court building, argued in a piece in WorldNetDaily that "Muslim Ellison should not sit in Congress." Prager apologized. I have yet to hear anything from Judge Moore.

There are differences between the communities, of course, principally around the conflict in the Holy Land. But the truth is that the American Jewish and American Muslim communities are not as far apart as one might guess on this matter. The Muslims I know support and accept Israel's existence, though many take issue with certain decisions made by the Israeli government with regard to the occupied territories. But, needless to say, there is a world of difference between objecting to some of a state's policies and objecting to that state's right to exist.

At the same time, many American Jewish groups have raised concerns about Israel's blockade of Gaza, the expansion of settlements in the West Bank, roadblocks, check points, and so on. American Jews overwhelmingly support a two-state solution. And Christian groups such as Churches for Middle East Peace have been vocal concerning peace in the Holy Land. That is why the debate around Israel and Palestine is not a conflict between Muslims and Jews (it bears mentioning that some 10 percent of Palestinians are Christians). The debate is complicated and nuanced, with people of all faiths taking various positions.

Of course there will always be people like Daniel Pipes, whose article "Islamism 2.0" described me, and other Muslims who believe in liberal democracy, as a "greater threat to western civilization" than Osama Bin Laden.[1] Every community has its fringe, including the Muslim community, wherein characters such as Anwar Awlaki, the Yemeni American cleric and propogandist for al-Qaeda, have openly called for American Muslims to attack their own country.

In the end, America is better for its diversity. It welcomes all colors, all cultures, and all faiths, and this includes Muslims and Jews. But this culture of tolerance and exclusion is not set in stone. Like a garden, people of good will must cultivate it by committing themselves to interfaith dialogue, interfaith service, and frank discussion. Only through this approach will our country move toward its true potential.

Note

1. Daniel Pipes, "Lion's Den: Islamism 2.0—An Even Greater Threat," *The Jerusalem Post*, November 24, 2009, www.jpost.com/Home/Article.aspx?id=161310, retrieved July 31, 2010.

CONTRIBUTORS

Imam Feisal Abdul Rauf is chairman of Cordoba Initiative, having founded the organization in 2004. In 1997, he founded the American Society for Muslim Advancement (ASMA), the first Muslim organization committed to bringing American Muslims and non-Muslims together through programs in academia, policy, current affairs, and culture. As imam of Masjid al-Farah, a mosque located twelve blocks from Ground Zero in New York City, he preaches a message of understanding between people of all creeds. Additionally, Imam Feisal sits on the board of trustees of the Islamic Center of New York and serves as an advisor to the Interfaith Center of New York.

Salam Al-Marayati is president of the Muslim Public Affairs Council, a nonprofit organization that aims to make Islam and Muslims a positive, integral part of American pluralism. For the past twenty-one years, Salam has had the opportunity to speak to congregations at community-sponsored events, temples, synagogues, churches, high schools, and college campuses. He has written extensively on Islam, human rights, democracy, Middle East politics, and U.S.-Muslim world relations. His articles and interviews have appeared in prominent newspapers and have been featured in major radio talk shows and television programs. Salam also works as an advisor to several interfaith, political, civic, and academic institutions seeking to understand the role of Islam and Muslims in America and throughout the world.

Debbie Almontaser is the founding and former principal of the Khalil Gibran International Academy. As a twenty-year veteran of the New York City public school system, she has taught special education, inclusion, trained teachers in literacy, and served as a multicultural specialist and diversity advisor. Currently, she is a doctoral student at Fordham University's Graduate School of Education in the Urban School Leadership Program, and is the board chairperson of the Muslim Consultative Network. Debbie frequently gives presentations on conflict resolution, Arab culture, and Islam at universities, libraries, museums, churches, and synagogues in national and international settings. Cofounder of Brooklyn Bridges, the September 11th Curriculum Project, and We Are All Brooklyn, founding board member of The Dialogue Project and the Brooklyn Borough President's new Diversity Task Force, board advisor for the Same Difference Interfaith Alliance, Youth Bridge NY, and member of the board of directors of Women in Islam, Debbie is also the "go to" person on cultural and religious diversity issues for the New York City Mayor's office of Immigrant Affairs, the New York City Police Department, and numerous New York City members of the City Council.

Reza Aslan is an associate professor of creative writing at the University of California, Riverside. His books include *No God but God: The Origins, Evolution, and Future of Islam* (2005), *Beyond Fundamentalism: Confronting Religious Extremism in the Age of Globalization* (2009), and *Tablet and Pen: Literary Landscapes from the Modern Middle East* (2010). He is also a current and founding member of the Board of Directors of Abraham's Vision, a conflict transformation educational organization working with Muslims, Jews, Palestinians, and Israelis.

Rabbi Amy Eilberg directs interfaith dialogue programs in Minneapolis and St. Paul, MN, including at the Jay Phillips Center for Interfaith Learning and the St. Paul Interfaith Network. In addition to serving as the chair of J Street Minnesota, Amy teaches the art of compassionate listening in venues throughout the United States and is deeply engaged in Israeli-Palestinian reconciliation efforts, as well as with issues of conflict within the Jewish community. She is at work on a book on Judaism and peacemaking.

Rabbi David Ellenson is president and I.H. and Anna Grancell Professor of Jewish Religious Thought at Hebrew Union College-Jewish Institute of Religion.

Hannah Ellenson is a graduate student in conflict resolution and mediation studies at Tel Aviv University. A 2008 graduate of Wellesley College, she has been involved in Palestinian-Israeli and Muslim-Jewish dialogue since she was a teenager.

Congressman Keith Ellison (D-MN) is currently serving his second term in the U.S. House of Representatives, representing the Fifth District of Minnesota, which consists of Minneapolis and surrounding suburbs. He is the first Muslim congressman in the history of the United States.

Hebah H. Farrag is project manager for the University of Southern California's Center for Religion and Civic Culture. She is a graduate of the American University in Cairo (AUC), receiving a master's degree in Middle East studies and a graduate diploma in forced migration and refugee studies. Hebah is interested in issues concerning religion, the politics of identity, nationalisms, and migration and has worked for and with organizations such as the Youth Policy Institute, Human Rights Watch—University, the Council on American-Islamic Relations (CAIR), and Casa Del Pueblo, traveling on delegations to conduct research in places such as Cuba, Egypt, Lebanon, Jordan, and Chiapas, Mexico.

Rabbi Reuven Firestone is professor of medieval Judaism and Islam at Hebrew Union College in Los Angeles. He has authored over seventy articles and seven books, including *Children of Abraham: An Introduction to Judaism for Muslims* (2000), *An Introduction to Islam for Jews* (2008), and *Who are the Real Chosen People* (2008). He is cofounder and codirector of the Center for Muslim-Jewish Engagement, a partnership between Hebrew Union College, the Omar Ibn Al-Khattab Foundation, and the University of Southern California College of Letters, Arts and Sciences (www.usc.edu/cmje) and lectures throughout the United States, Europe, and Asia on Jewish-Muslim relations.

Peter A. Geffen is the founder of the Abraham Joshua Heschel School (New York City) and KIVUNIM. He has been involved in many projects seeking greater understanding between Muslim Arabs and Jews since 1964. He is a founding member of the board of directors of Abraham's Vision, for whom he also served as board chair from 2007 to 2009.

Aaron J. Hahn Tapper is an assistant professor of theology and religious studies at the University of San Francisco, where he holds the Mae and Benjamin Swig Chair of Judaic Studies, and is the founding director of the university's Swig Program in Jewish Studies and Social Justice, the first academic program in the country formally linking these two fields. In 2003, he founded Abraham's Vision, a conflict transformation organization working within and between the Jewish, Muslim, Israeli, and Palestinian communities, for whom he has served as co-executive director since that time. Since September 2008 he has also served as the co-executive director of the Center for Transformative Education, a new educational initiative working to create empowering educational programs to transform societies into their potential, which he cofounded.

Aysha Hidayatullah is an assistant professor of theology and religious studies at the University of San Francisco, where she teaches classes in Islamic studies. Her research interests are in feminist theology and gender studies in Islam.

Rabbi Brad Hirschfield, the author of *You Don't Have To Be Wrong For Me To Be Right: Finding Faith Without Fanaticism* (2008), is a radio and TV talk show host. Listed as one of America's fifty most influential rabbis in *Newsweek*, and one of the top thirty "Preachers and Teachers" by Beliefnet.com, he cohosted the weekly radio show *Hirschfield and Kula*, and created two landmark series, *Building Bridges* and *American Pilgrimage*, on Bridges TV. President of Clal— The National Jewish Center for Learning and Leadership, a leadership training institute, think-tank, and resource center, he is a commentator for *The Huffington Post*, writes a weekly column for the WashingtonPost/Newsweek.com's "On Faith," and a daily for Beliefnet.

Rabbi Michael Lerner is editor of *Tikkun Magazine* (www.tikkun.org), chair of the interfaith Network of Spiritual Progressives (www.spiritualprogressives.org), rabbi of Beyt Tikkun Synagogue in Berkeley, California, and author of eleven books including *The Politics of Meaning* (1996), *Jewish Renewal* (1994), *The Left Hand of God: Taking Back our Country from the Religious Right* (2006), *Healing Israel/Palestine* (2003), and with Cornel West, *Jews and Blacks: A Dialogue on Race, Religion and Culture in America* (1995).

Ingrid Mattson is professor of Islamic studies, founder of the Islamic Chaplaincy Program, and director of the Macdonald Center for Islamic Studies and Christian-Muslim Relations at Hartford Seminary (CT). She earned her PhD in Islamic studies from the University of Chicago in 1999. In 2006, Dr. Mattson was elected president of the Islamic Society of North America (ISNA), a position she held until August 2010; she previously served two terms as vice president.

Eboo Patel is the founder and executive director of Interfaith Youth Core (IFYC), a Chicago-based institution building the global interfaith youth movement. Author of the award-winning book *Acts of Faith* (2007), Eboo is also a regular contributor to *The Washington Post*, *USA Today*, and CNN. He served on President Obama's Advisory Council of the White House Office of Faith Based and Neighborhood Partnerships, and holds a doctorate in the sociology of religion from Oxford University, where he studied on a Rhodes scholarship.

Judith Plaskow is professor of religious studies at Manhattan College and a Jewish feminist theologian. Cofounder and for ten years coeditor of the *Journal of Feminist Studies in Religion,* she is author or editor of several works in feminist theology, including *Standing Again at Sinai: Judaism from a Feminist Perspective* (1990) and *The Coming of Lilith: Essays on Feminism, Judaism, and Sexual Ethics 1972–2003* (2005).

Omid Safi is a leading Muslim public intellectual. A professor of Islamic studies at the University of North Carolina at Chapel Hill, he specializes in contemporary Islamic thought and medieval Islamic history. He is the editor of the volume *Progressive Muslims: On Justice, Gender, and Pluralism* (2003). His most recent book, *Memories of Muhammad* (2010), deals with the biography of the Prophet Muhammad.

Saba Soomekh is a theological studies professor at Loyola Marymount University, where she teaches courses on world religions, women and religion, and the history of modern Israel and Iran.

Sayyid M. Syeed is the national director of the Islamic Society of North America (ISNA), a national umbrella organization that has more than three hundred affiliates all over the United States and Canada, based in their Washington, D.C. office. From 1994 to 2006 he served as secretary general of ISNA in their Plainfield, IA-based office. From 1980 to 1982 he served as president of the Muslim Students Association of the United States and Canada, pioneering its development into ISNA.

Rabbi Eric H. Yoffie is president of the Union for Reform Judaism. Among the hallmarks of his fourteen-year tenure are initiatives to enrich Torah study and adult literacy, religious education, worship, and camping within the Movement. He is a strong voice for social justice, interfaith dialogue, Israel advocacy, and the rights of Israeli Reform Jews. Rabbi Yoffie is the only rabbi to speak at Convocation at the late Rev. Jerry Falwell's Liberty University and address the annual convention of the Evangelical Lutheran Church in America. He was also the first major Jewish leader to address the annual convention of the Islamic Society of North America.

Taymiya R. Zaman is an assistant professor of history at the University of San Francisco. Her research interests include Mughal India, Islamicate empires, and postcolonial Muslim identities. She teaches classes on both South Asia and the Middle East.

Introduction

Reza Aslan

Call it a security fence, a separation barrier, a seam zone, an apartheid wall. Whatever term you choose, there is no more tangible symbol of the division and dissociation that exist between Jews and Muslims in the Middle East than the maze of concrete slabs, barbed wire, electrical fencing, sniper towers, and checkpoints that snakes its way loosely along the disputed border dividing Israel and the occupied Palestinian territories. For Jewish Israelis, the separation is necessary to keep Israel's citizens safe from Palestinian terrorists. For Muslim and Christian Palestinians, the divide is merely the most physical manifestation of what they view as Israel's policy of ethnic and religious segregation. Either way, the narrative on both sides of the barrier seems permanently fixed. In fact, these two competing narratives—the one that views Israel as a bastion of civilization amidst an ocean of barbarism; the other that views Palestinians as victims of government apartheid and ethnic cleansing— have long ago broken free of the boundaries of the Middle East and become embedded into the consciousness of Jews and Muslims virtually everywhere, such that the physical wall separating the two communities in Israel-Palestine has become a metaphorical wall dividing Jews and Muslims across the globe. It is this metaphorical wall, and the distinct and often creative ways in which American Jews and American Muslims have tried to breach it, with which the essays in this collection are concerned.

There are roughly equal numbers of Muslims and Jews in the United States. Both communities boast higher-than-average levels of education, literacy, and income; both struggle with similar concerns when it comes to matters such as cultural assimilation, political representation, and media attention; and both share a common history of bigotry and marginalization as immigrant communities in the United States. One would think that these shared values and experiences would make American Jews and American Muslims natural and sympathetic allies, particularly in a country like the United States, by far the most religiously diverse nation in the world.

It is certainly true that American Jews and American Muslims consistently engage each other—whether directly or indirectly, constructively or not—in ways that often elude their coreligionists in other countries. This has partly to do with America's ethos as a "melting pot" of different religions, ethnicities, and cultures. The American experience, and in particular the American commitment to the values of pluralism and individualism, has allowed Jews and Muslims to develop unique and innovative forms and interpretations of their respective religious traditions that one rarely experiences in other parts of the world. The familiar tripartite division of Judaism into Orthodox, Conservative, and Reform communities may have its origins in Europe, but it is in the American context that all three have flourished and evolved side by side with common legitimacy. Likewise, an argument can be made that there is no other country in the world—certainly no Muslim-majority country—in which Muslims have the freedom and opportunity to practice their faith and traditions in whatever way they see fit.

It is also true that the common struggle of Jews and Muslims as minorities in the United States has created a bond between the two communities, one strengthened by a shared experience of persecution and prejudice. Consider this: while polls in the United States consistently show Americans expressing negative attitudes toward Islam and Muslims (more than 40 percent admit to feeling at least "a little" prejudice toward Muslims, while nearly one-third say their opinion of Islam is "not favorable at all"),[1] by far the strongest predictor of American prejudice against Muslims is whether the person polled holds similarly negative feelings toward Jews.[2] As more than one commentator has noted, the derogatory terms and negative images currently used to describe Muslims in the United States—foreign, exotic, *other*—seem wholly swiped from the words and images that were once commonly used to describe American Jews (and American Catholics, for that matter).

Yet, despite this shared historical trajectory, and regardless of America's proud tradition of religious and ethnic diversity, the essays in this collection demonstrate that, try as they might, Jews and Muslims in the United States cannot remain unaffected by the same global events that, over the last half-century, have widened the chasm between their coreligionists in the rest of the world. Indeed, whether it is the continuing conflict between Israelis and Palestinians, the attacks of 9/11 and the so-called War on Terror, the domestic battles over security and immigration, or even the political divide in America between Republicans and Democrats, American Jews and American Muslims often find themselves on "opposite sides of the wall," as it were, struggling to connect with one another as Americans while remaining true to the needs and concerns of their respective religious communities.

This book is an exploration of the sometimes contentious, sometimes conciliatory, and often complex relationship between Jews and Muslims in the United States. Each essay discusses a different episode from the recent twentieth- and current twenty-first-century American milieu that has either linked these two communities together or torn them apart. Some essays deal with case examples of local intercommunal interaction, such as "dialogue groups." Others focus on national trends, thus providing greater insights into individual incidents. Still others tackle the impact of global events, especially in the Middle East, on America's Jewish and Muslim communities. What binds all of the essays in the collection together is the fervent desire by the authors to break through the simple stereotypes and hollow platitudes that so often characterize interreligious dialogue, and instead tackle head-on the challenges and opportunities that arise in building firm and lasting relations between Jews and Muslims in the United States.

Section one, *Case Examples: Lessons Learned?*, explores the real world implications of trying to bridge the gap between Jews and Muslims in the United States. Brad Hirschfield's essay "You Can't Handle the Truth . . . or Maybe You Can" reflects on the state of interreligious relations from his personal vantage point as the only rabbi host of a talk show for the now defunct Bridges TV, following the gruesome murder of the network's cofounder, Aasiya Zubair, by her husband (and cofounder), Mo Hassan. Omid Safi provides an eye-opening investigation into the controversial DVD "Obsession: Radical Islam's War against the West," which was distributed to a large number of national and international newspapers by a shadowy network of right-wing Jewish and Christian organizations bent on altering the 2008 presidential elections. Amy Eilberg's "Children of Abraham in Dialogue" outlines the significant challenges that arise in Jewish-Muslim encounter programs, particularly when it comes to confronting one another's sacred scriptures. And finally, Debbie Almontaser recounts her emotional experience as the founder and first principal of the Khalil Gibran International Academy, America's first English-Arabic public school. Almontaser's searing account of being caught in the middle of the firestorm between Jewish and Muslim groups who used the school, and her leadership of it, as the stage upon which to play out their grievances against each other provides the most obvious illustration of the enormous obstacles that must be overcome if American Jews and American Muslims are to come together in peace and harmony, a pattern some have argued is once again being played out in the controversy surrounding the construction of an Islamic Community Center two blocks from New York City's "Ground Zero."

Section two, *Identity Formation: Muslims, Jews, and the American Experience*, begins with an instructive essay by Imam Feisal Abdul Rauf on the ways in which American Muslims can rely on the experiences of their Jewish (and Catholic) predecessors in dealing with the difficult hurdles they currently face on their journey toward societal integration in the United States. The coeditor of this volume, Aaron Hahn Tapper, traces the rise in intercommunal tensions in universities across the United States since 2000 and how certain events in the Middle East, particularly the Israeli-

Palestinian conflict, have manifested on America's college campuses. Taymiya Zaman builds upon Hahn Tapper's study by looking into the ways in which institutional accommodation of Muslim religious practices, such as the installation of footbaths and prayer rooms on university campuses, has raised troubling questions about the separation of church and state in the United States, which were not raised when Jewish students, especially those affiliated with privately funded Jewish groups such as Hillel, requested similar ritual spaces. Section two ends with Hannah and David Ellenson's report on the impact on the political scene of the new political action committee J Street, and its efforts to redirect the political conversation among both Jews and Muslims in the United States regarding the Israeli-Palestinian conflict.

Section three, *Challenges and Opportunities in Reaching across the Divide*, highlights the attempts of Jews and Muslims in the United States to build greater understanding of each other's communities. We begin with the historic speeches made by Rabbi Eric Yoffie, head of the Union for Reform Judaism, and Dr. Ingrid Mattson, president of the Islamic Society of North America, at one another's annual conferences. The challenges and opportunities of interreligious cooperation that these two speeches touch upon are explored in more intimate ways in Saba Soomekh's essay on the relationship between Iranian Jews and Iranian Muslims in Southern California. Soomekh provides a fascinating insight into how the perception these two communities had of each other in Iran has, or has not, shifted after their mass migration to the United States following the 1979 Iranian Revolution. The political challenges and opportunities of interreligious cooperation are brought to light by Salam Al-Marayati, the president of the Muslim Public Affairs Council, in his report on his professional experiences over the last decade with both supporters and detractors from the Jewish American community.

The final section of the book, *Toward the Future: New Models in Jewish-Muslim Relations*, looks toward the horizon, exploring new and novel paradigms for dealing with interreligious relations between Jews and Muslims in the United States. These prototypes begin with the necessity of inserting the often marginalized voice of women into the dialogue, as witnessed by a powerful and honest conversation between Aysha Hidayatullah and Judith Plaskow on the trials and tribulations of being doubly marginalized as Muslim and Jewish women. Eboo Patel, founder of Chicago's Interfaith Youth Core, presents a new model for America's Jews and Muslims to think about their relationship to the Israeli-Palestinian conflict, while Reuven Firestone and Hebah Farrag report on the success of a "Muslim-Jewish Text Study Program," a novel project that uses religious texts to foster intergroup dialogue between Jews and Muslims. We end with Rabbi Michael Lerner's impassioned plea to replace the current worldview that divides American Jews and American Muslims—the metaphorical wall with which we began—with a new one founded upon compassion, love, and a shared recognition that we must all rely on one another to create a more stable, more compassionate world.

Ultimately, it is our hope that the essays in this collection will not only reframe the perception that American Jews and American Muslims have of each other, but also will lay the ground for a fuller, more honest conversation about the issues of faith and identity that has for too long pitted these two communities against each other.

Notes

1. Gallup Poll, "In U.S., Religious Prejudice Stronger Against Muslims," www.gallup.com/poll/125312/ religious-prejudice-stronger-against-muslims.aspx, retrieved July 30, 2010.
2. Michelle Boorstein, "Americans' Bias against Jews, Muslims Linked, Poll Says," *Washington Post*, Thursday, January 21, 2010, www.washingtonpost.com/wp-dyn/content/article/2010/01/20/AR201 0012004488.html, retrieved July 30, 2010.

PART I

Case Examples: Lessons Learned?

CHAPTER ONE

You Can't Handle the Truth . . . or Maybe You Can

Rabbi Brad Hirschfield

Introduction

A Few Good Men could well describe more than a famous movie starring
Tom Cruise, Demi Moore, and Jack Nicholson about U.S. Marines and
their struggle to balance what they experience as the competing demands
of fealty to "the Corps" with their obligations as human beings separate from the military. It could also describe, with the addition of a few
good women, the struggle of interreligious relations, which all too often
is a struggle to balance these same competing demands. The best-known
line in the script is voiced when a young attorney demands the truth
from Nicholson's character, Colonel Nathan R. Jessup. Believing that his
experience commanding troops in Guantanamo Bay is too complex to be
properly understood by his examiner (an irony I will not examine here),
Jessup angrily screams back, "You can't handle the truth!"

In this instant, two things become clear to the viewer. First, however
painful it may be, the truth must always come out. The inability to shine a
light on the dark corners of the communities we love most ultimately weak-
ens and even destroys them. This is what happened with Colonel Jessup
and the Marines under his command. Second, it becomes clear that what
one understands as "the truth" is very much rooted in personal experience,
something that demands respect. And yet, respect for the personal context
that shapes the understanding of truth must not be used as an excuse for less-
than-forthright discussions of even the most difficult issues.

Colonel Jessup, fully consumed by his own personal experience and the
narrative that both shapes and is shaped by it, is not so different from any
one of us. Yes, he is an extreme example of what can happen when our
guiding narratives become entirely self-referential, lacking a mechanism
to be kept in check. But more importantly, he represents the impulse to

cover up those things we do not want to confront. Jessup also embodies the belief that the tough stuff cannot be fully explored with those outside one's community because not only will such outsiders fail to appreciate "the truth," they will use any newly acquired information shared by insiders to harm those who were brave enough to risk divulging it.

With only a few names changed, this entire discussion could easily describe the state of interreligious relations in much of the United States, especially between Jews and Muslims. This essay explores the current state of affairs between these two communities—our two communities—and how we might improve them.[1] I should point out that to even speak of the Jewish or Muslim community, especially in contemporary America, is a misnomer. There is no single Jewish or Muslim community in the United States or elsewhere. But there are organizations representing large segments of each community, as well as media, advocacy, and educational institutions that are seen as indicative, if not fully representative, of Jews and Muslims in America.

While I believe that there are as many ways to be either Jewish or Muslim as there are people who identify as such, these institutions and organizations often present themselves and/or are perceived of as being synonymous with Jews, Judaism, Muslims, and Islam. Since, as is often remarked, the biggest difference between perception and reality is that perception is more difficult to change, it remains useful to use the language of Jews, Muslims, and communities herein. Yet I do so with the acute awareness that these are terms of convenience and not in any way exhaustive of the ideological and spiritual range claimed by all Jews or Muslims.

The bulk of this essay explores the ethical obligations that devolve upon both individuals and the institutions that claim either to represent them or speak in the voice of their traditions. How do we keep from becoming Nathan Jessup? How do we build our capacity to "handle the truth?" How do we nurture this capacity in others? How do we become more honest about the challenges within our own communities and make it safe for members of other communities to do the same? Only when these questions are fully addressed will we find ourselves on the path of maximizing the relationships between America's Jewish and Muslim communities.

We must begin by raising the bar on our expectations regarding interreligious encounters. We must not confuse feel-good moments of mutual affirmation, which too often pass for genuine interreligious dialogue, with accomplishing the harder work of recognizing genuine differences between communities. It's not that the so-called kumbaya experiences do not have their place, but they are not enough. Such experiences bring people together without actually being inter-anything. They are simply opportunities for mutual self-congratulation about that which is already shared. Yes, the identification and celebration of shared values remains a critical component of peace-building work. But time and again we have seen that without a healthy capacity to examine and address the moments of breakdown between groups, things quickly devolve into ugly rhetoric and even into violence.

And while the process of seeing others as embodiments of what we already mean by Jewish or Muslim may be helpful for those who can barely imagine the other as human, the process of seeing ourselves in others is certainly no substitute for the kinds of experiences that build our capacity to withstand the pain, frustration, hurt, and even betrayal that are inevitable parts of long-term relationships. If we cannot get to this place of understanding, then we are never more than a single misstep away from shattering all that we think we have built in terms of interreligious relations.

Many examples come to mind, including a 2009 incident that occurred in the midst of a highly publicized and very public conversation between the imam of one of New York City's largest mosques and a rabbi very much involved in Jewish-Muslim affairs. With no malice and no obvious desire to be provocative, the imam questioned whether Israel, as a Jewish-specific state, was such a good idea. The rabbi stormed from the stage, accusing the imam of both gross insensitivity and anti-Semitic leanings. As one who considers himself a religious Zionist[2] and who has had lengthy conversations with the same imam, I assure you that neither is true. So what happened? Having departed from the expected script of mutual affirmation, the rabbi (though it happens just as often in reverse) experienced difference as denigration and disagreement as betrayal; as such, he chose to walk away. The cycle of disappointment followed by rupture must be broken. Yet the only way to do so demands that we become increasingly forthright about the problems in our respective communities and increasingly vigilant about the concomitant obligation to not exploit such moments of honesty by those in other communities. While this mandate is clear, achieving it is far more difficult, as I hope my own personal experience will show.

Bridges TV: Its Birth and Death

Beginning in 2005, I had the privilege of creating and hosting programming, including two different talk shows, for Bridges TV. Dubbed the American Muslim TV network, Bridges TV provided programs primarily to the North American Muslim community. So how did a rabbi come to be so deeply involved? The credit—or, if one is so inclined, the blame—for this goes largely to the network's cofounders, Mo Hassan and Aasiya Zubair.

In the wake of 9/11, Mo, a banker in Buffalo, New York, and his wife Aasiya, a stay-at-home mom with professional degrees of her own, founded Bridges TV. With walls going up all over the world, Mo and Aasiya believed that it was more important than ever to build a few bridges, and that television was a critical medium to utilize in pursuit of this endeavor. They hoped that Bridges TV would foster greater awareness and understanding—for Muslims specifically and the larger non-Muslim American milieu generally—of the American Muslim community, its beliefs, struggles, and successes. In the wake of other media work I had done, Mo contacted me and asked if I was open to working with them.

Frankly, my initial response was somewhat guarded. But the more I looked into it, the more I appreciated the importance of what they were doing and the genuine interreligious sensitivity with which they were doing it. To be sure, I did not agree with everything that I saw or did at Bridges TV. If I had, though, what "inter-ness" would there have been? If we were already in perfect agreement then this would not be a genuine experiment in building bridges any more than getting two people, one of whom likes vanilla and the other chocolate, to enter an ice cream parlor at the same time. I suppose one could argue that such an exercise in ice cream experiences may be an accomplishment, but it would hardly be worthy of a national television program. So, while fully aware of those things about which we did not agree, it was hard not to be deeply impressed by a Muslim television network not only inviting a rabbi to create and host programming, but even doing so when it was not always in accord with what they believed!

One of the shows, *Building Bridges: Abrahamic Perspectives on the World Today*, became the network's most popular series, second only to the daily news. Mo, Aasiya, and I were really building something. And although it was Mo who originally reached out to me, it was Aasiya, in her role as program director and executive producer, with whom I worked most closely. Things were truly amazing for the next four years.

But then, in February 2009, the whole thing came to a sudden and tragic end: Mo was charged with murdering Aasiya in their Buffalo office. According to authorities, Mo beheaded his wife in response to ongoing marital troubles including Aasiya's desire to seek a divorce. I was sick with grief. I was also besieged with calls seeking my response to the tragedy. After reaching out to the family, and taking a day to digest the initial shock and horror, I began to respond. And in responding as I did, I brought down the wrath of both Muslims and Jews by inviting us all to rise above the Nathan Jessup syndrome and actually try and handle some truth.

The Dearth of Communal Introspection

My response then, as it remains to this day, is that tragedies of this kind demand both courage and understanding, precisely the kind of courage and understanding that should define all interreligious work. I know that's hard to do. We live in a society in which soul-searching and self-critique are often viewed as betrayal of one's community, while compassion and understanding on the part of victims is seen as dangerous naiveté at best, and self-hatred at worst. This dynamic, present in every community, is seriously pronounced in both the Muslim and Jewish communities (perhaps not to the same degree, and perhaps not practiced with the same frequency, but this debate is pointless since each community always thinks that they do better than the other).

For example, at the time of Aasiya's murder the Muslim community needed to find the courage to seriously address the inevitable questions about the role of religion in this crime, the extent to which Islam was a factor, the connection between domestic violence and traditional cultures of any kind that arises with cases such as these, and so on. Without raising such questions no internal growth can take place and outside detractors have the freedom to critique the "other" to their hearts' content. And even if some of these critics are not coming from a place of earnest commitment to human rights and justice, it is not enough to cry "Islamaphobe" when such questions are merely raised.

By the same token, it is neither accurate nor appropriate when those who genuinely do harbor malice against, or fear of, a particular community or religion circle around stories such as Aasiya's murder like sharks around an injured swimmer. Instead of working the story for the angle that "proves" what they already believe, as most people do at such moments, they need to hold back and resist making rhetorical use out of other people's tragedies. In this case, both sides needed to go a bit deeper. They needed to learn to handle some truth. It is simply too convenient, and ultimately too dangerous, to claim that Aasiya's murder had nothing to do with Islam. Yet when I made this very point, I was called a hater and was even threatened with violence. On the other hand, although I understand that it is dangerously convenient to use one woman's murder as "proof" of who and what Muslims "really are," because I chose not to condemn Islam or Muslims I was told by more than a few people that I was not only a fool but was actually committing treason against both America and the Jewish people.

Of course, there is no single demon to blame in Aasiya's death. There is no dragon for shining knights—be they defenders of secularism or religion—to slay and make the whole problem of domestic violence go away. There is no simple explanation for this atrocity. It would be so much easier if there were; indeed this is the appeal that fairy tales all have. But there is not.

Yet at the same time, let us be clear. This case did have to do with religion in general and Islam in particular. This was after all, a beheading—a ritualistic form of murder, albeit not one either unique to or imposed by Islam. Whether this act was or was not the product of good religious jurisprudence is not the issue. If Aasiya had been shot numerous times with a family-owned gun, it would be appropriate to discuss the problems associated with the prevalence of guns in American culture. Given that her death reflects a specific set of religious and cultural issues within Islam,

however marginal, it is appropriate to examine these notions. Simply saying that this has nothing to do with Islam and/or religion, as too many
religious leaders have done, is not acceptable. In fact, such an approach
creates the very space utilized by those who use their religion in despicable ways. Defining a problem out of existence does not make it go away.
It is only when practitioners take responsibility for the religious elements
or underpinnings of those actions they abhor that they can help keep such
abuses from happening.

February 2009 was the precise time to embrace the possibility that this
was a so-called honor killing, not because we knew then or now with
absolute certainty that it was, but rather because Aasiya's death looked like
one and invited our attention to the five thousand women each year who
are murdered by men in this fashion (a low-end estimate according to the
United Nations).[3] February 2009 was the precise time to focus on the
connection between religion and violence, not because we immediately
knew that faith was the primary motivation in the murder, but rather
because too many people die each year in the name of God, and only the
faithful can make this stop. To be sure, nobody knows to this day what
was in the murderer's mind or soul when Aasiya was beheaded. But we
do know that nothing provides cover for violence against people as effectively as belief in God or some equivalent redemptive ideology. February
2009 was the precise time for religious leaders who are more concerned
with the black eyes given to women by members of their own faith community than the black eyes given to the faith itself when practitioners beat
their wives or commit acts of violence in God's name.

In February 2009 we needed to see religious leaders who did more
than explain away the connections between faith and fighting, in the
home or in the world. Sadly there was little of that kind of leadership to be found. Of course, demonstrating such courageous leadership demands a context in which it is reasonably safe to do so. Leaders
needed to know that their efforts at genuine communal reflection and
reform would not be viewed as betrayal from within the community
itself or even used to justify the irrational hatreds of their community
by others, which does exist in some places. February 2009 was also a
moment that made demands upon critics of Islam in general and of the
American Muslim community in particular, upon the hard secularists,
and upon all those who wrote about Aasiya's death as proof of the futility of all interreligious bridge-building efforts with Muslims, and what
is still falsely presumed by many to be their inherently violent culture.
By responding with seeming delight at events that "proved" what they
had always believed, and relishing what they believed was their moment
to say "we told you so," such detractors made it increasingly difficult
to instigate the self-critique and reform that they claim is so necessary.
Consciously or not, these fearmongers, haters, and cynics helped to create the reality that they most vocally oppose. They made it virtually
impossible for Muslim leaders to publicly ask the tough questions that

needed to be asked. In so doing, they bear a portion of the guilt for the absence of public self-critique in the Muslim community.

In effect, the behavior of both positions—"this has nothing to do with Islam" versus "this only occurred because of Islam"—tended to perpetuate the status quo. Too many Muslims deflected the real and legitimate challenges that arose with Aasiya's murder by leveling the charge of Islamophobia at those who raised them. And at the same time, too many who really do hate Muslims exploited a tragedy in order to score political points. If we hope to be more than Nathan Jessup we must give up such behavior.

To be sure, the problem of introspection exists in the Jewish community as well. The readiness, willingness, and even casualness with which charges of anti-Semitism are tossed about are beyond disturbing. A recent tussle between Abe Foxman and Andrew Sullivan is a good case example. Speaking at the 2010 Jewish Council on Public Affairs' national meeting in Dallas, Anti-Defamation League director Abe Foxman lashed out at writer and pundit Andrew Sullivan, calling him a good example of an educated anti-Semite. Sullivan is many things. But an anti-Semite? Someone who loathes Jews? This just doesn't wash. I do think that Sullivan's analysis of the conflict between Israelis and Palestinians often substitutes easy moral equivalence for the more complex reality in which there is blame enough to go around, without claiming that all bad acts are equally bad. But be that as it may, weak analysis does not an anti-Semite make, especially since the latter is a claim about a person's inner beliefs, and such beliefs cannot be measured by a few comments, no matter how objectionable Mr. Foxman or anybody else finds them. Yet rather than take on Sullivan based on his understanding of the facts, Foxman chose to label him a Jew-hater.

Perhaps even more troubling is how the easy use of this charge devalues the ugly phenomenon of real anti-Semitism and the fact that Foxman, one of the nation's leaders in the fight against anti-Semitism, also leads the process of its devaluation as either a meaningful term or a genuine challenge. In doing so, an important man becomes the boy who cried wolf. In a world where real wolves remain, this not only makes Foxman look foolish but also feeds the belief that *every* claim of anti-Semitism is ridiculous. After all, people will reasonably conclude, look who's making the claim, *again*! If Jews are genuinely concerned about real anti-Semitism, they should stop tossing out this charge every time someone does something that any Jew finds disagreeable. The label of anti-Semitism is powerful, which is why people love to use it. But it is powerful precisely because it describes an ugly state of mind and the potentially deadly actions that flow from it. If regularly used to describe anything else, the term, like the boy's cries of wolf, will lose its potency, including at those moments when real wolves approach.

The same is true for those who insist that anyone challenging Muslims and/or Islam is guilty of Islamophobia. Like anti-Semitism, this is also a powerful charge, but will remain so only if it used as something other than a charge meant to silence all critics at all times. In fact, it would be interesting to see what would happen if Jews and Muslims agreed to abandon the terms anti-Semite and Islamophobe in all cases except for those of physical violence, overtly claiming hatred of the respective groups as their motivation. I sometimes wonder if this would move both communities toward greater success in combating actual hate.

Moving toward Deeper Intercommunal Introspection

Three significant factors contribute to the current state of affairs in which moving toward deeper intercommunal introspection is so difficult. Our willingness to address these factors in substantive ways will be crucial to raising the level of health both within and between the Jewish and Muslim communities. One of the three factors seems equally to affect both communities, while the other two are present in each separately but not in the same measure.

The shared challenge is the common presumption that communal strength and unity are built upon uniformity (or at least the portrayal of it) and the refusal to engage those with whom we may most deeply disagree because of the fear that doing so will "legitimize" them. Rather than encouraging bold attempts to reach across communal boundaries to those with whom relations are most strained, there is an internal vetting process that predetermines who is and who is not an "authentic" partner for interreligious dialogue. All too often, the primary criterion for allowing someone into this club is an assessment of who is most likely to say that which one wants to hear and least likely to say what one doesn't. The fear that such encounters legitimize the so-called other side is also absurd if for no other reason than the fact that the "other side" does not imagine that their legitimacy flows from those who are withholding their approval.

This approach is both profoundly unsophisticated and potentially dangerous. The lack of sophistication lies in the inability to see that diplomacy—be it cultural, spiritual, communal, or political—always demands multiple approaches and tactics. It may be called back channel, second track, or third way, but breakthroughs are made when communities engage each other on multiple fronts. The prequalifying approach is also dangerous because when things get particularly bad between members of different communities there is no apparatus in place for reaching out to those deemed by each side to be most problematic. Having focused on efforts with those with whom we most commonly agree, we successfully avoid those issues that are most likely to cause us genuine difficulties and contact with those who have the greatest capacity to address them— hardly an enviable position for any community to find itself in.

Then there are the issues that, though present in each community, are more specific to one or the other. The issue among Muslims, in my experience, is the insistence on the perfection of Islam and the lack of real capacity for shared responsibility. Among Jews it is the obsession with victimhood.

The propensity of Muslim leaders to disconnect Islam from the way Muslims live is a genuine and ongoing challenge. Time and again I have encountered imams, teachers, and other communal leaders who insist that there is no problem with Islam—by definition it is perfect. Along with others, I have been told that the problems are not with Islam the "religion" but with Islam the "culture," as if there is some clear line between the two. Perhaps more troubling is that in such a context the term "culture" is deemed to be problematic whereas "religion" is not. This creates a double wall of insulation against the very questioning that keeps any religious tradition from becoming dangerously self-referential and self-serving.

I once asked a group of Muslim leaders what in their tradition, if anything, caused them pain or shame. It was literally impossible for most of them to comprehend the question, let alone offer an answer. When I offered to share elements of my own tradition—one I love very deeply, one that structures my life in virtually every way—they thought I was joking. "How," one of them asked, "could you give yourself over to a faith that was flawed?" When I responded that my love for Judaism was not based on it necessarily being perfect, but upon finding it to be perfect for me, they were even more surprised. To make my position more understandable, I tried the following analogy.

I asked them if they were married and had children. They all responded with a "yes" to both questions. "Do you," I asked, "need to believe that your spouses and children are perfect in order to love them with all of your heart and believe with that same heart that it is God's will that they be in your life?" They all said that they did not. I suggested that it was the same with our faith traditions. We do not need to insist to either ourselves or to others that our respective religious traditions are flawless in order for them to be worthy of our love and devotion. While they did not all jump to share my conclusion, they understood that the need to assert perfection can actually get in the way of the deeper love that comes with greater honesty.

A similar kind of honesty about the nature of shared responsibility would also go a long way in getting us to richer and more productive levels of interreligious encounter. But, as I have discovered, what I call shared responsibility is often thought of as collective guilt among Muslim intellectuals and religious leaders. The best example of this from my experiences was an interview I conducted with Professor Jamal Badawi, one of North America's most prominent and popular teachers of Islam. We were taping for Bridges TV in Halifax, Nova Scotia, where Dr. Badawi is Professor Emeritus at St. Mary's University. At some point in our conversation, I asked the professor about "Islamic Terror." Becoming annoyed, he shot back, "there is no such thing."

"But professor," I pressed, "when people commit crimes in the name of Islam, crimes that you yourself describe as mass murder, how can you tell me that there is no such thing as Islamic terror?"

Now visibly disturbed, Professor Badawi went on the offensive. "Would you describe the man in the mosque in Palestine . . . I don't recall his name or the exact details, but would you call him a Jewish terrorist? Was that Jewish terror?"

"His name," I responded, "was Baruch Goldstein. He murdered 29 innocent Muslims in the Ibrahimi Mosque in Hebron, traditionally understood by both Muslims and Jews to be the burial place of Abraham, Sarah, Isaac, Rebecca, Jacob and Leah. And yes, he was a Jewish terrorist who committed acts of Jewish terror."

"But that," the professor almost shouted at me, "is collective guilt." I responded by saying that it was nothing of the kind. "I loathe collective guilt," I continued, "and this is not collective guilt. It is collective responsibility."

We all need to distinguish between collective guilt, in which an entire group is pushed to mimic the behavior of a select few, from collective or shared responsibility, in which those who share a claim to a particular community or tradition in good times feel the burden of the bad times and take steps to correct them. Collective guilt is something that is imposed from without. Collective responsibility is something that is assumed from within. The former is unethical to say the least. The latter is necessary to keep the former at bay and build solid relationships across communal boundaries.

While Jews are not generally held back by either an insistence on the perfection of Judaism or an inability to assume collective responsibility, we have our own issues that must be addressed for us to become better interreligious partners. We need to give up a belief held by many in the Jewish community: the belief that Jews are the most victimized people in the world. Even if it were true, a debate into which I will not engage herein, it is hardly a productive frame for encountering the world. To be sure, Jews have suffered mightily over our history. The fact that Jews suffered less living under Muslim rule than under Christian rule does not excuse the oppression that occurred under either of them. I also appreciate the fact that the Holocaust of sixty years ago was a genocide where six million Jews were murdered, two out of every three Jews in Europe and one out of every three in the world. Six decades is not enough time to absorb this calculated and unthinkably vicious event. In this sense, it is not crazy that a large segment of the Jewish people still see the world through the lenses of victimization.

But understanding this dominant worldview is not an excuse. Moreover, we Jews cannot allow ourselves to remain so imprisoned by the memory of past suffering that we make it virtually impossible to build new and better realities. Is that kind of ideological imprisonment the norm in Jewish life? I would say it is not. But to imagine that we are not burdened by at least some measure of it is not true either. At its worst, the mantle of victimhood serves as the justification for becoming the victimizer in situations when we Jews have power. In its less toxic forms, it becomes the excuse for being less than sensitive to the needs of others who suffer. (The thinking, albeit sometimes unconscious, goes, "however much 'those people' have suffered, it's not as bad as we have had it.") We Jews must figure out how to raise questions and concerns about other groups and communities without quickly assuming that those differences and disagreements are motivated by deep hatred of Jews. We must be willing to confront our own failings without the fear that in doing so we empower a world that wants nothing but our destruction.

Conclusion

Ultimately, Jews and Muslims share much more in common than they do not, especially in the United States of America. The challenges that arise between our communities are not, primarily, a function of the absence of shared needs, desires, or even traditions. They are not even a function of the very real differences that do exist between our communities. The challenges lie in the fears and protectionism that I have examined in this essay. I believe that none of these communal dominant narratives is endemic or inherent in what it means to be either a Jew or a Muslim. I maintain that all of them can be addressed in honest and safe environments.

Nathan Jessup was wrong, at least for most Muslims and Jews. We actually can handle the truth. But to do so, we need to remain mindful of the ways that we insulate ourselves from doing so. With this awareness, we can nurture our capacity to handle the truth about the things we love most, and about the good that is found even among those with whom we may most deeply disagree. When this is accomplished we may not always get along, but we will know a greater measure of peace, understanding, and respect between our two communities.

Notes

1. Though I will make reference to other religious communities in the course of this piece, the focus will be on the Jewish and Muslim communities, largely due to my personal experiences.
2. By religious Zionist I mean one who sees the establishment of a Jewish state, in at least some portion of the ancient land of Israel, as part of the religious destiny of the Jewish people. I also see it as a mandate to assure maximal freedom and dignity to all inhabitants of the region, because that too is part of the same religious system to which I subscribe.
3. United Nations Development Fund for Women (UNIFEM), "Facts and Figures on Harmful Traditional Practices" (2007), section on violence against women (VAW); also cited by the Amnesty International project on Violence against Women (2010).

CHAPTER TWO

Who Put Hate in My Sunday Paper?: Uncovering the Israeli-Republican-Evangelical Networks behind the "Obsession" DVD

OMID SAFI

Introduction

In September 2008, something strange showed up inside the Sunday edition of the *New York Times* newspapers of millions of Americans. Alongside comics, coupons, and advertisements for local stores, readers found a controversial DVD called "Obsession: Radical Islam's War against the West." Around twenty-eight million copies of this DVD were distributed for free in this fashion. In some ways the scale of this campaign, and its ideological venom, were unprecedented; many newspapers have since stated that they had never previously distributed free DVDs as inserts, let alone something with such charged content. The copies were distributed in specific "swing states": Colorado, Florida, Iowa, Michigan, Ohio, Pennsylvania, Wisconsin, and so on, all of which were understood to be "toss-ups" in the November 2008 presidential election between Senator John McCain and then-senator Barack Obama. It was obvious to all that someone was trying to influence the American electorate by playing on the themes of fear and hate. But who? Who was behind this massive, multimillion dollar campaign?

Answering that question proved more difficult than one might think, as the groups behind this DVD worked hard to hide their tracks. The connections, which were partially concealed in the DVD as well as the distribution campaign, involved a slew of right-wing groups, from Israel-based organizations to self-identified pro-Israel American lobby organizations to Christian American evangelical groups to Neoconservative think-tanks. Since September 2008, the "facts" presented by "Obsession" have been refuted in several detailed presentations

and articles. Therefore, rather than make a point by point refutation of
the contents of the DVD, the intention of this essay is to explore the
networks that were behind the production and distribution of this DVD,
and illustrate that their goal was to influence the 2008 presidential election toward the Republican nominee, John McCain, using incredibly
destructive and divisive means.

In this day and age, all politics are both local *and* global. This is particularly the case in the United States. The distribution of the DVD affected
me and my family at an intimate, local level: approximately 160,000 copies of this propaganda piece were distributed throughout our community
in North Carolina. The newspaper of the nearby city of Charlotte distributed another 200,000 copies. Upon contacting the local newspaper, the
Raleigh-based *News and Observer*, and asking why such a hateful piece of
propaganda was being distributed for free to all the paper's subscribers, the
response of the paper was less than impressive. Jim McClure, vice president of Display Advertising for the *News and Observer*, said, "Obviously,
we have distributed other product samples, whether it's cereal or toothpaste." Really? Is this where we are? A DVD that includes seventy-seven
minutes of propaganda footage slicing together videos of violent Muslims
with those of Nazis, suggesting that Muslims are out to destroy Western
civilization, is comparable to cereal and toothpaste?

Some of the "facts" of the DVD, which claims to be an educational
product and part of a nonprofit production, are as follows:

- The world in 2008 stands as it did in 1938. Radical Islam is as great
  a threat, if not greater, than the Nazis. Unspecified action must be
  taken.
- Attacks taking place in Iraq, Palestine, Chechnya, and Iran present a
  global Muslim conspiracy against Israel and "The West."
- Radical Islam is intricately linked to destroying the state of Israel.
  Most of the figures who are paraded in the DVD, whether they are
  Jewish, Christian, or Muslim, are all passionate pro-Israel speakers
  who have a long history of speaking out against Palestinians, Arabs,
  and Muslims in general. The list includes such luminaries as:
  - Nonie Darwish, who runs the tell-all website www.arabsforisrael.
    com. Darwish neglects to mention that she is a Christian convert
    from Islam and an ardent supporter of Israel.
  - Caroline Glick, a member of the Israel On Campus Coalition.
  - Daniel Pipes, arguably the best-known critic of Islam in the United
    States, who is also the director of the pro-Israel think-tank, "The
    Middle East Forum."
  - Walid Shoebat, who claims to have been a "former PLO Islamic
    terrorist" turned Christian Evangelical Zionist. (Never mind that
    the *Jerusalem Post*, among others, has already dismissed the factual-
    ity of his "terrorist" claims.)

One could go on and on, but the list here gives some indication that contrary to what the official website of the DVD claims the "experts" found on the film are far from impartial. They have an extremely biased point of view born of a hatred of Islam and a passionate defense of Israel at all costs, even if that cost happens to be truth and facts.

Who Made This DVD?

Let's return to the claim of my local newspaper that the distribution of this product is qualitatively no different from giving customers a free sample of toothpaste. For the sake of argument, let's follow this reasoning. How many of us would receive an unmarked package of toothpaste and brush our teeth with it if it did not have an official label, lacked information regarding the manufacturer, and made no mention of whether or not an agency has vouched for its safety? If we do not take unmarked material to our teeth, why would we take a product like "Obsession" and likewise ingest it into our homes, schools, churches, synagogues, mosques, and civic institutions when the DVD doesn't disclose the network behind it?

The "Obsession" DVD states that it is made by the Clarion Fund. What does the Clarion Fund stand for and who are they? Their intentions are made a bit clearer through the use of their registered website, www.radicalislam.org. Yet what exactly does "radical Islam" constitute? Who stands for it and who opposes it? We are not told, aside from this: "Radical Islam poses a significant threat to the Western way of life. The Islamists' ultimate aim is conversion and domination of the West, which they see as the root of all evil that must be eradicated." This type of general labeling is as unhelpful as accusations of being a "Communist" in the 1950s or, more recently, the terms "unpatriotic" and "un-American." It is a catch all, bogeyman argument masquerading as sophisticated analysis.

What about a specified individual producer of the "Obsession" DVD? On the DVD's website, the producer is identified as Raphael Shore, "a documentary producer and founder of Clarion Fund, Inc., a new non-profit organization dedicated to educating the public about national security threats." So, Raphael Shore is the founder of Clarion Fund, and the producer of "Obsession." But who is Raphael Shore? This required a good bit of background research. Shore is part of a Jewish Israeli missionary group called Aish HaTorah (fire or flame of the Torah),[1] whose goal is to call "assimilated" Jews to ultra-Orthodox Judaism.[2] Their international headquarters is located in the Jewish Quarter section of the Old City of Jerusalem, a plot of Boardwalk-esque land that overlooks the renowned "Western Wall," given to them by the Israeli government after the June 1967 war. (Their founder, Rabbi Noah Weinberg, has been honored by a number of different mayors of Jerusalem.) It turns out that Shore, a Canadian-born Aish HaTorah-ordained rabbi, is also the director of the international wing of Aish HaTorah. His business card is even available online.[3]

So does the "Obsession" DVD fall within the purview of Aish HaTorah's "outreach?" Given the interconnected nature of the political and the religious in Israel it seems that Aish HaTorah has gone from evangelizing to Jews to waging a global propaganda campaign against Islam and Muslims. They worked hard to cover their tracks in this process, as the connections between Aish HaTorah and the Clarion Fund run deep. According to paperwork filed with the state of Delaware, the Clarion Fund uses the same New York address as Aish HaTorah. In 2006, the two directors of the Clarion Fund were Shore and Jacob Fetman, the latter Aish HaTorah's former chief financial officer. In 2007, the Clarion Fund had three directors: Shore, Rabbi Henry Harris (the educational director for Aish HaTorah), and Rebecca Kabat, another Aish HaTorah employee.

Hasbara Fellowship and Honestreporting.com

Shore is also the director of Hasbara Fellowships, whose website is www.israelactivism.com, another organization run through Aish HaTorah. Their activism on behalf of Israel is worn like a badge of honor. But like the Clarion Fund and yet another new group, the Jewish University Online (which Shore is likewise involved with), one has to conduct intensive research to uncover the connection between the Hasbara Fellowships and this ultra-Orthodox missionary organization.[4] So how is it that a group with the stated goal of "Israel activism" is responsible for distributing twenty-eight million copies of a DVD warning Americans about the danger of "radical Islam?" In many of the screenings of this DVD, the audience was even required to sign up for receiving material from the israelactivism.com website. Why did seventy U.S. newspapers accept and distribute this DVD without knowing the source of this propaganda?

Hasbara Fellowship's own website includes the following pieces of information about their history and mission. All of the following are direct quotes:

- "Hasbara Fellowships, a program spearheaded by Aish International, educates and trains university students to be effective pro-Israel activists on their campuses."
- "Started in 2001 in conjunction with Israel's Ministry of Foreign Affairs, Hasbara Fellowships brings hundreds of students to Israel every summer and winter." This is perhaps the most intriguing connection and startling confession because Israel's Ministry of Foreign Affairs acts as the country's official and national center to disseminate state-approved information.
- "So far, Hasbara Fellowships has trained over 1,400 students on over 250 campuses, providing its participants with the information, tools,

resources, and confidence to return to their campuses as leaders in the fight for Israel's image." Interestingly, college campuses formed the primary site of the distribution of the "Obsession" DVD before the newspaper campaign. The primary audience on college campuses have been Jewish organizations (i.e., Hillel) and, perhaps not surprisingly, student College Republicans.

Shore has previously written at length about his passionate advocacy on behalf of Israel in a number of Aish HaTorah newsletters. His earlier works were produced alongside an entity called "Honestreporting.com," founded by Shore's twin brother, Ephraim,[5] with the following self-description: "Israel is in the midst of a battle for public opinion—waged primarily via the media. To ensure Israel is represented fairly and accurately 'HonestReporting' monitors the media, exposes cases of bias, promotes balance, and effects change through education and action." In other words, Honestreporting.com sees itself as a media advocacy organization working on behalf of Israel, with the requisite "fair and balanced" claims. Honestreporting.com has worked with the Clarion Fund and Aish HaTorah in producing additional monolithically pro-Israeli government policy material.

The Israeli newspaper *Ha'aretz* reports that "Obsession" is described as "Honest Reporting's newest documentary film."[6] Honestreporting.com's own website confirms this: "HonestReporting is proud to have been a former marketing partner during the initial production of this award-winning documentary."[7] Perhaps recognizing that the credibility of his message would be undermined if its connection to these organizations was revealed, Shore told *Ha'aretz* that they "have told Honest Reporting to take [this relationship] off their site 'a dozen times.'"

One of the other elements that the producers of the "Obsession" DVD may not want the public to know about is their clear political agenda, as related specifically to *American* politics. An article previously published on the "Obsession" website reads, "McCain's policies seek to confront radical Islamic extremism and terrorism and roll it back while [Barack] Obama's, although intending to do the same, could in fact make the situation facing the West even worse."[8] The Clarion Fund's spokesperson Gregory Ross did not deny that this article appeared on their site. It seems that he was only upset that they had been caught with it. Established as a 501(c)3, as opposed to a 501(c)4, it is illegal for a nonprofit organization such as the Clarion Fund to endorse one political candidate over another. National Public Radio (NPR) reported on this illegal action, as well as the possibility of a forthcoming FEC probe.[9]

Who Is Paying for "Obsession" and Who Distributed It?

The answers to these questions have yet to be confirmed. Aside from the Clarion Fund stating that their organization paid for the production and distribution of the DVD, not much else is known. They admit that the names they give for the funders on their material are bogus aliases.[10] For example, Shore has said that 80 percent of the funding for the "Obsession" DVD has come from one source, "Peter Mier." Yet he adds that this name is an alias.[11] In other words, it is hard to know for sure who is paying for the production and, even more importantly, the distribution of what the Endowment for Middle East Truth (EMET), the main distributor for "Obsession," refers to as the "Obsession Project." Given that EMET estimates that this project cost tens of millions of dollars,[12] the evidence seems to point to someone such as Sheldon Adelson, the Jewish Republican billionaire.

According to the *New York Times*, when Shore and Co. could not find any traditional distributor for their film, they formulated a strategy of working with neoconservative organizations such as the Heritage Foundation, College Republicans, and a few specific Jewish organizations.[13] Then, according to NPR, EMET (lit. translated as "truth") stepped into the fray.[14] Like Honestreporting.com, the "Middle East Truth" being propagated here is another self-described pro-Israel group whose perspective is in line with that of the current ruling Israeli political party, Likud. In fact, with the stated mission of support for Israel to oppose any "concessions" as part of a peace agreement with the Palestinian Authority, such as the 2005 partial withdrawal from occupied Gaza, EMET's positions are much more conservative than even Likud's, more akin to the dominant voice of ideological Jewish Israeli settlers living in the occupied West Bank.[15] EMET also has an overt connection to the Republican Party, which they seem to parade on their website: "EMET was also requested to help the Republican Policy Committee with a Sense of the Congress resolution talking about Israel's inherent right to defend itself..." In other words, the Clarion Fund claims to be nonpolitical, but uses a pro-Israel ally of the GOP to distribute its product.[16] It is important to reiterate that it is illegal to fund U.S.-based groups supporting foreign governmental policies—like Israel's—that have a U.S. 501(c)3 status. This becomes even more problematic when such policies are positions that run contrary to those of the American government.[17]

EMET has a cozy relationship with Sheldon Adelson, who has a proven track record of using his wealth to push both the agendas of Likud and the American Republican party. Adelson has a long-standing public relationship with current Israeli prime minister Benjamin Netanyahu.[18] A recent investigative piece in the *New Yorker* illuminated many details of Adelson's political agenda in both the United States and Israel. He is also a longtime contributor to the Zionist Organization of America (ZOA), the previous employer of Sarah Stern, EMET's current director. Through EMET, Stern has sponsored lectures and seminars on Capital Hill in Adelson's name: "EMET would like to thank the Adelson Family Foundation for their generous support in enabling these critically important seminars to take place."[19]

Adelson commonly makes *Forbes Magazine*'s annual list of wealthiest Americans (he ranks as the third richest person in the United States[20]), to say nothing of being one of the wealthiest people in the world, reaching twelfth position in 2008. His personal wealth, largely gained through Las Vegas business ventures, is estimated as exceeding $20 billion. *The Washington Post* reports that he has already given over $200 million to Jewish and Israeli causes. He has been a major donor for the Taglit-Birthright Israel program, to which he makes a $25 million annual contribution.[21] To put Adelson on the political spectrum, it is important to recall that he has described himself as a critic of AIPAC *from the right*. In other words, he feels that the American Israel Public Affairs Committee has been too compassionate in dealing with the Palestinian community.[22] Adelson has also been a longtime contributor to Republican causes, including both campaigns of President George W. Bush. He was personally chosen to accompany then president Bush on his 2008 visit to Israel to celebrate the sixtieth anniversary of Israel's founding.[23] Initially, he had designs of spending $250 million dollars to set up an organization called "Freedom Watch" to keep President Obama out of the White House. Conceived of as the conservative right's answer to Moveon.org, Freedom Watch continues to be a meeting place for Jewish Republicans and former officials of the Bush administration.[24]

As for a list of those who serve on the board of EMET—it is a virtual who's who of Israeli officials and U.S. conservative Zionists[25]:

- Ambassador Yossi Ben-Aharon, a former chief of staff for Israeli prime minister Yitzchak Shamir, and previous deputy director general of Israel's Ministry of Foreign Affairs.
- Lenny Ben-David, a former deputy chief of mission at Israel's embassy in Washington, D.C., who held previous posts in AIPAC for twenty-five years, in both Israel and the United States.
- Ambassador Yoram Ettinger, a former minister for congressional affairs at Israel's Embassy in Washington, D.C., Israel's consul general in Houston, and director of Israel's Government Press Office.

In addition to Israeli officials, the EMET Board includes[26]:

- Neoconservatives such as Ariel Cohen (affiliated with the Heritage Foundation), David Dalin (affiliated with the Heritage Foundation and the Hoover Institute), Frank Gaffney (previously awarded honors by the ZOA), and R. James Woolsey.
- Pro-Israeli government policy lobbyists such as Caroline Glick, Daniel Pipes, and Meyrav Wurmser (former director of MEMRI, founded by members of the Israeli Defense Forces).
- Many of the so-called experts found in "Obsession," such as Walid Shoebat.

- Christian Zionists, such as Rev. James. M. Hutchens, the founder of the Jerusalem Connection International.

Other connections to pro-Israel organizations responsible for the distribution of "Obsession" include the following:

- Extreme fringes of the Christian evangelical movement, including, above all else, Christians United for Israel (CUFI), which mailed out copies of the DVD from their mailing center. CUFI's founder and national director is John Hagee, renowned for claiming that Islam is an evil religion and that the Holocaust happened because Adolf Hitler was directed by God to drive Jews out of Europe and into Israel in order to bring about the return of Jesus Christ.[27]
- Such anti-Obama organizations as "Our Country Deserves Better." According to NPR, a political consultant named Joe Wierzbicki, who also serves as the public affairs coordinator of this organization, screened "Obsession" on September 11, 2008, in Dearborn, MI. According to their website, "Our Country Deserves Better than Barack Obama—and with your help we can ensure that Barack Obama is defeated on November 4th."[28]
- The Republican Jewish Coalition (RJC), who worked in partnership with CUFI to distribute copies of a book entitled *Standing With Israel* to a large number of American rabbis and other leaders of the Jewish community, a package that also included a copy of the "Obsession" DVD and a letter of approval from a former Israeli ambassador encouraging them to strengthen connections with Christian Zionists.[29] On their website, the Republican Jewish Coalition states that Barack Obama and Joe Biden and their supporters "have handed Ahmadenijad [*sic*] a big win."[30]

Ha'aretz notes that "Obsession" "has a largely Jewish and pro-Israel distribution network, though Shore is trying to expand the film's appeal."[31]

Islam or Radical Islam?

Before concluding it is important to add a word about the distinction between Islam and radical Islam. In the last few years, we have indeed seen a number of terrorist acts around the world, which have resulted in the death of thousands. While the bulk of these have not emanated from Islamic organizations, many have. (And, of course, the majority of the victims of acts of terrorism, even in these latter cases, have been Muslims.) No doubt, a critical look at the ideology of terrorist groups is more than called for in today's political climate. What many would object to, however, is painting all Muslims and all of Islam with the same brush.

The "Obsession" DVD opens by making a sharp distinction between Islam and radical Islam. The producers of the documentary state, adamantly, that they are not anti-Islam or anti-Muslim, but that they are only against "radical Islam." Leaving aside for a moment the debates over what constitutes "radical Islam" and how pervasive or marginal it actually is, there is an uncomfortable disconnect between this claim, also found on their website, and the claims made during the movie itself. The people paraded as so-called experts do not express a distinction between Islam and "radical Islam." Instead, the many speakers found in the DVD make blanket statements against Islam—all of Islam—and all of Muslims.

Let's take one example, the very first speaker shown on camera, Walid Shoebat. Shoebat's claim to fame is his contention that he is an ex-"Islamic terrorist" turned Christian Zionist. Aside from the criminal implication being a former terrorist presents, let's examine Shoebat's track record regarding some of his more audacious claims about Islam (not just "radical Islam"):

- "Obama is a Muslim." Yes, that old myth again. Sadly, according to a *Wall Street Journal* poll, some 13 percent of American citizens believe this to be the case,[32] in spite of the fact that Obama is a committed Christian. Who knows how many more people have been moved against Obama due to this rumor.
- "The Arabic speaking communities in America, however, do indeed support Osama bin Ladin and Hamas...The less they know about Islam the more peaceful they are." In other words, when Muslims are peaceful it is not because of Islam, but in spite of Islam, whereas "radical Muslims" are radical and violent precisely because of Islam.[33]
- "Islam is not the religion of God—Islam is the devil."[34]
- Shoebat's solution to the Palestine-Israel problem, as told to the Israel National News, the voice of the settler movement in the occupied West Bank, is as follows, "Tear down the Dome of the Rock, and re-establish Solomon's Temple on the Temple Mount."[35]

For a second example, let's look at another figure from the movie, the Lebanese Christian Brigitte Gabriel, who appeared at the July 27, 2007, CUFI conference and opined,

The difference, my dear Christian friends, between Israel and the Arab world is quite simply the difference between civilization and barbarism. It's the difference between good and evil and this is what we're witnessing in the Arabic and Islamic world. I am angry. They have no SOUL! They are dead set on killing and destruction. And in the name of something they call "Allah," which is very different from the God we believe in, because our God is the God of love.[36]

It would be unfair to take Gabriel's hateful words as authoritative teachings of the Christian tradition, or as exemplifying Christian love. And yet the producers of "Obsession" want the viewers to take Gabriel as an authoritative expert on Islam and Muslims. When Gabriel describes the whole "Islamic world" as having "no soul," it is difficult to think that their claim to only be talking about Muslim radicals is deserved. Perhaps this is why the *New York Times* described Gabriel to be a "radical Islamophobe."[37]

Conclusion

The massive scale of the "Obsession" campaign raises a number of disturbing questions: Should it really be that easy for a non-American organization to propagate mass hate speech in the United States, especially through actions that can potentially sway U.S. presidential elections? Why has mainstream American journalism been so slow to pick up on these networks, all of which are publicly available and require minimal investigation? Is the American milieu ready to fuel a poisonous political climate, where demonizing an entire ethnic or religious community is seen as acceptable? America's history clearly speaks to severe discrimination against other groups, such as African Americans, Hispanics, women, gays and lesbians, and many others. But perhaps no community in the West has been the victim of millennia-long persecution and "othering" campaigns as have the Jews.

This leads to an incredibly poignant final question: Why are Jewish American and Jewish Israeli organizations deploying the same "othering" strategies that were leveled against Jews for millennia? And where is the voice of dissent from within the Jewish community itself? Indeed, "Obsession" has torn down bridges of dialogue between Muslim and Jewish groups across the country, connections that took years to establish. Jews and non-Jews alike readily admit that Israel remains both a rallying cry and a source of tension within the Jewish American community itself. One can point to many Jewish Americans who have taken the lead in criticism of Israeli human rights violations against Palestinians. But there are important fissures in the Jewish American community over all sorts of issues, not just those related to Israel. And from the civil rights movement of the 1960s through today, Jewish Americans have often had an exemplary legacy of peace and justice activism. So why is the Jewish American community relatively silent when it comes to such blatant attacks on Muslims? Will future screed against Muslims be met with equal silence from this important American minority?

Last, it is important to add that from historical experience we know that campaigns like this tend to increasingly lower the bar of what is deemed acceptable speech as opposed to "hate speech." Make no mistake about it—there will be follow-up projects.[38] One shudders at the thought of the hate these pieces of propaganda are producing against members of the Muslim American community. We can either keep going down this slippery slope of accusations and blanket generalizations, or bond together and rise up to say "Enough!" The point is not only that Muslims are being targeted. Rather, it is the very poisoning of our cultural discourse and our hopes for a pluralistic American society that can welcome and embrace pluralism. To quote Dr. Martin Luther King, Jr., "Returning hate for hate multiplies hate, adding deeper darkness to a night already devoid of stars."[39] What we need now is less of the hateful heat of "Obsession" (and its networks) and more light from everyone committed to a just and pluralistic future for all of us.

Toward that day, starting today.

Notes

This essay, in a slightly different form, was first published at omidsafi.com/index.php?option=com_content &task=view&id=42&Itemid=9 (retrieved July 20, 2010) on September 29, 2008. The opinions here are the personal opinions of the author, and do not reflect those of the University of North Carolina or the American Academy of Religion.

1. Since that time, Shore has claimed that he no longer works for Aish HaTorah.
2. In addition, although Aish HaTorah presents itself as a pluralistic, nondenominational Jewish organization in much of their literature, it is clear that they affiliate with ultra-Orthodoxy, as opposed to modern Orthodoxy. Yet, similar to the Lubavitch rabbis affiliated with Chabad, Aish HaTorah is a unique ultra-Orthodox institution in that they interact with the non-ultra-Orthodox world on a daily basis. See note 6 in Aaron J. Tapper, "The 'Cult' of Aish HaTorah: Ba'alei Teshuva and the New Religious Movement Phenomenon," *Jewish Journal of Sociology*, Vol. 44: 1 and 2 (2002), 5–29.
3. For an in-depth analysis of the cult-like behavior of this multimillion dollar missionary organization, which has branches in tens of countries throughout the world, see Tapper, "The 'Cult' of Aish HaTorah."
4. See Shmarya Rosenberg, "Aish HaTorah Masks Involvement Of Online Jewish 'University' Meant To Lure Unwitting Students To Orthodoxy" (August 25, 2009) found at failedmessiah.typepad.com/failed_messiahcom/2009/08/exclusive-aish-hatorah-masks-involvement-of-online-jewish-university-meant-to-lure-unwitting-students-to-orthodoxy-345.html, retrieved July 20, 2010.
5. Ironically, Shore was so concerned that his brother had become involved with Aish HaTorah that in 1992 he went to Israel to "rescue" his brother from what he seems to have regarded as a "big hoax" and a cult-like milieu. Instead, Raphael also became part of Aish HaTorah (www.npr.org/templates/archives/archive.php?thingId=1 27308933, retrieved July 20, 2010).
6. www.haaretz.com/magazine/anglo-file/obsession-stokes-passions-fears-and-controversy-1.223820, retrieved July 20, 2010.
7. www.honestreporting.com/articles/45884734/critiques/new/Reviewers_Reject_The_Israel_Lobby.asp, retrieved July 20, 2010.
8. www.washingtonpost.com/wp-dyn/content/article/2008/10/25/AR2008102502092.html, retrieved July 20, 2010.
9. www.npr.org/templates/story/story.php?storyId=95076174, retrieved July 20, 2010.
10. www.haaretz.com/magazine/anglo-file/obsession-stokes-passions-fears-and-controversy-1.223820, retrieved July 20, 2010.
11. Ibid.
12. www.emetonline.org/index.html, retrieved July 20, 2010.
13. www.nytimes.com/2007/02/26/movies/26docu.html?_r=1&scp=1&sq=obsession+islam+jewish+shore&st=nyt, retrieved July 20, 2010.

14. www.npr.org/templates/story/story.php?storyId=95076174, retrieved July 20, 2010.
15. www.emetonline.org/about.html, retrieved July 20, 2010.
16. Formerly found on www.emetonlineblog.com; it has since been removed.
17. See Gal Beckerman, "Group Paying IDF Soldiers to Refuse Duty May Be in Violation of U.S. Tax Law," *Forward* (December 25, 2009), 1.
18. www.newyorker.com/reporting/2008/06/30/080630fa_fact_bruck, retrieved July 20, 2010.
19. www.emetonline.org/, retrieved July 20, 2010.
20. www.forbes.com/lists/2008/10/billionaires08_Sheldon-Adelson_ER9O.html, retrieved July 20, 2010.
21. www.ynetnews.com/articles/0,7340,L-3361888,00.html, retrieved July 20, 2010.
22. www.newyorker.com/reporting/2008/06/30/080630fa_fact_bruck?currentPage=all, retrieved July 20, 2010.
23. www.jweekly.com/article/full/35012/on-its-60th-israel-embraces-bush/, retrieved July 21, 2010.
24. www.washingtonpost.com/wp-dyn/content/article/2008/01/19/AR2008011902309_pf.html, retrieved July 20, 2010.
25. www.emetonline.org/index.html, retrieved July 20, 2010.
26. Ibid.
27. www.huffingtonpost.com/2008/05/21/mccain-backer-hagee-said_n_102892.html and www.huffingtonpost.com /2008 /05/22/unapologetic-hagee-says-h_n_103081.html, retrieved July 20, 2010.
28. www.ourcountrydeservesbetter.com/whoweare/index.html, retrieved July 20, 2010.
29. www.jewsonfirst.org/08a/cufi_obsession.html, retrieved July 20, 2010.
30. www.rjchq.org/Newsroom/newsdetail.aspx?id=bdb8c4cf-4a3a-4325-a30c-d4825660b8ec, retrieved July 20, 2010.
31. www.haaretz.com/magazine/anglo-file/obsession-stokes-passions-fears-and-controversy-1.223820, retrieved July 20, 2010.
32. online.wsj.com/public/resources/documents/WSJ-20080312-poll.pdf, retrieved July 20, 2010.
33. www.israelnationalnews.com/News/News.aspx/56867, retrieved July 20, 2010.
34. www.prnewswire.com/news-releases/ncis-tells-cair-anti-islam-film-not-ok-for-training-93433244.html, retrieved July 20, 2010.
35. www.israelnationalnews.com/News/News.aspx/56867, retrieved July 20, 2010.
36. www.pbs.org/moyers/journal/10052007/transcript5.html, retrieved July 20, 2010.
37. publiceditor.blogs.nytimes.com/2008/08/21/a-radical-islamophobe/?scp=1&sq=brigette%20gabriel&st=cse, retrieved July 20, 2010.
38. As of fall 2008 the Clarion Fund had already declared that its next project was to be a documentary titled "The Third Jihad." The film's synopsis is as follows: "How is radical Islam operating inside the West? Is a subversive 'cultural jihad' underway? How does radical Islam plan to bring America to its knees? What is the endgame?" This self-described documentary was released in October 2009. In other words, if "Obsession" is about the danger of Radical Islam over *there*, "The Third Jihad" makes the case that this same threat exists over *here*. For the propaganda-based website associated with this new film, see thethirdjihad.com/, retrieved July 20, 2010.
39. www.drmartinlutherkingjr.com/mlkquotes.htm, retrieved July 20, 2010.

CHAPTER THREE

Children of Abraham in Dialogue

RABBI AMY EILBERG

Introduction

The field of North American and Western European Jewish-Christian dialogue has reached maturity; by one estimate, it has been going on for approximately seventy years.[1] At the same time, the nascent field of Jewish-Muslim dialogue is just starting to flourish. One might feel a measure of sorrow that the need for such programs is so great, as the perception of conflict between Muslims and Jews around the world grows more desperate and the need for reconciliation is perceived as increasingly urgent. But there is much to celebrate in the heartfelt desire of so many people contributing to the cause of peace by building programs of learning and fostering relationships of respect and affection between Jews and Muslims around the world.

This essay offers reflections on the field of interfaith relations from the perspective of a rabbi and practitioner.[2] Most of my interfaith work takes place in the Twin Cities of Minneapolis and St. Paul, Minnesota, where I work in two primary contexts. One environment is the Jay Phillips Center for Interfaith Learning of St. Thomas University, where I created and currently direct the Center's Interfaith Conversations Project, a congregationally based interfaith trialogue project that pairs synagogues, churches, and Islamic centers for a variety of programs of learning and relationship-building. At the same time, I am also a leader in a grassroots interfaith dialogue network called the St. Paul Interfaith Network (or "SPIN"), created and sustained by volunteers in cooperation with the St. Paul Area Council of Churches. SPIN sponsors a wide variety of programs of interfaith learning, conversation, and relationship-building. While most of my experience takes place in the community in which I have lived for the past six years, the motivation for my work lies far away, in the Middle East. In recent years I have grown increasingly anguished by the Israeli-Palestinian conflict, the conflict closest to my heart, and subsequently have shifted the focus of my work to cultivate positive, trusting relationships between Muslims and Jews in Minnesota—my attempt to contribute to the cause of peace.

This essay explores two major challenges that arise in Jewish-Muslim encounter programs: the Israeli-Palestinian conflict and differences in theologies of revelation. The first issue plays a significant role as a threshold issue, affecting the decision of Jews and Muslims to even participate in programs of interreligious learning. It also predictably arises, whether as an unspoken concern or as an explicit dynamic, whenever Muslims and Jews develop relationships with one another. The second issue involves the differences between the two communities' views of the authority of their sacred scripture. My experience suggests that the difference between theological traditionalists and liberals may be a greater divide between the groups—and a greater challenge to mutual understanding—than the fact of religious difference alone.

The Israeli–Palestinian Conflict

More often than not, the Israeli-Palestinian conflict plays a role when American Muslims and American Jews enter into a relationship with one another. Generally speaking, I have found this to be true to a greater or lesser extent even for Muslims and Jews who do not have direct personal or familial ties to Palestine or Israel. Thus, this issue serves as a potent threshold for individuals when deciding whether or not to participate in such programming. Some, assuming that the conflict will be the subject of every program of Muslim-Jewish learning, imagine the programs are going to be aggressive sparring matches or fruitless, repetitive debates across irreconcilable political divides. For others, there is fear about entering the other's place of worship and suspicion regarding the genuineness of the partner group's desire to learn about its own community.

In my experience, most practitioners of interfaith dialogue agree that the wisest course for dealing with the conflict is to focus the initial, entry-level programming on the process of learning about one another's beliefs, practices, and personal commitments, thus building a strong foundation of relationship by celebrating similarities and respectfully exploring differences. Once this foundation is built, contentious issues can then be explored constructively without endangering relationships. At the same time, leaders must be both flexible and skillful enough to respond to the issue of the conflict if and when it arises spontaneously. Ultimately, it is my belief, and that of many participants, that intercommunal conflict is a key positive reason to engage in such encounters. Once relationships are strong enough to be sustained in the presence of conflicting views, Jewish-Muslim dialogue may hold its greatest promise.

I offer here three vignettes from my experience, all of which poignantly illustrate ways in which the Israeli-Palestinian conflict can impact programs of Muslim-Jewish relationship-building.

Encountering the Space of the "Other." A Jewish woman enters an Islamic Center, her first time in a mosque, to attend an Iftar meal (held each evening during Ramadan to break a practitioner's fast) sponsored by an established program of interfaith learning. At the door to the building's social hall she expresses gratitude for the opportunity to participate. The decorations in the hall include a large collection of national flags. This is part of the Center's effort to showcase and celebrate the unique cultures and heritages of its members—Muslims from Somalia, Ethiopia, the Middle East, South Asia, and Turkey, as well as African Americans. Hence the flags festooning the social hall represent a message of welcome and respect, inviting an intracommunal celebration of both the commonalities and differences among Muslims from many different parts of the world.

Within moments, the Jewish participant approaches me in distress. Upon entering the room, she had immediately scanned the many flags in the room and recognized that the Israeli flag was not displayed. "Why is the Israeli flag not included?" she asks painfully. Entering the Muslim space, she had instinctively surveyed the room to evaluate whether the space was "safe" for her as a Jew and lover of Israel. The absence of the Israeli flag confirmed her worst fear—that to step into a Muslim space is to enter a place that is anti-Israel. She cannot engage in the evening's program until this pain is addressed.

Engaging Contrasting Narratives. Leaders of the synagogue, church, and Islamic Center participating in the Interfaith Conversations Project have been working closely together for two years when the team meets to plan a program on justice in the three religious traditions. Following the template developed successfully in other programs, they decide that a leader from each community will offer brief comments on the subject of justice in his/her religious tradition, followed by facilitated small-group conversations among the participants. The team works to fine-tune the topic and attend to logistical details.

With a few minutes remaining in the meeting, our Muslim colleague quietly asks the rabbi slated to be the Jewish speaker how he imagines he would respond if someone from the audience asked him, "Given what you have said about the centrality of justice in the Jewish tradition, how do you understand Israel's treatment of the Palestinians?" I am stunned because I have heard this colleague on many occasions articulate the view that the purpose of our programs is not to explore geopolitical realities, but to learn about our religious commonalities and differences.

The emotional temperature of the room spikes. Jewish team members sit in anxious silence. Our Muslim colleague recognizes that his question has caused tension and immediately moves to allay fears, assuring his Jewish colleagues that he did not mean to suggest that the question would be raised in a hostile or adversarial way. He simply wants to suggest that the rabbi consider how he might respond to such a question. Seeing that his gentle words have not allayed the sense of fear in the room, our Muslim colleague turns to me and whispers, "Can you explain why my question made everyone so uncomfortable?"

Dialogue in Times of War. The planning team from the second scenario (given earlier) meets for its regularly scheduled meeting in January 2009, in the midst of Israel's war in Gaza.[3] As meetings are rotated among the host institutions, this particular meeting happens to take place at the Islamic Center. As we gather, all of us are aware that we are meeting as conflict rages in Gaza and Israel.

Greeting each other as warmly as ever, we agree that we should begin by checking in regarding our thoughts and feelings on the violence. Going around in a circle, each person has a chance to speak without interruption, sharing feelings of pain, outrage, fear, shame, and ambivalence. The sharing is honest, heartfelt, and connected. It is not an easy conversation. But at the end, it confirms what we all intuit: the time of external conflict makes our work more urgent and meaningful, our relationships with our colleagues are precious to us, and the connections to one another are unquestionably strong enough to hold the pain of sitting with deeply felt, divergent views. In fact, we feel closer to one another than ever before, more devoted to our shared work as a result.

On my way out of the building, members of the office staff of the school operated by the Islamic Center strike up a conversation with me, having recognized me as a rabbi involved in interfaith work. Some share that they are quietly pained about the war, aware of the number of children in their school with relatives in Gaza who are waiting in fear for news about their loved ones. Others are angry about Israel's conduct in particular. We talk about how the school is handling these challenges with their students. I do not seek to persuade them of the dominant Jewish perspective justifying the war. Rather we talk, I listen, and they have an experience of dialogue with a rabbi who can hear and hold their pain unflinchingly.

These three vignettes illustrate three different levels of impact that the Israeli-Palestinian conflict can have on programs of Jewish-Muslim learning and dialogue. The first is the threshold issue of whether or not feelings and perspectives regarding the conflict prevent Muslims and Jews from engaging with one another at all. This scenario is striking because, in the presence of international flags, the Jewish woman understood herself to have physical evidence to evaluate whether or not the Muslim space was a safe and appropriate place for her as a Jew and a Zionist. While this experience is generally navigated in more subtle, indirect ways, such a scenario poses the question of safety based on seemingly concrete evidence: Can I engage with "these" people without compromising who I am? Are these Jews/Muslims enemies of "my" people? Can I engage in relationship with them without betraying my convictions or my identity?

Members of both Muslim and Jewish communities commonly question the appropriateness of engaging with the "other." Jews sometimes begin by asking whether their potential Muslim partners believe in a two-state solution to the conflict, or renounce terror, or support charitable organizations connected to Hamas. Occasionally such individuals demand that the desired answers to these questions be supplied as a precondition for their participation. More frequently, such people stay away from these programs altogether, quietly (or publicly) judging its leaders as naïve and uninformed at best, or traitors to the community at worst.

Similarly, my Muslim colleagues report that some in their community feel uncomfortable entering a synagogue, while others feel too angry about what they understand to be Israeli injustice against the Palestinians to want to engage in any way with American Jews, whom they associate with the Israeli government. For example, I had been tentatively invited to speak at a "Palestinian Cultural Night" at an Islamic Center on the assumption that it would be good for members of the Muslim community to encounter a rabbi who had a compassionate understanding of the dominant Palestinian narrative of the conflict. But in the months following the Gaza war, Muslim leaders felt it best to postpone my appearance, since at that time they felt their community's emotions ran too high to experiment with such a challenging dialogue.

The second level of how the conflict impacts Muslim-Jewish engagement is the challenge of how to enter into dialogue about the conflict, even in the midst of programming that aims to focus on issues having nothing to do with Israel and Palestine. Many fear that topics that would otherwise be natural candidates for Jewish-Muslim programming (e.g., peace, justice, nonviolence, etc.) will trigger discussion of the conflict, which could then engender contentious and provocative comments painful enough to compromise relationships. (I have certainly experienced such difficult moments, such as when a charged question about Zionism was asked in the context of a community-wide interfaith series on "Peace and Violence in Religious Traditions.")

The second vignette, wherein the conflict made its way into what was intended to be a discussion of justice from religious perspectives, illustrates the fact that group leaders must be prepared to respond when the conflict unexpectedly makes its way into Muslim-Jewish programming. It was precisely because strong relationships had been carefully built in the course of pursuing Jewish-Muslim learning programs that the difficult issue could be dealt with when it arose. In fact, the Muslim colleague's question led to a remarkable follow-up conversation filled with learning and mutual respect, where we pondered the difference between the dominant Palestinian and Israeli narratives and the ways that they are understood by each of our communities. The encounter turned out to be fruitful, moving, and full of promise.

The third and deepest level of impact invites participants in Muslim-Jewish dialogue to hold both their own narrative and that of the "other" simultaneously, with respect and genuine desire for learning. This is most likely to occur as it did in the vignettes presented here, when skillful listening, strong relationships, and well-facilitated conversations produce deep learning about the "other's" perspective. In so doing, participants learn that the members of the other group are not a single, undifferentiated monolith. Generalizations begin to break down as members of the group come to be known as separate, unique human beings and canned, rhetorical stereotypes of the "other" are replaced with real, embodied, human information. They realize that members of the other group are different from one another, with different views, life experiences, and communication styles. Participants thus gain a body of potentially transformative experiences, displacing previously held prejudice and misinformation.

Such experiences are not only powerfully significant for those who participate in them, but the participants in such encounters begin to communicate differently, challenging ethnocentric and prejudicial attitudes within their own communities. Knowing members of the other group, one can no longer hear stereotyped rhetoric ("Muslims think X" or "Jews think Y") without picturing members of the group with whom one is in relationship. As I have frequently heard dialogue activists report, "When I hear a terrible news report about your group, I see your face." The group formerly seen as "the enemy" now includes people known and valued as conversation partners, even as friends.

There are many reasons to engage in encounter work, ranging from a desire to know one's neighbors to a need to live out one's theology of pluralism to a conviction that intercommunal coalitions serve as the best foundation for social justice and environmental work. As I have indicated, my own dedication to the work of Jewish-Muslim dialogue is grounded in the desire to reach the precise level of peace-building work discussed here. When conflict erupts among program participants or in the Middle East region itself, the "elephant in the room" is seen and named, allowing different perspectives to be respectfully explored. In such moments, there is commonly a palpable sense of gratitude, relief, and even awe that relationships can deepen in the course of exploring painfully divergent perspectives. These are moments of peace-building, which encourage hope in participants that such experiences are possible in the world at large as well as in personal relationships. Further, the hope exists that ever-deepening relationships among Muslims and Jews in North America may have ripple effects among friends and family members elsewhere in the Jewish and Muslim world.

Differences in Theological Approaches

I turn now to the second of the issues I wish to consider: a divide between contrasting theologies of revelation and different approaches to sacred texts in one's own religion. As I began my serious engagement in Jewish-

Muslim work, I felt thrilled by the opportunity to know Muslims and learn about Islam. I had a palpable sense that each hour spent together was an hour of building a more peaceful world. It soon became apparent that the Muslims I was meeting were traditionalists in their attitude toward the Qur'an, God, and the teachings and leaders of Islam. As such, I was preparing to invite Muslims who were theological traditionalists into dialogue with Jews who were theologically liberal. I began to see that this difference would likely represent a greater divide among the participants than the difference between their actual religions. Here are two episodes that elucidate this issue.

Criticizing One's Sacred Texts. A group of community members gathers to plan an interfaith Passover Seder, sponsored by a community interfaith network. The event's goal is to present an authentically Jewish Passover Seder, while also highlighting interfaith reflections on the Seder's themes of liberation and transformation. Progressive Jewish and Christian members of the lay planning team express painful discomfort at the violent dimensions of the Exodus story that are embellished and explored in the Passover Seder. I bring to the leadership meeting the suggestion that we focus the "Four Questions" section of the Seder on a single question: "How are we to understand the violent actions of God in the Exodus story?" Discussion ensues, yet without comment from our Muslim colleague, a professional with deep and broad dialogue experience. After some time, he expresses his growing discomfort with our critical attitude toward the story. "You are talking about criticizing your sacred text! I do not feel comfortable with this." The rabbi and the Methodist minister, both strong feminists and progressives, are taken aback.

Questioning God. A local synagogue and mosque partner for a weekend of sacred study. The imam and a number of Muslim community members come to the Conservative synagogue on Shabbat morning and speak to a packed room about Qur'anic verses describing the near-sacrifice of Abraham's son. This presentation is followed by responses from a rabbi and vibrant questions from synagogue members. The following day, the rabbis and a number of synagogue members go to the imam's weekly Qur'an class at the Islamic Center, where I speak on the Torah's narrative of this same event. I express my own deep and ambivalent relationship to this sacred text, including horror that God would even ask Abraham to sacrifice his beloved, long-awaited son. I portray this critical approach as common among contemporary Jews. In the lively discussion that ensues, a Muslim participant asks in a provocative tone what sort of religion could possibly allow us to question God.

Because Jewish tradition, even as practiced by the Orthodox, tolerates and even celebrates a kind of wrestling with God and creative reinterpretation of sacred texts,[4] some Jewish participants are puzzled and disturbed by such questions as posed by the Muslim participant.[5] For liberal-minded Jews, for whom Enlightenment values of pluralism and respect for difference are passionately held, the notion of a perfect religion is met with incredulity. Worse still, Jews may at times judge the attitude of their Muslim partners as fundamentalist. This perception subsequently has the potential to dovetail with political questions regarding radical Islam, even reinforcing stereotypes about Islam that the dialogue fundamentally aims to deconstruct.

By contrast, the Muslim dialogue partners may meet their theologically liberal Jews with negative judgments of their own. They may be confused or unnerved by their Jewish partners' apparent irreverence, silently wondering what kind of religion Judaism is if it fails to teach its adherents a deep respect for God. They may find themselves judging the Judaism they are encountering as theologically superficial, or simply fatally wounded by the much-celebrated Western Enlightenment.[6] This largely unspoken set of contrasting assumptions may impede understanding between the two groups.

This difference in theological perspectives parallels other imbalances in the Muslim-Jewish dialogue, magnifying its effect.[7] Since 9/11, for example, Muslims interested in dialogue often keenly feel the responsibility to dissuade Americans of stereotypes nourished by sensationalist news media. As such, even dialogue-minded Muslims may feel that they are on the defensive from the very beginning, making them even less likely to discuss the human limitations of their tradition and their community. Jewish dialogue participants, generally committed to learning about and supporting their Muslim partners, may find such perceived defensiveness frustrating.[8]

Learning in the Midst of Challenge

How are facilitators to work with these challenges, moving participants from stereotypes and judgments to mutual understanding and deepened connection? It is my assumption that interreligious learning moves forward through the following three stages.

Stage One

Entry-level programs of interfaith dialogue aim to bring people into the room together so that participants can experience the humanity of the "other" and the joy of connecting across intercommunal boundaries. This is the time for exploring ways in which religions, values, cultures, and life experiences are similar, ways in which the perceived "other" is more like "us" than we might have thought. While this may seem a minimal set of goals, it is no small thing in today's world. At this stage of work, generalizations and stereotypes begin to break down and personal relationships begin to develop. The "other" now has a name, a face, and a story. Members of each community begin to introduce a different view of the other into internal conversations within their own communities.

For some programs, especially residential ones, a few hours of ice-breaker exercises may suffice to meet the goals of this first level of engagement. In other cases, particularly in community settings in which attendance at events is sporadic and relationships grow much more gradually, this stage may last for many months. But at a certain point, participants can and should be led past the polite stage of focusing only on similarities, beyond sharing the proverbial "humus and pita," delighting in similarities between Arabic and Hebrew, and declaring that all religions are really the same at their core.

Stage Two

When relationships are strong enough to sustain themselves in the midst of conflict it is time to explore differences. At such a point leaders may find it wise to make use of the many structured facilitation techniques in the field to help create an atmosphere conducive to respectful listening. Well-designed structures and exercises can help participants experience compassionate and open-minded encounters even in the presence of conflicting perspectives. For example, in some situations all that is required is a reminder of the listening posture needed to support successful conversations. Alternatively, the simple structure of passing a "talking stick" and imposing a "no crosstalk" rule can sometimes allow each person to speak without fear of interruption and others are reminded to focus on attentive listening. In other situations, when conflict is more intense and threatening, it is wise to employ more elaborate communication guidelines and facilitative structures.[9] It takes courage to press beyond the initial good-hearted embrace of one another into areas of pain and challenge. Facilitators' skills can be essential in guiding participants through delicate conversations such that relationships will be strengthened rather than endangered. It might be important to point out to the group that this is the deeper work of peacemaking, a place where individuals continue to explore relationships even when listening is painful and frightening. Staying at the table in the midst of such encounters not only strengthens relationships, but also offers participants valuable training in everyday reconciliation that they can use elsewhere in their lives.

Stage Three

For some groups, stage two may stretch participants' capacities to their limit. For others, there is a still higher goal. Whereas the work of the first stage is to explore commonalities (i.e., ways in which "the other is like me"), and the second stage explores areas of difference (i.e., ways in which "the other is different from me"), there is a third possibility. Stage three is when one opens oneself up to being changed by the encounter with the "other." In the case of interreligious difference, this is "leaving room for holy envy,"[10] allowing oneself to longingly admire an area of emphasis in another religion that is underdeveloped in one's own, or a way in which an image, ritual, or concept of the "other" can lead one to experience one's own religious life more deeply. In the case of the Israeli-Palestinian dimension of Jewish-Muslim dialogue, this is the stage of reaching an empathic understanding of the other side's narrative, even to the point of transforming one's own perspective on the conflict to incorporate multiple truths. As a friend of mine imagines it, one learns the difficult skill of watching the action on both screens of a split-screen broadcast at the same time. In the case of religious difference, the sense of "we" or collective religious identity expands beyond the confines of one's own group to include many other people of faith and those who profess no faith.

Dialogue should not be a polemic or debate, and so does not necessarily require a change of opinion. Yet dialogue at the deepest level does imply an openness to being changed by the experience, a willingness to learn about oneself and one's own tradition, culture, and perspective in new ways by virtue of encountering the "other." To put it another way, stage three is when we think about our own traditions and perspectives in the presence of the "other."[11] It requires both courage and humility—grounding in one's own religious perspective and radical respect for diversity—to share one's own doubts and struggles in the presence of the "other," acknowledging that the "other" may embody parts of the truth that one's own community lacks. In such honest conversations, people can learn things they could not learn in any other way. They stretch their identities beyond that of their immediate group to a sense of global citizenship, opening themselves up to learn a broader spectrum of truth than any one group can possess on its own.

Conclusion

In sum, the two issues I have named can certainly be overcome in the course of Muslim-Jewish encounter. In fact, when these issues arise and are explored openly and respectfully, the educational impact of this work becomes magnified. Facilitating new understandings between American Jews and American Muslims about these complex issues is a *mitzvah*, holy work that may well contribute to the cause of peace.

In closing, I am reminded of the biblical tale of conflict in the original Abrahamic family. Sarah and Hagar, the mothers of Isaac and Ishmael, respectively, rather than bonding together as women in a patriarchal household, fall prey to mutual envy. Hagar is even banished. Jewish biblical commentators tell us that although Abraham's sons, Isaac and Ishmael, played together as children, in later years they became enemies. Abraham cultivates intimacy with God but tolerates the breakdown of his family. But strikingly, when Abraham dies, the biblical text tells us laconically that Isaac and Ishmael come together to bury their father. How are we to imagine this final encounter between Isaac and Ishmael, after years of separation and alienation? Did the brothers meet in hushed silence, sharing their grief but seething with old resentment? Did they work shoulder to shoulder burying their father, pretending that nothing separated them? Did they sit down after the burial and wrestle through old issues, becoming family again? Or somehow, in death, did the past melt away, leaving only loving connection? All those who labor in the field of Muslim-Jewish relations invest much time and passionate energy in the hope of fostering real reconciliation between tragically estranged members of an ancient family. Such work does not come easily. But it is the only way to peace.

Notes

1. Consider, e.g., the recent conference, "A Time for Recommitment: Jewish–Christian Dialogue Seventy Years After War and *Sho'ah*," sponsored by the International Conference of Christians and Jews in Berlin in July 2009.
2. I generally describe my work as "interfaith" or "interreligious" dialogue, encounter, or learning because I work as a rabbi with other religious leaders in the context of religiously based institutions. In this essay, while I reflect on the presence of nonreligious, intergroup, or intercommunal elements in the interfaith conversation, the interreligious context is primary in my work. I also use the terms "interfaith" and "interreligious" interchangeably.
3. Or, as it is commonly known among Jewish Israelis, "Operation Cast Lead."
4. As explicitly depicted in the Torah, biblical figures from Abraham on question and argue with God. Further, traditional rabbinic rules of interpretation allow for significant freedom in the process of textual exploration, even when determining legal rulings. See, e.g., Babylonian Talmud, Baba Metzia 59b.
5. This dynamic is not exclusive to Jewish-Muslim dialogue, of course. I recently attended a session of interfaith dialogue in which a Catholic presenter refused to acknowledge widely held concerns about church officials' recently stepping back from the commitment to interfaith respect and dialogue enshrined in *Nostra Aetate*. When participants were unable to pierce the presenter's defensiveness during the discussion time, they left the session deeply frustrated.
6. Many Muslims, especially traditionalists, may view the European Enlightenment tradition with suspicion, and for good reason, since the Enlightenment came to the Muslim world in the context of Western colonialism.
7. For the most part, Jewish participants in American-based dialogue programs are long settled in the United States, frequently three–four generations removed from the immigrant experience, a time when many Jews struggled for acceptance in America. By contrast, the Muslims in the dialogue are frequently new immigrants. Even those who are middle-class professionals are relative newcomers to the United States, seeking to acclimate to American culture with their religion and traditions intact.
8. There are certainly groups where significant numbers of Orthodox Jews participate in interfaith dialogue, bringing a theological perspective more similar to that of traditional Muslims. Several Orthodox rabbis, both in the United States and in Israel, are prominent international leaders of such Jewish-Muslim dialogue efforts. Consider, e.g., Rabbis David Rosen, Michael Melchior, and Irving "Yitz" Greenberg, to name but a few. In addition, in some communities Muslim dialogue participants have more liberal attitudes, whether grounded in their Islamic training or in their experience of the changing nature of Islam in America. Still, anecdotal evidence suggests that, in the current reality, my experience of theological mismatch between Muslim and Jewish dialogue partners is not unique. Further study needs to be conducted in order to verify this hypothesis.

CHAPTER FOUR

The Khalil Gibran International Academy—Lessons Learned?

Debbie Almontaser

Introduction

Muslim, Arab, and Jewish relations in the United States have played out in dynamic ways throughout the last decade. As an educator I have committed myself to building relationships between these communities in New York City. This chapter outlines my personal experience at the center of one of the most intense recent flashpoints in these relations, the founding of the Khalil Gibran International Academy (KGIA). This is my first attempt to put down, in a focused way, my thoughts about the lessons I learned from the episode. As such, it is meant as a personal reflection rather than a rigorous academic article or political polemic. Although the KGIA situation included many different players, here I am writing specifically about my relationships with the Jewish community. This piece does not explore the relationship that the KGIA affair had to the larger Arab and Muslim communities, let alone some of the pedagogical and other educational issues that played out during this process.

Healing through Dialogue

I began my bridge-building work as the first American Muslim of Arab heritage to participate in the "Dialogue Project," an organization established in Brooklyn in 2001 to create a space for constructive discussions for Muslims, Jews, and other Americans wanting to overcome divisions created by the Israeli-Palestinian conflict. As an avid supporter of dialogue and healing through storytelling, I began to recruit members from the Arab and Muslim communities to join the group. Slowly, the Dialogue Project gained its footing to become an established organization; I was privileged to serve as a member of the board of directors for its first five years.

Just a few months after the organization was founded, the country was profoundly tested by the tragedy of the 9/11 attacks. Through my work with the Dialogue Project I had already formed numerous relationships with members of the Jewish and Christian communities, alliances that were quickly strengthened in the collective trauma that followed the attacks. In response to the backlash, detentions, and deportations, I soon found myself speaking about Islam, Muslims, and Arabs at synagogues and churches across the country. I also began to organize interfaith and cross-cultural education events and know-your-rights trainings with the help of clergy, the Christian Children's Fund, and organizations such as Jews for Racial and Economic Justice (JFREJ).

Some of these activities became annual events, allowing me to work alongside rabbis, ministers, and imams who were collaborating to bring our communities together throughout New York City by sharing rituals, traditions, and what our faiths taught about peace and justice. One example was a Ramadan and Yom Kippur break-fast dinner jointly organized with members of B'nai Jeshurun Synagogue and The Church of St. Paul and St. Andrews, which has become an annual interfaith dinner. Such experiences showed us we had much in common.

I am especially proud of the Children of Abraham Peace Walk, which I cofounded with Rabbi Ellen Lippman of Temple Kolut Chayeinu in 2003. The impetus for this event was a sermon that Rabbi Lippman and I copresented to a synagogue audience of well over five hundred people on Rosh Hashanah, the Jewish new year. In our joint sermon, Rabbi Lippman and I promised one another to find ways to continue our one-on-one dialogues within both of our communities. We also promised not to let the Israeli–Palestinian conflict stifle our partnership. At the sermon's end, the congregation responded enthusiastically. The Children of Abraham Peace Walk is now in its seventh year. Since its founding, Rabbi Lippman and I have regularly checked in with each other when violence has erupted in the Middle East, sharing our pain, exchanging information, and reaffirming our commitment to this bridge-building work.

During this same time, I also engaged in work focused on hate crimes and bias incidents with various mainstream Jewish organizations. For example, in Brooklyn, we created a coalition called We Are All Brooklyn (WAAB), composed of over thirty organizations working together to educate and train immigrant communities on reporting bias incidents and other rights violations. As a result of my work with WAAB, the Jewish Community Relations Council (JCRC) invited me to sit on the board of Youth Bridge, an organization focusing on youth leadership. I also worked closely with Mayor Michael Bloomberg's office on bias and hate crime incidents, as well as building bridges between his office and the Arab and Muslim communities. This work earned me citywide recognition and gave me the opportunity to become a Revson Fellow at Columbia University.

The Khalil Gibran International Academy

As I continued this work, I began to explore ways to more fully incorporate my bridge-building activities into my "daytime" professional vocation at the New York City Department of Education (DOE). In 2005, I led an informal feasibility study, introducing community leaders, politicians, and multifaith clergy to the concept of a dual-language English-Arabic public school that could give students from different communities the background and critical-thinking skills to become leaders in building bridges domestically and globally. This school was intended to develop global citizens through a rigorous academic program that offered students the opportunity to become fluent in Arabic while preparing them to become experts on the "Arab world."

The school's concept received broad support from many communities, including Jewish leaders such as Rabbis Roly Matalon of B'nai Jeshurun and Bob Kaplan of JCRC. With such support, I began the search for a partnering agency and design team to create the first dual-language English-Arabic public school in the United States, ultimately partnering with New Visions for Public Schools, which was directed to me by the mayor's office and the DOE. Two years later, in February of 2007, KGIA was approved by the DOE and was publicly announced in the *New York Times*. I became its founding principal; my dream seemed to be on the verge of coming to fruition.

The Rise and Fall of KGIA: DOE Caves in to Communal Pressure

For a moment we reveled in KGIA's approval from the DOE and the mayor's office. Unfortunately, a few days later a number of right-wing-affiliated, neoconservative bloggers began to editorialize in opposition to the school in general and to me specifically, as its founder. Leading the charge were numerous individuals who lived outside New York City, such as Daniel Pipes, the controversial blogger and noted critic of Islam, who seemed to hold nothing back. On the local front the opposition was led by an organization called Stop the Madrassa Coalition (STM), led by, among others, Jeffery S. Wiesenfeld, a board member of JCRC and of the City University of New York. For seven months these people relentlessly attacked KGIA as a "jihad school," and me personally as an "Islamist" and a "9/11 denier" who had used my positions in the DOE to "promote Islamic propagation projects under the guise of educational programs."[1]

In response to these attacks, I formed an advisory council for KGIA comprised of clergy and community leaders, later called the Friends of KGIA. On numerous occasions New York City rabbis, imams, and ministers defended KGIA and my leadership of it as did other members of the Christian, Arab, Muslim, and Jewish communities. One voice that consistently rang loudly from the progressive Jewish community was that of Rabbi Andy Backman of Congregation Beth Elohim. Also, in May 2007, the Anti-Defamation League's (ADL) New York City chapter president Joel Levy wrote a letter to the *New York Sun* in support of the school.[2] While the ADL's letter of support calmed the waters momentarily in some Jewish quarters, the attacks continued throughout the summer.

The assaults reached a climax in August of the same year, when a reporter from the *New York Post,* Rupert Murdoch's New York City tabloid, wrote an article that linked me to a T-shirt being sold at an Arab Heritage park festival bearing the words "Intifada NYC."[3] The supposed connection was that this T-shirt was produced by Arab Women Active in the Arts and the Media (AWAAM), an organization working with Arab girls that leased space from an organization upon whose board I sat.

When an STM member found out about the T-shirt, STM sent out a press release calling on DOE chancellor Joel Klein to fire me for my alleged connection to AWAAM. The *Post* reporter was insistent on interviewing me after receiving the press release. I was apprehensive of speaking about an issue that had no direct relationship to KGIA or my role as principal. I was especially reluctant given the *Post*'s prior hostile reporting on issues concerning Arabs and Muslims. However, the DOE insisted that I do the interview.

A DOE press person joined me on the entire phone interview, during which time I firmly stated that the T-shirt had nothing to do with KGIA or with me. At the end of the interview, the reporter asked me for the Arabic root of the word "intifada." Though I was concerned that this was a setup, I was also worried that if I declined to answer the question the reporter would claim that I had "refused" to do so, as had happened previously in an interview with the equally hostile *New York Sun*. Wearing my "teacher hat," I responded that the root word in Arabic means "shake off." I added that over time this word evolved to mean "uprising," and had developed a negative connotation for many due to its connection to the Israeli-Palestinian conflict. Further stating that the word holds different meanings for different people, I concluded by saying that I condemn violence in all shapes and forms. One of the reporter's last "questions" was a statement that the young women selling the "Intifada NYC" T-shirts were planning to engage in a Gaza-style uprising. I responded that I didn't believe these inner-city girls were going to engage in any violence, adding that AWAAM's goal is to empower girls to confront female exploitation caused by stereotypes found in the media.

The following day's *Post* headline read "Principal Revolting." I was portrayed as minimizing the historical context of the Intifada. The reporter had distorted and decontextualized my words. In the crescendo of attacks that followed, I was branded a violent extremist who aimed to establish a radical *madrassa* in the heart of Brooklyn. A number of conservative pundits and politicians called for my resignation. On STM's website, NYC assemblyman Dov Hikind announced a protest that was planned

outside DOE headquarters. He was quoted as stating, "I have personally spoken with scores of New Yorkers who are very concerned about
where a school like this would go. They legitimately want to know if
school projects would laud Hezbollah leader [Sheikh Hassan] Nasrallah?
Would Israel's Independence Day be treated as Yawm al-Nakba, a cat-
astrophic anniversary?"[4] In reality, KGIA's team and faculty had, from
the very beginning, been quite clear that when addressing different conflicts in the world, including Israel and Palestine, our intention was to
give students access to multiple perspectives, helping them develop the
critical-thinking skills needed to analyze issues while developing their
own informed opinions.

By week's end, the DOE charged Robert Hughes, president of New
Visions for Public Schools, with the task of forcing me out of my position as KGIA principal, giving me the ultimatum that "it's either you
[go] or the school will not open." Refusing to accept this directive from
a partner, I demanded to speak to DOE's Chancellor Klein. In his place, I
met with Deputy Mayor Dennis Walcott, who stated that his instructions
were coming directly from the mayor. He told me that the mayor was no
longer interested in going forward with the school if I remained principal.
I was told to submit my resignation letter by 8 a.m. the following day in
order to give the mayor enough time to prepare his announcement of my
resignation on his radio show.

"In the End, we will remember not the words of our enemies, but the silence of our friends"
—Dr. Martin Luther King, Jr.

In the days after my resignation, I received calls, e-mails, and letters from
individuals within the Jewish community offering support and apologies,
as well as from members of other communities. I heard from organizations such as JFREJ, who had been supportive from the beginning, and
leaders such as Rabbi Michael Paley, affiliated with the UJA-Federation
of New York, who was quoted in the *Jewish Week* only a few days after my
forced resignation, characterizing what happened to me as a "high-tech
lynching."[5] Rabbis Ellen Lippman and Roly Matalon and their congregations were outspokenly supportive, as was Rabbi Michael Feinberg of the
Greater New York Labor-Religion Coalition. Longtime Jewish community activist and cofounder of JFREJ Donna Nevel was, and continues to
be, an extraordinary source of support.

However, the silence from mainstream Jewish organizations was deaf-
ening; in the days following my resignation, it became even more so.
Within weeks, as chronicled in the *Jewish Daily Forward*,[6] Rabbi Paley
was instructed by the UJA Federation to refrain from publicly speaking
in my defense. That was followed by ADL president Abraham Foxman's
public statement that he no longer supported my leadership of KGIA.[7] I

was deeply pained that colleagues at institutions such as JCRC chose to stand on the sidelines rather than refute the erroneous charges made about me. In fact, I was shocked that JCRC allowed a board member to attack me without comment, especially in light of my long-standing working relationship with the organization.

Colleagues at these normative Jewish institutions were people with whom I had shared grief when members of our respective families had died. They knew me and they knew that the attacks were baseless and, equally seriously, that they fomented anti-Muslim and anti-Arab hatred. Those members of the Jewish community who chose to stand on the sidelines despite the slanderous attacks against me, thinking that by not taking a position on my forced resignation they could remain "neutral," chose a position by not choosing.[8] I was devastated that individuals who I thought were my friends—professionally and personally—turned their backs on me at an unbearable time.

In the weeks following my forced resignation from KGIA, relations among the Muslim, Arab, and Jewish institutions of New York City grew intense. When Muslim and Arab institutional and individual leaders brought up the injustice of my ousting, in hopes of working together to form a united response, many Jewish institutional leaders refused to engage with them. Sadly, it appeared that because I was being portrayed as "anti-Israel," which therefore made me an "unacceptable" partner, there was no constructive space to discuss what happened to me and KGIA with mainstream Jewish organizations. Years of bridge-building were instantaneously negated.

Fortunately, after my forced resignation I saw new bridges being built among members of the Jewish, Arab, Muslim, and other communities based on shared principles and mutual respect. Grassroots leaders, activists, educators, and New York City residents demanded answers from Mayor Bloomberg and the DOE. In less than two weeks, a coalition called Communities in Support of KGIA (CIS-KGIA) was established. Composed of over forty organizations, it publicly declared support for the vision of the school, spoke out against anti-Arab and anti-Muslim racism, and fought for justice in the public education system. The CIS-KGIA steering committee was composed of AWAAM, Brooklyn for Peace, Center for Immigrant Families, Greater New York Labor-Religion Coalition, JFREJ, and the Muslim Consultative Network. Coalition leaders included Elly Bulkin, Adem Carroll, Mona El-Dahry, Michael Feinberg, Carol Horwitz, Donna Nevel, and Ray Wofsy.

On August 20, 2007, this coalition organized an amazingly diverse demonstration. Individuals from multiethnic, multiracial, and multireligious communities coalesced in front of the DOE. Never in my wildest dreams did I imagine being at the center of a social justice issue with so many supporters speaking out for my reinstatement as principal of KGIA. In the sea of people there were demonstrators who held such signs as "Jewish UFT-er for Debbie Almontaser." I was deeply touched by the passion and dedication to KGIA's mission. This demonstration reaffirmed my commitment and deepened my conviction to continue strengthening relations and building bridges of understanding between Muslims, Arabs, and Jews.

CIS-KGIA quickly developed a website, www.kgia.wordpress.com. It then initiated a sophisticated organizing campaign to hold the mayor, the DOE, and Randi Weingarten—then president of the United Federation of Teachers (UFT), who attacked me in the *Post*—accountable for capitulating to a campaign steeped in anti-Arab and anti-Muslim racism. They demanded my reinstatement. Strategies included rallies, petitions, press conferences, media outreach, educational forums, and engagements with a broad array of political leaders, community members, and academics.

As we developed a legal case to challenge my forced resignation, this unified political voice called out for justice. My legal team was led by longtime civil rights attorney Alan Levine, a social justice activist who was also a founding member of JFREJ. CIS-KGIA remained steadfast at every turn for four years, until we won the determination from the Federal Equal Employment Opportunities Commission (EEOC) that my forced resignation was discriminatory on account of my "race, religion and national origin" and that the DOE had "succumbed to the very bias that creation of the school was intended to dispel." The EEOC declared that I "had no connection whatever" with the T-shirts and that "a small segment of the public succeeded in imposing its prejudices on DOE as an employer."[9] Such a movement shows that we can stand up to anything and anyone if we are united under the umbrella of social justice and respect for all.

KGIA and the Israeli-Palestinian Conflict

It was clear that the lack of support I received from mainstream Jewish organizations was a result of their unwillingness—in the name of support for Israel—to confront those who attacked me, no matter how unjustified and unprincipled the attacks. Unfortunately, I believe that this critical failure in courage and commitment has left me little room to address the underlying issues that continue to impact the Muslim, Arab, and Jewish communities in the United States. In this sense alone, we have all truly lost an important opportunity.

On the other hand, I think that the majority of those from the Jewish community who publicly supported me are also individuals and organizations who have engaged openly in the search for a just solution to the Israeli-Palestinian conflict. They have not made their litmus test of potential partnerships with others dependent on support for Israeli government policies, deciding accordingly which Arabs or Muslims are therefore considered "safe." I do not think this is a mere coincidence.

On a personal level, at this time I find it viable only to participate in collaborative activities with Jewish (and other) organizations in settings where there is an acknowledgment that people are coming to the table with diverse viewpoints on the Middle East, that Israeli-Palestinian human rights and governance issues are legitimate and important topics for discussion, and that racists and bigots in all communities must be challenged. It is also essential, from the very beginning, for the power dynamics and inequalities between the groups to be openly discussed and acknowledged, and to recognize that communities must come together intentionally as equals. Without these values, as well as this courage and commitment, dialogue and cooperation will be limited. Ultimately such superficial activities have little value.

An example of this unequal treatment is illustrated by the contrast between what happened with KGIA and the experiences of the burgeoning "Hebrew charter school" movement. The Hebrew Language Academy Charter School (HLA), founded in 2009 in Brooklyn, whose mission is "to provide a nurturing yet rigorous dual language program committed to fostering academic excellence and a high degree of Hebrew language proficiency," has an explicit Hebrew-language component, comparable to KGIA's Arabic-language component.[10] HLA's board chair, Sara Berman, recently said that learning about Israeli culture through Hebrew-language instruction is no different from learning about Bastille Day and baguettes in French class. "This is a dual-language school, contextualized by a rich culture... To say that you can't learn about what it is like to go to a shuk in Jerusalem because it's too complicated or tied to religion or politics, that's just not the case."[11] Yet, this is the precise argument that was made against KGIA—that the very teaching of Arabic was inherently too religious and too political. Much more can be said on this topic. Perhaps what is most noteworthy here is not only that HLA was started in Brooklyn just a short while after I was removed as KGIA's principal, but that there has not been any ruckus surrounding its founding.

Conclusion

I have drawn both personal and political lessons from my deepened understanding of the importance of mutual respect, courage, commitment, and openness to genuine intercommunal dialogue. I have also drawn lessons from the intensely searing experience of being unjustly attacked, leading me to discover who was and was not my true friend and ally. When I think about the KGIA saga, and the larger, macro situation in Israel-Palestine, I feel a great deal of pain and grief. But I also take pride in my efforts and the efforts of many friends and colleagues—Muslims, Arabs, Jews, Christians, and others—who have worked together to educate, to build bridges, and to defend human rights. I hope and pray that in our lifetime the Israeli-Palestinian conflict will be resolved in a way that furthers peace and justice for all peoples, and that Muslim, Arab, and Jewish communities in New York will be able to engage in genuine intercommunal conversation and collaboration in the days ahead.

Notes

I want to take this opportunity to thank my husband and children for their unconditional support over the last six years—they are my inspiration and hope. I also want to thank the following people: my lead counsel, Alan Levine, and his entire legal team for their incredible representation; Donna Nevel for her political insights, emotional support, and availability night and day, which helped me survive this ordeal; the CIS-KGIA Coalition members for their tireless efforts to set the record straight; and last, Jon Moscow and Elly Bulkin for their amazing editing skills.

1. Militantislammonitor.org, "New York Set to Open Khalil Gibran 'Jihad' School—Connected to Saudi Funded ADC—Principal Won CAIR Award," retrieved July 29, 2010.
2. www.adl.org/media_watch/newspapers/20070507-NYSun.htm, retrieved July 30, 2010.
3. Chuck Bennett and Anna Winter, "City Principal is 'Revolting,' Ties to 'Intifada NYC' Shirts," *New York Post* (August 6, 2007), www.nypost.com/p/news/regional/item_UerzwvF7fcSQY8YOP1ln4K, retrieved July 31, 2010.
4. stopthemadrassa.wordpress.com/2007/08/page/4/, retrieved July 31, 2010.
5. Larry Cohler-Esses, "Jewish Shootout Over Arab School," *Jewish Week* (August 17, 2007), www.thejewishweek.com/features/jewish_shootout_over_arab_school, retrieved July 31, 2010.
6. Nathan Guttman, "JCPA Approves Effort to Build Dialogue with Muslim Groups" (March 13, 2009), www.forward.com/articles/103606/, retrieved July, 30, 2010.
7. Cohler-Esses, "Jewish Shootout Over Arab School."
8. As it says in the Babylonian Talmud, considered a sacred text by many in the Jewish community, *shtikah k'hoda'ah*, or "silence is tantamount to consent" (BT Yevamot 87a). This citation was introduced to me by Aaron Hahn Tapper.
9. Andrea Elliott, "Federal Panel Finds Bias in Ouster of Principal," *New York Times* (March 12, 2010), www.nytimes.com/2010/03/13/nyregion/13principal.html, retrieved July 31, 2010.
10. www.hlacharterschool.org/About_HLA/index.php, retrieved June 30, 2010.
11. Jennifer Medina, "Success and Scrutiny at Hebrew Charter School," *New York Times* (June 24, 2010), www.nytimes.com/2010/06/25/nyregion/25hebrew.html, retrieved July 31, 2010.

PART II

Identity Formation: Muslims, Jews, and the American Experience

CHAPTER FIVE

Evolving from Muslims in America to American Muslims: A Shared Trajectory with the American Jewish Community

IMAM FEISAL ABDUL RAUF

Jewish–Muslim Partnerships in the United States: Historical Precedent and Contemporary Need

In 2004, I wrote a book that expressed the following notion: "The crucial need of our day is to find ways to accelerate the process whereby American Muslims will be able to establish their Islamic identity not apart from or in spite of their American identity, but precisely in and through it."[1] Any student of American immigrant history recognizes that the path to integration in the United States has always been painfully difficult. As a result, it is important that as Muslims struggle to establish themselves within the context of the broader American society,[2] they learn successful lessons from the American Jewish community's historical integration, which will likewise open a space for meaningful partnership between these two communities. As American Muslims forge such relationships, I am convinced that we can *both* solidify Muslims' presence within the American mainstream and initiate a fresh chapter in global Jewish–Muslim relations, one that echoes the best chapters of the historical reality of Jewish–Muslim harmony.

The Abrahamic Ethic: A Foundation for Partnership

Though focused on issues of immigration and integration within a specific American context, Jewish-Muslim partnerships should be built upon the foundation of what I call the "Abrahamic Ethic,"[3] named after the figure revered by Jews, Christians, and Muslims alike. This ethic is the necessary outcome of the two major commandments that underscore the Abrahamic religions: First, to love God with all our hearts, minds, souls. And second, to love each other as we do ourselves. Once we move the love for our brother and sister to the larger context of brotherhood, sisterhood, and humanity, we are able to move away from the divisive structures we impose against others. The Abrahamic Ethic destroys those barriers that keep us from loving one another as God has intended. Thus, the essence of the Abrahamic Ethic is the understanding that all human beings stem from the same ancestors, making all of humankind innately equal.

The monotheism that Abraham taught was not only *theologically* radical in that it decried polytheism as false, but it was also *socially* radical. This revolutionary idea implies two significant things about humankind. First, it means that *all humans are equal*, simply because we are born of one man and one woman.[4] In other words, showing preference for one human over another on the basis of accidents of birth such as skin color, caste or class structure, tribal or family belonging, or gender is unjust and therefore has no place within a proper *human* worldview. Second, because we all have equal human status and have been given free will by God, we all have certain inalienable liberties, the most significant being the choice to accept or reject the very Creator that brought us into existence. According to the Muslim tradition, as stated in the Qur'an, God created humans with this critical element of free will.[5] Human free will, the liberty to make individual choices—and individual mistakes—is essential to human dignity. Only if humans have free will can we be held individually accountable for our choices and actions. But individuals can and do freely exercise their will in ways that also sow inequality and limit the liberties of others, thus freely choosing to engage in unjust and tyrannical behavior. Jews, Christians, and Muslims interpret strict sensibilities of right and wrong behavior from this ethos, embodied in a particularly strong sense of social justice.

The oneness of God and the oneness of humankind define the Abrahamic Ethic. This code of morality constitutes the essential core of Abrahamic religions, which led to later iterations and reformations of the Abrahamic religions we know today as Judaism, Christianity, and Islam. The Abrahamic Ethic requires that each society allows its individual members the freedoms appropriate to human dignity, such as the freedom to stand before God and exercise individual choices without coercion. This ethic speaks not only to theology—that is, that our ideas about God should be built upon the idea of God's oneness, transcendence, and ineffability—but also to issues of sociology and politics, about how society should be structured on the basis of human equality, human liberty, and social justice.

It is this Abrahamic idea upon which the history of Jewish-Muslim harmony has rested and the United States was developed. The American Declaration of Independence reads, "We hold these truths to be self-evident, that all men are created equal, and endowed by the Creator with certain inalienable rights," thereby acknowledging both the existence of a single God and the equality of humankind. The American social contract and existential worldview incorporates the principles of the Abrahamic Ethic. It is this same ethic, therefore, that forms the basis upon which American Muslims can ground their collaboration not only with American Jews but with Americans from all religious denominations.

A Common Path to Integration for American Jews and American Muslims

American Muslims currently face difficult hurdles on their journey toward integration, similar to what their Jewish (and Catholic) predecessors experienced approximately a century ago.[6] Like the American Jew of the early twentieth century, and to some extent today, the American Muslim is often viewed with suspicion; his patriotism and commitment to American values are habitually questioned. In reaction, some Muslim and non-Muslim leaders have attempted to separate their "Muslim-ness" from their "American-ness," rendering an increased interpretation for one identity to be a direct threat to the other. Yet despite these and other impediments, similar to the history of American Jews, Muslims in the United States are fostering a burgeoning American Muslim culture and identity, drawing from the diversity of its immigrant and African American backgrounds.

In other words, most American Muslims are unaware that they are currently in the midst of a transformation of *sociological*, not *religious*, means, a process that is repeating the experience of previous American immigrant populations, those who came to the United States prior to the last three decades. For this reason, it behooves Muslim leaders to study these other American immigrant narratives if for no other reasons than to better predict what American Muslims' future might look like, and to expedite the process of integration to the degree that they can. Likewise, blended with lessons gleaned from Islamic history in other lands and times, American Muslims should learn from their earlier non-American experiences to help them more rapidly navigate the struggles, diversity of opinions, moments of deep despair, and enormous challenges along the road to societal integration into a non-Muslim-majority country.

Migrating Religious Communities: How a Religious Community Becomes Native

Though the American Jewish community is not without struggle even to this day, American Muslims regard the Jewish community as having reached an advanced stage of assimilation, acceptance, and integration into American society, especially when compared to Jews' first experiences in this country. This said, with help from and collaboration with American Jews the American Muslim community can move this process forward. For starters, neither Judaism nor Islam was founded as an "American" religion. Likewise, though Christianity did not initially emerge from the Roman community, after Emperor Constantine I made this new religious tradition the official religion of the Roman Empire in the fourth century CE, Romans began to consider Christianity a *Roman*—not a Palestinian or Greek—religion. Analogously, when American communities see their respective religious traditions as *American*, this implicitly means that they have arrived at a major milestone in the "Americanization" of their religion, leading to a fuller level of integration of their community into the larger American milieu.

By the "Americanization" or "nativization" of a religion, I mean to convey that every religion is revealed in a particular society with a distinct set of legal, social, and institutional norms. As a religious community migrates from one society to another, from one land to another, the religion undergoes a transformative "fitting in" within a broader context, one that includes various histories, cultures, and traditions from the dominant "other." Though a religion's theological core commonly remains the same, through this process its sociological edges become trimmed, often shedding as the religion's adherents delineate cultural expressions from the religion's foundation. For example, when Judaism spread from Judea-Samaria to other places in the Near East, and later Europe, it took on different cultural forms in each new society, a process some have called "cross-fertilization."[7] Judaism became Yemeni or French, Indian or Ethiopian. Likewise, as Christianity expanded out from Roman-controlled Palestine, newly established churches adopted local cultural expressions and institutions of their non-Christian neighbors. Thus, the Coptic Church was formed in Egypt as *both* Christian and Egyptian, the Greek Orthodox Church in Greece as *both* Christian and Greek, the Anglican Church in England as *both* Christian and English, and the Baptist Church in the United States as *both* Christian and American. Each religious tradition integrates itself into its new "home," simultaneously maintaining core beliefs while also establishing new forms of culture. This has happened with all religions. Islam is no exception.

When Islam swelled from its original source in the Arabian Peninsula to ancient and wholly disparate civilizations around the globe, Muslims restated the religion's core principles in such contexts as the Byzantine Empire, Egypt, Persia, South and South East Asia, sub-Saharan Africa, and beyond. Indeed we can acknowledge shades of difference between Egyptian Islam and Senegalese Islam, between Turkish Islam and Iranian Islam, between Indo-Pakistani Islam and Malay or Indonesian Islam—not in the essential theology but through the various sociological expressions, laws, customs, and religious institutions that flowed from the preexisting norms of each society through the new Muslim communal incarnation.

Cultural Assimilation and the Role of Interlocutors: Can Islam Be Indigenized?

How are those that carry a religion to a new place—in contemporary vernacular, better known as immigrants—able to acculturate their religion and their communities? How can they restate their religious customs, jurisprudence, and institutional forms from the "old country" to their new home? And how, in particular, do religious communities become "Americanized"?

In the case of the American Jewish community, after migrating to the United States (primarily from Europe and Russia), they quickly coalesced around ethnic-cultural enclaves of German Jews, Russian Jews, and Polish Jews. Later on they reconceptualized themselves more broadly either as Ashkenazi or Sephardic (generally speaking), particularly when Sephardic Jews began emigrating to America in the mid-twentieth century, each specific community with its own synagogues.[8] (The same differentiation happened with Polish Catholic churches, Italian Catholic churches, and Irish Catholic churches.) Like many American Muslim communities today, these American Jews initially clung to their particular cultural and religious identities before choosing to shed aspects of these labels. Instead of adopting those American practices that were consistent with their religion, some Jews maintained the "old world" form of their practice with their *particular* immigrant culture, preserving previous traditions despite the fact that they clashed with the values of their new American society. This recreation of a community's identity continues to exist as a barrier to fuller societal integration, something that all American religious immigrant communities have experienced.

This challenge is most commonly solved through interlocutors who learn to mediate between their immigrant religious tradition and the new culture. These interlocutors—both individuals and organizations—engage in a process of creative discernment and contextual restatement that takes place in every arena: dress, architecture, music, jurisprudence, and the relationship between its faith community and the state.

While ethical norms in terms of religious mandates to love both God and one's neighbor are shared between American Muslims and American Jews and Christians—some form of these commandments is common to all three of these religions—the problem lies in discerning the core of a religious tradition's ethics, how to separate a community from its "old world" societal packaging while repackaging itself into the new. This requires knowledge of the proper limits and applications of context, as well as the boundary between a religion's core and the larger societal context. It points to the need for acute intellectual and religious leadership to emerge from the community, a group of individuals who must understand and acknowledge both the core aspects of the religion and the nature of their new society. These leaders must identify what is perennial and authentic to the religious tradition—those central aspects of its theology, ethics, and jurisprudence—and translate it into the equivalent norms of the new milieu.

To give an illustration of this tension, consider an ethical question that all communities must eventually deal with: What is appropriate attire in terms of the parts of the body that can and should be shown in public? Though all religious traditions affirm the importance of modesty, how should this manifest in actual terms? The simple answer is that there are many possible ways to address this complex question. For example, when Muslims first migrated to India, Muslim women decided to adopt the Indian *shalwar qameez*, a unisex dress similar in manner to shirts and pants worn by both women and men in the West, thereby translating the Islamic ethic of modesty into the native sartorial norms of their new South Asian culture. Had these Muslim immigrants insisted on Arabian-style clothing, this would have most likely made Islam much more of a foreign religion to South Asia, arguably never allowing Muslims to become accepted as *Indian*. Another example can be found in the contemporary controversy surrounding a Muslim woman's choice to wear a *hijab*, a headscarf, in France. Perhaps the best way to have approached this challenge would have been for Muslim women who feel that they must cover their heads to explore ways to make the *hijab* more French. Though having fallen on deaf ears as of yet, I continue to suggest to French Muslim and non-Muslim fashion designers to create attractive head coverings that both satisfy Islamic requirements and are distinctly *French*, similar to the Indian *shalwar qameez*. This is one potential way to bridge such a divide, "Francophizing" Islam, if you will, and neither necessitates a prohibition of those who believe it is their religious obligation to wear a *hijab*, nor does it ignore the need for French Muslims to integrate their customs, to some degree, into the larger French milieu.

Take another example. In 2009, the Swiss Parliament passed a controversial law that banned *minarets*, the towers commonly attached to a mosque. Similar to the case of wearing a *hijab* in France, once again I continue to argue that this issue should have been reframed from its inception. *Minarets* are not a requirement in Islam. In fact, in the beginning of Islamic history they were not even present. Certainly there is nothing wrong with placing a *minaret* on a mosque. But the mosque-*minaret* association is purely cultural and technological; it was a solution for laypeople without clocks or loudspeakers to know when it was time to pray. It is not, nor has it ever been, a theological requirement of Islamic law for a mosque to have a *minaret*. While Muslim minorities must surely enjoy the right to practice their religion, these communities should also attempt to adapt to the society in which they live, in particular when such a community's majority is non-Muslim. I hold that mosques and other houses of worship in Switzerland should function optimally in a *Swiss* environment and look like they belong in Switzerland, just like in the Arabian Peninsula they should look *Arab* or in the United States *American*.

Similarly, consider how Islamic music always takes on a unique and often hybrid form depending on its context. Perhaps the most famous example in the West is that of the Iranian British singer Sami Yusuf, one of the Muslim community's biggest rock stars.[9] A blend of Western and Middle Eastern traditions, Yusuf's rock music features Islam-themed songs such as "The Creator," "Muhammad," and "Hasbi Rabbi." Similarly, the genre of music referred to as Qawwali emerged in the South Asian subcontinent from a distinctly Indian genius and culture. Though it sounds Indian and its words are rooted in Muslim-centric ideas, it is not like other music from the Muslim-Arab World. Qawwali is the product of Indian Muslims having made Islam an *Indian* religion.

"Americanizing" Islam, Fostering New Identities

The transformation of a religious community has never been easy. The acculturation of any immigrant religious community results from a dynamic process that transpires across time, in and through a number of generations. In American immigrant history in particular, it is the members of the second or third generation—with no recollection of the previous homeland—who tend to assimilate, seeing themselves as American *before* any other communal identity. When Americanization takes place within a given ethnic enclave, a central shift in the community's dominant attitude takes place. What was once considered iconoclasm becomes innovation; a lack of concern for one's heritage and such cultural identifiers as dress or language—or even more contentious issues such as living outside the community or intermarriage—all fade in importance, giving into the greater assimilationist ethos of "fitting in." For example, over many generations immigrant American Muslim women have become less likely to dress in their traditional *jalabiya*, the traditional robe, or *shalwar qameez,* choosing instead to wear full-length dresses, pant suits, or jeans, since these latter forms of clothing are part of American sartorial norms while also being in accordance with Islamic law.

As immigrant communities become Americanized they foster unprecedented identities that coalesce, by definition, what it means to be both American *and* a member of a specific religious community. By the end of the nineteenth and into the twentieth century, for example, many American Jews had begun to cement their "Jewishness" as an inseparable element of their "Americanness" and vice versa. As they developed innovative cultural institutions and expressions to fit within the dominant non-Jewish American society, a number of uniquely *American Jewish* movements arose, including the denominations now known as Reform,[10] Conservative, and Reconstructionist.[11] Leaders of these movements were able to distinguish the theological from the sociological in an affirmation of both their Jewish religion and American customs. What emerged from this give-and-take process was an Americanization of Jewish religious institutions and traditions, a phenomenon reflective of far-reaching accommodation within broader patterns of religious life in the United States. For example, American Reform Judaism in particular came to mirror the American Protestant churchs' institutions and practices, echoing some of the same communal structures such as men's clubs, sisterhoods, junior congregations, youth groups, discussion circles, adult education projects, and more.

American Muslims are currently in the midst of a similar process. Just as Muslim communities have been cast in the institutional and cultural contexts of places such as Yemen, Senegal, and Indonesia, so too are they now re-inventing themselves in the United States. This process is essential to Islam's development in the United States because, for example, Islam as practiced just as it is in rural Pakistan simply does not work in the milieu of urban Chicago. This advent also resonates within the larger history of Islam and the adaptability of Muslim communities for centuries. Indeed, despite real challenges, many of which stem from complex geopolitical realities, American Muslims are *already* developing a unique American-Islamic identity; Islam is *already* being practiced in a distinctly American manner. As an imam of a New York City mosque and a former immigrant myself, I have witnessed this first-hand.

Let's briefly examine a particularly important issue for the Muslim community, one that is relevant for all religious immigrant communities in this country: the relationship between institutions of religion and institutions of the state. Whereas previous generations of American Muslims assumed a role for the government in the mosque, Muslims today are able to more effectively navigate the American "church-state relationship" by recognizing that unlike the Ministries of Religious Affairs (also known as religious endowments) in Muslim-majority communities and countries the U.S. government cannot support houses of worship in the same way due to American church-state distinctions. Therefore, the American Muslim community is fully running these American mosques. In other words, after a number of generations, American Muslims are now beginning to manage their affairs in an *American* way, rather than as they did in the "old country."

The 2007 Pew Research Center report "Muslim Americans: Middle Class and Mostly Mainstream" confirms this phenomenon. Its findings are summarized as follows: "[Muslim-Americans] are decidedly American in their outlook, values and attitudes."[12] In fact, American Muslims can be considered totally within the mainstream of American society in terms of religiosity and a number of other indicators. The 2008 Pew report "U.S. Religious Landscape Survey" offers illuminating data that demonstrate this second point. Take, for example, the following:

- 82 percent of Americans said that religion is either "very important" or "somewhat important" in their lives, compared with 90 percent of American Muslims;
- 40 percent of Americans who affiliate with a particular religious tradition see a "conflict between religion and modern society," compared with 32 percent of American Muslims;
- 27 percent of Americans are "very or somewhat satisfied" with the American political system, compared with 25 percent of American Muslims.[13]

Moving from Assimilation to Integration

It is obvious from the preceding paragraphs that, like American Jews before them, a unique American Muslim consciousness and identity is now taking root and beginning to prosper. That said, cultural assimilation does not necessarily lead to immediate and full integration or acceptance. Immigrant communities must develop interlocutors that are well-equipped to mediate between their community and public society. For instance, even as American Jews began to assimilate they continued to suffer from both official and unofficial discrimination and rejection emanating from the larger fabric of non-Jewish America. Ultimately, their integration can be traced to the development of interlocutors that were (and still are) able to effectively engage within the hallways of normative American political power, media, and civil society, advocating for their community on issues such as politics and civil liberties, representation in the media, and interfaith relations.

Within the last three decades, the American Muslim community has begun to develop institutions parallel to the American Jewish community in order to advance their own interests. It is critical that as inheritors of the American Jewish legacy, American Muslims continue to replicate their counterparts' successful strategies, especially as Muslim integration is still resisted by many elements within American society at large. Each of the following relatively new Muslim institutions shares a Jewish predecessor in its diverse work:

- The American-Arab Anti-Discrimination Committee (ADC), founded in 1980,[14] and the Anti-Defamation League (ADL), founded in 1913, are civil rights organizations that advocate for religious freedom and combat bigotry.
- The Islamic Society of North America (ISNA), founded in 1981, and the Union for Reform Judaism (URJ), founded 1873, are religious institutions that provide a wide range of leadership, outreach, and programmatic support to their respective congregations and communities.
- The Muslim Public Affairs Council (MPAC), founded in 1986, and the Jewish Council for Public Affairs (JCPA), founded in 1944 as the National Community Relations Advisory Council, are advocacy and lobbying groups that build consensus within their respective communities and develop responses on key issues.
- The Council on American-Islamic Relations (CAIR), founded in 1994, and the American Jewish Committee (AJC), founded in 1906, are advocacy groups that advance positive images of their community in the public sector, defend their civil rights, and promote democracy and pluralism.

These newly formed American Muslim institutions are best understood alongside the development of another American immigrant population, namely American Jews, as this better contextualizes the nascent stage of organizational development of American Muslims.

Another important force in the integration of American Jews was the twentieth-century growth of Jewish Community Centers (JCC) throughout America's urban hubs. Unlike their Christian forerunners, these centers were founded with a mission to do more than preserve inveterate cultural traditions. As a result, the JCCs helped transition a community of immigrants to one of integrated Americans with a robust awareness of their Jewish identity and traditions alongside their new American identity and practices. American Muslims have yet to develop similar institutions. For this reason, my own organization, the Cordoba Initiative, is beginning to establish a number of new and unique community centers called "Cordoba Houses," which will offer diverse programming in the arts and culture, education, religion, global engagement, and recreation. Like JCCs before them, Cordoba Houses will serve as a go-to-place for generations of Muslim immigrants, fostering a strong sense of American Muslim culture.

American Immigrants Transforming Their Global Community

As immigrant communities elbow their way into mainstream American society, finding their American legs and becoming grounded, their unprecedented experiences always transform the thought and practice of the global religious community with whom they identify.[15] Some of my rabbi friends have noted that the United States was the first country in which Jews lived in nonsegregated communities. Through newly formed coexistence with other religious communities, Judaism experienced a separation between its spiritual and cultural expressions, whereas previously, cultural and religious traditions had been deeply interwoven and no such separation existed. Analogously, as American Muslims integrate their identities within the democratic, pluralistic American milieu, they too will begin to have a tremendous impact on the global *ummah*, or Muslim community.

We can already see the rise of significant American movements in terms of academic research related to Islam and Muslims. Such American Muslim scholars as Khaled Abou El Fadl, Seyyed Hossein Nasr, Amina Wadud, and others are transforming the discourse on some of the most important issues affecting Muslims around the globe, such as governance (how should Muslims self-govern?), gender (how should Muslims define the respective roles and responsibilities of men and women in society?), and interfaith relations (how should Muslims relate to other religious communities?). It is my conviction that this impact will only intensify in the years to come, largely due to the absence of political pressures within the United States. Consequently, the view that Islamic theology and jurisprudence demand democracy, gender equality, pluralism, and harmonious relations between religious communities will be further cemented in the United States.

This impact is not restricted to theology or jurisprudence alone. Rather, owing to their position as both Americans and members of larger global communities, American immigrants have also acted as indispensable players on key political concerns of their coreligionists across the globe. For example, American Jews advanced their community in the United States while simultaneously they strove to protect Jewish interests outside the United States. Through such institutions as the AJC, JCPA, and the American Israel Public Affairs Committee (AIPAC), American Jews played an instrumental role in the founding and strengthening of the state of Israel, garnering necessary support from American and non-American governments in their effort.

Likewise, especially in a post-9/11 environment, American Muslims are now called upon to engage in improving U.S.-Muslim world relations. Given the United States' long history of engagement with the Muslim world, coupled with the reality that this presence has not always been helpful either for the United States or for Muslim-majority countries, American Muslims need to increase their active participation in framing U.S. geopolitical priorities in the Muslim world in a manner that is consistent with the interests of both Americans and Muslims worldwide. Furthermore, because American Muslims understand the aspirations of each community, they have a central role to play in mediating, building trust, and brokering interreligious and intercultural partnerships. With a foot in both the East and West, American Muslims are singularly positioned to carry out these increasingly momentous tasks in such hotspots as Afghanistan, Iraq, Iran, Israel-Palestine, and elsewhere.

This is precisely what the Cordoba Initiative aims to do through programs focusing on leadership development (Muslim Leaders of Tomorrow or MLT), women's empowerment (Women's Islamic Initiative in Spirituality & Equality), and Islamic law and governance (Shariah Index Project). Building a coalition of diverse partners and stakeholders, the Cordoba Initiative seeks to create a tipping point in relations between the West and the Muslim world over the next decade. My organization maintains that American Muslims must be catalysts in this work. For those American Muslims who work and live at the intersections of America and the Muslim world, there is no higher calling than to heal this relationship.

Collaboration in Action: Two Examples of American Muslim/American Jewish Coalition Building

I have stressed that American Jews and American Muslims must draw upon their shared histories and values to confront the challenges of immigration and integration still faced today. Such strategic partnerships are already forming between these two communities, and the Cordoba Initiative is highly involved in these efforts. For example, as part of our MLT program, we facilitate relationships between young, civic-minded Muslims and leaders of other religious communities, both in the United States and across the globe. Through this work, we are nurturing a new generation

of Muslim leaders eager to partner with American Jews on such issues as
Muslim integration in the United States as well as global issues such as
achieving political peace in the Middle East. I am personally convinced
that older generations of American Muslims—my generation—can no
longer solve our nation's or the world's most intractable problems. Instead,
it is the younger generations that will bring about justice and peace, first
by building friendships and relationships of trust.

The following are two examples of ways that Muslim youth can take
the mantle and move the American Muslim community forward, actions
already taken with success by the American Jewish community:

Adopting Shared Media Strategies. At a recent MLT media training conference, small groups of Muslim leaders met with a diverse range of local
media representatives, organizations, and other outlets in order to learn
practical lessons in covering the issues that concern them. One of these
"learning journeys" took place at the American Jewish Committee (AJC)
Media Center, where MLTs and their Jewish counterparts discussed models of media engagement from the past fifty years of the American Jewish
experience and how emerging Muslim civil society organizations could
potentially replicate these models. A particularly promising example
involved the AJC's targeted—and ultimately successful—media campaign to insert the word "Judeo" before mentioning the United States
as a "Christian" nation.[16] This symbolic transformation of a "Christian"
nation to a "Judeo-Christian" one has profoundly impacted the discourse
surrounding Jews in this country.

I believe that such a practical media campaign can be replicated by
American Muslims today. Imagine if American Muslims, in partnership
with American Jews, led a similarly targeted campaign to further extend
the core American religious identity to include Islam and Muslims. Just
as the Judeo-Christian ethic became ingrained in twentieth-century
American consciousness and American Muslims' own self-identity, so
too can the "Abrahamic Ethic"—encompassing the Christian, Jewish,
and Islamic traditions—become part of twenty-first-century American
discourse.

Jewish Council for Public Affairs Responds to Islamophobia. The second example is a model for collaboration between American Jews and American
Muslims around common priorities of these two minority communities: civil rights and tolerance of diversity. In 2009, the JCPA released
a remarkable document titled, "Task Force Concern on Jewish Muslim
Relations." Passed by a large organizational majority, this text stresses the
importance of dialogue and coalitions between American Muslims and
American Jews. Take, for example, the following passage:

> We recognize with concern that there have been incidents of ste-
> reotyping, scapegoating and bigotry directed at Muslim Americans
> for no reason other than their religious identity, and we deplore such
> incidents and the attitudes that give rise to them. As Jews, we are

especially sensitive to these immoral acts and recognize their cor-
rupting influence on our society. The JCPA applauds the progress
that has taken place in Muslim-Jewish relationships, including local
and national dialogues that have deepened mutual understanding,
that have advanced shared commitments to social justice and equality...While we vigorously support the efforts of law enforcement
to combat terror, we recognize that some Muslim-Americans have
been the target of efforts that have, at times, been overzealous. Jewish
and Muslim Americans, where appropriate, should work in coalition
to advance our common commitment to civil liberties, the struggle
against all forms of terrorism, racism, anti-Semitism, anti-Muslim
prejudice, or any other form of discrimination or stigmatization
against any racial, religious, or ethnic group...[17]

This resolution offers an important model for coalition building between
Americans. The development of strategic, focused initiatives around specific issues that affect both of these American minority communities will
have tremendous positive impact in the years to come. This is especially
true given the false perception that Jews and Muslims cannot get along,
let alone establish positive alliances. Such partnerships must be the future
of Jewish-Muslim relations in the United States and around the world.

Why I Remain Optimistic

Despite many challenges, my perspective remains decidedly optimistic.
Yet it is an optimism firmly grounded in historical reality. As an Italian
American recently told me, "Americans have a love-hate relationship with
immigrants." On the one hand, we Americans seriously restrict immigration, even often unfairly implicating immigrants in national problems. On the other, we have cultivated indelible national narratives based
entirely upon our various immigrant foundations and diverse, multicultural compositions. We are a country of immigrants. Such successes as the
American Jewish community attest to this fact.

I believe that this mixed American legacy will continue to fall on the
side of embracing our immigrant communities and facilitating the healthy
integration of these multiple identities. As American Muslim organizations and institutions build coalitions with American Jews in order to
learn from each other's experiences, to leverage each other's work, and
to partner in peace efforts, I am confident that the American Muslim
community can become the latest American success story. Building on
our parallel immigrant histories in this country—as well as our shared
values and historical interdependence, friendships, and partnerships—can
transform the relationship between Muslims and Jews globally, serving
as the impetus to shape a new world order based on peace, harmony, and
respect.

Notes

1. Feisal Abdul Rauf, *What's Right With Islam is What's Right With America: A New Vision for Muslims and the West* (San Francisco, CA: HarperSanFrancisco, 2005), 221.
2. I should make a preliminary clarification regarding the specific communities I am discussing in this essay. My basic premises apply to American Muslim immigrants and their descendants and not African American Muslims or American converts to Islam. Muslim immigrants represents over two-thirds of the composite American Muslim population.
3. Ibid., 14–27.
4. As it says in the Qur'an, "O humankind, surely we have created you from one male and one female and made you into tribes and clans [just] so that you may get to know each other. Those noblest of you with God are the most devout of you" (49:13).
5. See such Qur'anic verses as the following: "There shall be no coercion in religion; the right way is clearly distinct from error" (2:256) and "The Truth is from your Lord; so let whomever wills, believe, and let whomever wills, disbelieve" (18:29).
6. Though some of the first Jews came to the United States in 1654, and a great wave of Jewish immigration took place in the 1800s, my analysis herein addresses the majority of Jews who arrived in the United States at the turn of the twentieth century.
7. See, e.g., the self-narrated script in the video of Frederic Brenner's acclaimed photography project, *Diaspora*.
8. In the twentieth century, the dominant way that American Jews began redefining themselves was as either Ashkenazi or Sephardi, despite the fact that many Jews labeled Sephardic were of Middle Eastern descent with no historical ties to fifteenth-century Spain or Portugal.
9. Lindsay Wise, "Meet Islam's Biggest Rock Star," *TIME Magazine* (July 31, 2006 and January 20, 2010), found at www.time.com/time/world/article/0,8599,1220754,00.html, retrieved July 30, 2010.
10. Although Reform Judaism originated in nineteenth-century Germany, it was in the United States that it grew into its current state of being the world's largest Jewish denomination.
11. In fact, the vast majority of American Jews today belong either to Reform or to Conservative Judaism, as opposed to the Orthodox Judaism of their European ancestors.
12. "Muslim Americans: Middle Class and Mostly Mainstream," Pew Research Center (May 22, 2007).
13. "U.S. Religious Landscape Survey: Religious Beliefs and Practices: Diverse and Politically Relevant," The Pew Forum on Religion & Public Life (June 2008).
14. Though not focused exclusively on Muslim communities and issues, the work of this American-*Arab* civil rights organization, with over forty chapters in the United States, overlaps with the interests of the American Muslim community. Furthermore, around a quarter of all Arabs in the United States are Muslim.
15. The impact of Americanized religions has perhaps been most evident within the Catholic community. As American Catholics successfully developed a unique American Catholic identity and practice, they played a critical role in mediating between the American and global Catholic Church. One important example is the Second Ecumenical Council of the Vatican, better known as Vatican II, which was opened under Pope John XXIII in 1962 and closed by Paul VI in 1965. The original Vatican II meeting had a strong presence of American Catholic bishops, something that arguably had a major impact on this important document, which in large part reflects American Catholic scholarship, especially American ideas on the separation of church and state.
16. This was reminiscent of the "salting it in" media campaign during World War II, a period of rising anti-Semitism in the United States when Jews engaged in a wide-scale effort to encourage non-Jewish organizations and media outlets to present favorable messaging regarding the American Jewish community. For example, this campaign promoted a notion of national unity that explicitly included American Jews [see "The American Jewish Committee's Fight against Anti-Semitism: 1938–1950," American Jewish Committee Archives (December 22, 2009), found at www.ajcarchives.org/AJC_DATA/Files/RS-16.pdf].
17. "Task Force Concern on Muslim Jewish Relations" (December 22, 2009), found at engage.jewishpublicaffairs.org/t/1686/blog/comments.jsp?blog_entry_KEY=394&t=, retrieved July 30, 2010.

CHAPTER SIX

The War of Words: Jews, Muslims, and the Israeli-Palestinian Conflict on American University Campuses

AARON J. HAHN TAPPER

Introduction

To some degree, all conflicts are about the relationship between power and identity.[1] As individuals and communities, we enact a constructed sense of identity, or self, primarily through our behavior and experiences, which in turn is shaped by cultures, value and belief systems, histories, and narratives. Conflicts commonly intensify when a person's or group's identity is taken away, threatened, or violated.[2] The Israeli-Palestinian conflict is an example of such a struggle, a contemporary battle over power and identity. But like many other international contests, this conflict does not play out solely among communities in the Middle East. On the contrary, this is a conflict that has been exported to and relived in different countries around the world, such as the United States.

Since September 2000—after the failure of the so-called Camp David peace accords, the start of the second Palestinian *Intifada*, and the subsequent increase in violence between Jewish Israelis and Palestinians—American universities have seen a sharp spike in on-campus tensions between student groups identifying with the Israeli-Palestinian conflict. This essay explores this phenomenon, approaching such campus episodes of conflict as elements of a national trend taking place on- and off-campuses, a fever pitch that reflects macro-communal narratives, particularly those emerging among Muslim Americans and Jewish Americans.[3] This analysis is based on research carried out between September 2004 and May 2010, during which time I conducted more than one hundred interviews with university students, faculty, and on-campus staff at more than twenty-five university campuses across the United States.[4]

The Rise in Intercommunal Tensions on
University Campuses

In September 2000 American campuses across the country saw a rise in confrontations between student groups largely identifying as either pro-Israel or pro-Palestine.[5] But tensions between these on-campus groups did not emerge in a vacuum, nor were they a mere derivative of the increase in violence between Jewish Israelis and Palestinians during this same period. Rather, this friction ignited dormant, isolated undercurrents that had not yet emerged as a nationwide phenomenon. On some campuses this tension surfaced precisely in September 2000, whereas other campus communities did not see an increase in student demonstrations until fall 2001, following the September 11 attacks of the same year; winter 2001–02, following the U.S. military's actions in Afghanistan; spring 2002, following the Israeli military's actions in the West Bank town of Jenin; winter 2002–03, following the U.S. military's actions in Iraq; or fall 2005, when American public opinion began to shift away from supporting the U.S.-government-sanctioned war in Iraq.

In other words, since 2000 there have been a number of occurrences in the Middle East (and surrounding areas) that have been perceived by American university student groups as antithetical to their particular value system(s), events that have manifested in on-campus student demonstrations and other noticeable activities.[6] Many of these episodes were reported in the media.[7] Though the number of incidents on campuses has varied, and there have been a few documented incidents of physical violence against students and/or property, almost all of the violence has been verbal.[8]

Sometimes these intercommunal conflicts have occurred as a result of controversies that seem to have had no overt connection to the Israeli-Palestinian conflict. For example, one situation involved a public university agreeing to pay for washing stations to accommodate their Muslim students' ritual observances.[9] A second incident occurred at a private university, where a small group of female Muslim students asked the administration to set aside hours in a school gym to accommodate their religious observances related to modesty.[10] There are two important things to mention about such examples. First, in each one Muslims and non-Muslims both felt that their respective identities were being threatened. As a result, the groups involved (re)acted as if they were under attack. Although Muslim Americans have starkly different historical and sociological experiences than other minorities in the United States, like all communities they feel the need to enact their communal identity. This has led to reactions among non-Muslims, some of whom have felt that their identity was endangered by Muslims asking to make modifications to their campus environment.[11] Second, among the most vocal opponents of university accommodations to Muslim students have been Jews, almost all of whom have identified with conservative, pro-Israeli government positions in regard to the Israeli-Palestinian and who have tended to interpret these on-campus events through the lens of the Israeli-Palestinian conflict.[12] It is more than likely that these opponents reacted because they experienced a threat to their identity.

Making matters more complicated, some administrators on these campuses have made public statements regarding these incidents, which have fostered the impression that they have "taken sides" with one community over another. For example, over the last decade the student body at one school has received a great deal of media coverage regarding their on-campus tensions, which have taken place largely between a small number of campus organizations: GUPS (General Union of Palestinian Students), Hillel's Israel Coalition, and the College Republicans, with the last two groups commonly pitted up against the first. In early November 2004, the university's president wrote a letter to the campus community chronicling the previous week's on-campus tensions. Part of the letter reads as follows:

> On November 1, four members of the campus College Republicans staffing a table were approached by four students who began to voice their intense anger about Bush policy and the war in Iraq. Tempers flared on both sides, but the only physical exchange occurred when a College Republican attempted to slap away the hand of a student leaning over the table and pointing at him. In response, she slapped his shoulder. Campus Public Safety intervened and interviewed the two students on the spot. When asked whether they wanted to press charges against each other, both declined. However, both have now been referred to the campus discipline office for possible violation of the student code of conduct.[13]

By definitively stating what happened, the school's president de facto chose a particular perspective, thereby marginalizing and disempowering those perspectives that did not fall in line with his own. Even though much of his statement focused on the ideals for a democratically based community where people do not resort to physical violence but take advantage of their freedom to engage in verbal debate and/or discussion, because this president also recounted the event according to a particular narrative—factual or not—this inevitably placed him in a particular place on the political spectrum vis-à-vis GUPS and Israel Coalition/Hillel/College Republicans.[14] No doubt university administrations must take stances on particular campus issues. But when such action is taken this subsequently places them in a particular political camp, regardless of whether this is accurate, because identifying with one community's micro-narrative is commonly perceived as supporting that community's macro-narrative.[15]

The Dominant Narrative of Muslim Americans

At first glance it may seem problematic to say that any community, especially one as diverse as the American Muslim community, has a single narrative. But despite rarely having completely homogenous narratives, all communities have *dominant* narratives, especially those communities in conflict with others. Such communal discourse embodies opinions and stories that communities tell themselves and others, ideas that shift over time based on a number of ever-changing factors. Narratives are fluid, often altering according to time and place. Sometimes a community's narrative changes so radically that what is thought to be the truth at one point becomes fiction shortly thereafter. In this sense, a community's narrative is its *truth*, its perception of a given set of facts. Yet in actuality, there is not necessarily a direct correlation between a community's truth and facts on the ground.[16]

One way that a "group" of people becomes a "community" is when its membership reaches a critical mass. As such, the number of individuals in a community is important to a community's emergence into a larger society; size of a unit is often perceived in relation to power. For example, when the American Muslim community first began publishing its find-ings on its population (in particular over the last decade), a small group of non-Muslim American groups, many of whom identify as American Jews, challenged the conclusions. According to the first major nonpar-tisan study conducted on the American Muslim community, published in May 2007 by the Pew Research Center (PRC), there are 2.35 million Muslims in the United States.[17] But like years previous, even though the PRC is unaffiliated with a particular ethnic or religious community numerous American Jewish groups contested this figure, arguing that the American Muslim community is much less populated than what the PRC says.[18]

Some of these non-Muslim groups have gone beyond merely critiquing Muslim organizations' population studies, going to the extent of con-ducting studies of their own, something they have not done in regard to any other American minority other than themselves. In 2001, the American Jewish Committee (AJC) published a piece citing the popula-tion of the American Muslim community to be anywhere from 1.9 to 2.8 million individuals, claiming that the average figure cited by the media, 6.7 million, is erroneous.[19] In contrast, the Council of American–Islamic Relations (CAIR) thereafter estimated this figure at 7 million, something that was quickly refuted by the Middle East Forum's Daniel Pipes and AJC's Yehudit Barsky.[20] According to Pipes, such "militant Islamic orga-nizations" as CAIR inflate this number "because a larger number, even if phony, offers it enhanced access and clout. Convincing the Republican Party that Muslims number 8 million, for example, led to urgent calls from its chairman for 'meeting with [Muslim] leaders,' something which becomes less of a priority when the Muslim population turns out to be much smaller."[21] Various pundits have speculated why some in the Jewish American community have focused a disproportionate amount of time on the issue of Muslim American population studies.[22] Regardless of inten-tions, the fact that Jewish American organizations have challenged the

Muslim American community in this way is reflective of strained relations between these two groups.

Though American Jews are largely comprised of Ashkenazi Jews who are third, fourth, or fifth generation Americans, American Muslims are primarily first generation (at least 65 percent of Muslims in the United States are foreign born).[23] Moreover, Muslims are among the most diverse minorities in the United States, coming from more than sixty-eight countries; the number of different traditions, practices, doctrines, languages, and beliefs within the Muslim American community is staggering and, in terms of diversity, unlike any other minority community in the United States.[24] American Muslims are also significantly younger than non-Muslims; more than half of adult Muslims in the United States (56 percent) are between the ages of eighteen and thirty-nine.[25]

Aside from these statistics, in examining this community's dominant narrative (and its dynamic with the American Jewish community's narrative) it is also useful to look at opinion polls.[26] In relation to this essay's focus, four things from the PRC study stand out in particular[27]: (1) Though almost half (47 percent) of American Muslims think of themselves as Muslims first and Americans second, when broken into age groups this statistic spikes to 60 percent for American Muslims under the age of thirty; (2) a quarter of all American Muslims say they have been the victim of discrimination in the United States; (3) younger American Muslims—those under the age of thirty—are more religiously observant and more accepting of Islamic extremism than older American Muslims; and (4) most Muslims believe that a balanced solution to the Israeli-Palestinian conflict can be found. These data reflect feelings of alienation, deviation from dominant American ideologies, and disempowerment among young American Muslims.

But perhaps what wasn't included in the study is more telling. According to Zahid Bukhari, a former director of the Pew Foundation project "Muslims in the American Public Square" and current director of the American Muslim Studies Program (AMSP) at the Prince Alwaleed Bin-Talal Center for Muslim-Christian Understanding at Georgetown University, "Muslims have a universal belief that Jewish groups are controlling American foreign policy, at least in the Middle East. Half a century before achieving this 'status,' the Jewish intellectuals and activists were also instrumental in shaping the domestic agenda of President Roosevelt."[28]

The Dominant Narrative of Muslim
American University Students

The focus of the PRC study is the Muslim American community broadly speaking. But because they divide up much of their data based on age it is helpful, if not altogether necessary, to look at these statistics in order to understand Muslim student populations on university campuses. Before doing this, however, we must briefly discuss the history of Muslim student groups on American university campuses.

Muslim Student Associations[29] (MSAs) have been a part of the American university landscape since 1963, when the first one was established at the University of Illinois at Urbana-Champaign.[30] Historically, MSAs have generally aimed at providing a given university's Muslim student body an opportunity to observe religious services and rituals.[31] Indeed, they were set up by Muslim students decades before there were spaces on campuses for them to pray and perform communal rituals (something that actually exists on only an infinitesimal number of schools today). The funding for these first MSAs came from Saudi Arabia, a trend that lasted into the 1970s, and, by some accounts, continues to this day. Thus, many of the religious practices of these MSAs mirrored Islamic practices found in the Arabian Kingdom (e.g., early MSAs banned women from meetings, had men follow strict codes of prayer and fasting, and were held in Arabic). It is worth adding that these MSAs generally kept a low profile.[32]

Following the 9/11 attacks, many MSAs became more visible and active, engaging in intercommunal activities and bringing outspoken Muslim activists to their campuses.[33] On some of these campuses, American Muslim students became more empowered, reembracing the original intent of the MSA's first founders—that they should be "Muslims first, Muslims last, and Muslims forever."[34] Regarding this post-9/11 university-based phenomenon, one scholar notes,

> Their ranks are increasing from all directions: young Muslims who grew up in secular families are becoming members [of MSAs] in order to learn about their faith and to surround themselves with other Muslims; conservative students join because they want their ideas to dominate the organizations; and non-Muslims are entering those MSAs that will make room for them because they are curious about a religion and a way of life that is capturing the daily headlines.[35]

The increase in MSA participation has led to an internal struggle over chapters' identities vis-à-vis liberalism and conservatism. Though each individual MSA group enjoys autonomy in setting its own chapter's rules,[36] it is often the case that MSAs at private colleges tend to be more liberal than those at public universities. Some speculate that this is due to the fact that private colleges tend to draw students from more diverse geographical locations and worldviews whereas public universities are commonly attended by those living nearer to the university. (More likely, many Muslim students attend public universities over private ones because such students come from conservative families who do not want their children to travel too far from home.[37])

When looked at alongside the previously cited PRC statistics it is relevant to underscore the following facts about Muslim students on U.S.

campuses: (1) Because American Muslims are significantly younger than non-Muslims the population of Muslim students in American universities is increasing exponentially; (2) Muslim students do not have highly organized and active off-campus Muslim organizations to support them, certainly not in comparison to the Jewish community[38]; (3) in the same way that American Muslims are skeptical that Arab Muslims carried out the 9/11 attacks,[39] they are likewise reluctant to embrace authorities outside the Muslim community, such as university campus administrations, and, arguably, the U.S. government.[40]

The Dominant Narrative of Jewish Americans

When compared to the Muslim community, the American Jewish community is much more ethnically and ideologically homogeneous. Part of this is due to the fact that approximately one-third of the world's fifteen million Jews live in the United States,[41] 80 percent of whom identify as Ashkenazi (generally of European and/or Russian descent).[42] Historically,[43] this has played a significant role in attempts to formally shape the American Jewish community into an ideological and structural monolith, especially in relation to intercommunal relations, despite a great deal of intracommunal heterogeneity.[44] Ideologically, the most important issue[45] of concern for the Jewish community is survival, both physical and vis-à-vis identity (i.e., largely seen in discussions surrounding in-marriage versus intermarriage/out-marriage).[46]

One of the ways this community voices concern for its physical survival is through their protection of the state of Israel. This, however, is largely a generational trend. According to an August 2007 study,[47] there is a direct correlation between an American Jew's age and one's connection to Israel, with older Jews having a stronger connection to the Jewish state than younger Jews.[48] The study concludes by saying,

> [the fact] that each age group is less Israel-attached than its elders suggests that we are in the midst of a long-term and ongoing decline in Israel attachment. The age-related differences cannot be attributed primarily to family life cycle effects, if only because the age-related declines characterize the entire age spectrum from the very old to the very young.[49] Rather, we are in the midst of a massive shift in attitudes toward Israel...with all this said, caring for Israel among younger adult Jews has not evaporated entirely. Far from it. On a variety of measures, approximately 60% of non-Orthodox Jews under the age of 35 express a measure of interest in caring for and [having an] attachment to Israel.[50]

In other words, questions such as the following lie at the core of the American Jewish community's narrative: Will the state of Israel survive the twenty-first century or will it be destroyed? If Israel ceases to exist, will this affect the ability of Americans Jews to survive? Will Jews survive the contemporary world or will they intermarry to the point of no longer having a Jewish identity at all? Though some of this is rooted in the deep-seeded trauma of the mass genocide of Jews during World War II, and older generations of American Jews continue to express concern about the recurrence of a genocide aimed at Jews, the idea of disempowerment and persecution predates the twentieth century, rooted in the Jewish community's centuries-old experiences as a minority that has been discriminated against time and time again in countless different places.[51] The current American reality of empowerment has not rewritten this dominant communal orientation toward the 97.8 percent of the United States and 99.8 percent of the world that are non-Jews.

The Dominant Narrative of Jewish American University Students

While the first MSA was established in 1963, the first Hillel chapter was established on the same campus, the University of Illinois, Urbana-Champaign, forty-one years prior, in 1923.[52] Today, there are Hillel chapters on 531 campuses in the United States and Canada[53]; in 2006 their annual budget was over twenty-six million dollars,[54] whereas their current budget is approximately sixty-six million dollars.[55] The various forms of support that Hillel gives their Jewish students is enormous, providing such things as meals, lectures, and religious and cultural activities. In contrast to American Muslim students, who do not have anything akin to campus Hillels, Jewish university students are commonly supported by a range of Jewish organizations besides Hillel, many, if not most, of which focus their on-campus efforts on training students to support particular political positions in regard to Israel.[56]

The existence of these Jewish organizations—virtually all of which are based off-campus and almost all of which do not normally focus on activities relevant to university student populations beyond anything other than the state of Israel—is also reflective of the chasm between American Jews and American Muslims. It is partly for this reason that the American Muslim university community cannot accurately be compared to the American Jewish university community in terms of strength or organization, on or off the university campus. Further, off-campus American Muslim communities do not normally share ideas publically with on-campus student populations, especially those related to the Israeli-Palestinian conflict.[57]

Jews and Muslims on American University Campuses

It is imperative to see Jewish-Muslim student interactions through the lens of large-scale relations between these same groups. Whether arguing about population numbers or another issue altogether, struggles between these two communities, on- and off-campus, are representative of inter-communal strife in the United States and beyond. Whether an issue arises between these communities with regard to the building of a new Muslim community center[58] or on a university campus with regard to the Israeli-Palestinian conflict, these disputes arise as a result of communal assertions of identity, largely as they relate to one another. Whether this declaration emerges from a Muslim student group, a Jewish student group, or another group altogether, and whether it relates to religious ritual practices or sup-port for a nationalist cause, on-campus issues most commonly arise over a group's need to publicly express its identity.

No on-campus student body exists irrespective of its larger off-campus community. Though the Jewish and Muslim communities in the United States have starkly different historical and sociological experiences and his-tories, both continue to express a need to assert their identity. Particularly on university campuses, where the percentage of Muslims is higher than the national average, it is common to see American Muslims vocally expressing their opinions, such as over issues related to religious freedom in the United States or the suffering of Muslims abroad. So, too, we see the need to express communal identity among Jews on campuses that have sizeable Jewish populations.

As for Muslim student behavior specifically (whether or not related to the Israeli-Palestinian conflict), it is common for Muslim student groups to express distrust toward non-Muslims, something often seen in their rela-tionship with on-campus administrations. Part of this is a result of Muslim student groups' feelings of disempowerment.[59] Though the primary way they feel empowered is by carrying out on-campus demonstrations, when they get increased media attention or when campus administrations try to quell their on-campus demonstrations, situations that are usually both perceived negatively, thereby disempowering them, the Muslim students push back, perpetuating a vicious cycle.

Two recent events from spring 2010 reflect this phenomenon. In the first, student government representatives at one university voted against a measure to call for the campus' board of trustees to divest university monies from Israeli companies. After the episode gained an international audience, and following the Jewish community's intense mobilization, which included having official AIPAC (American Israel Public Affairs Committee) representatives meeting with student government represen-tatives, the bill was defeated. In the second, a campus' Muslim Student Union was suspended after a number of MSU members disrupted an on-campus talk delivered by the Israeli ambassador to the United States Michael Oren. Aside from the administration's choice to punish the MSU, off-campus Jewish organizations—such as Hillel, the local Jewish Federation, and the Zionist Organization of America—carried out intense campaigns threatening the school's administration with a boycott of Jewish donations to the university if the MSU was not punished.[60] Ironically, through such actions Muslim students fall prey to the precise stereotype those public personas such as Daniel Pipes and Bill O'Reilly portray, that they are political extremists who are anti-Israeli government, anti-American government, and have "anti-American values."[61]

In contrast to the phenomenon of American Muslim students' marginalization, on-campus Jews commonly express feelings of empowerment. This is a result of increased feelings of empowerment among American Jews more broadly, evidenced by their disproportionate representation in the power-spheres of academia, government, media, and pop culture (specifically vis-à-vis movies, music, and television). In addition, many of the campuses where the Jewish student body is publicly active have powerful Hillels, something that does not exist in the Muslim community. Off-campus Jewish organizations' involvement in on-campus issues adds to these feelings of empowerment.

Another case example of the stark communal differences in communal power between these two groups is as follows: Jewish-Muslim tensions at one school first made national press due to an event that took place in June 2004, when a handful of Muslim students wore green stoles around their necks at the university's graduation ceremony. The stoles all had the *shahada*, the traditional Muslim profession of faith that translates to "There is no god but God and Muhammed is God's messenger," written on them in Arabic. A number of on- and off-campus groups vehemently protested the students' decision to wear the stoles.[62] Though there are no precise numbers regarding how many of the organizations that protested the wearing of the stoles were Jewish, one of the most vocal protesters was the local branch of the Anti-Defamation League, which immediately published a press release decrying the stoles as symbolizing sympathy for violent extremists.

Issued on June 18, 2004, portions of the press release were as follows:

> The Anti-Defamation League (ADL) is deeply troubled that members of [the] Muslim Students Union (MSU) have chosen to wear a green graduation stole bearing the *Shahada*, a declaration of faith that has been closely identified...with Palestinian terrorist groups and that can be especially offensive to Jewish students...This is part of an ongoing pattern of vicious anti-Israel and anti-Semitic incidents on th[is] campus, many perpetuated by the Muslim Students Union...Green is the color of Hamas, and its activists and prospective suicide bombers wear the *Shahada,* a declaration of faith, on green armbands and headbands.[63]

Though the ADL retracted parts of the press release four days later, the apology was construed by many as too late.[64] By then Fox News' Bill O'Reilly had already done a number of segments about the incident on his show, "The O'Reilly Factor," including a "Factor Follow-up," where he accused the university's administration of "not being up front about the controversy."[65]

As for off-campus American Jewish organizations aside from the ADL, a large number of them have been vocal regarding on-campus issues related to the Israeli-Palestinian conflict. Sometimes there has even been a competition between these organizations as to who is "fighting harder" for a given university's Jewish students.[66] The fact that these Jewish organizations invest such time and energy into these on-campus issues reflects another disparity between American Jews and American Muslims.

The gulf between these two American groups becomes even broader when we examine how issues that are *not* deemed to be relevant to on-campus Jewish student populations are sometimes deemed to be important to off-campus Jewish organizations. For example, following ongoing tensions between Jews and Muslims on one campus, Jewish student leaders of the major on-campus Jewish organizations published a joint declaration thanking the administration's assistance in quelling the campus tensions.[67] Though their press release ended in saying that "verbal anti-Semitism spurred by controversial student groups unfortunately continues to exist on campus," it also praised the local Hillel and Jewish Federation while simultaneously censuring nonspecific off-campus Jewish organizations.[68] These off-campus Jewish organizations immediately responded by discrediting the students altogether, as if the off-campus organizations' positions were more important than those of the campus' Jewish students.[69]

A final point worth noting is that Jewish students' feelings of empowerment as they relate to the Muslim community often emerge through a general outspoken request to "dialogue"[70] with on-campus Muslim students, an effort rarely led by Muslim students in turn. Unfortunately, and despite good intentions, what is lacking from this effort is an understanding that there is seldom an equal desire by members of the Muslim community to engage in such activities precisely because of the disparity in power between the two groups. In other words, when two groups are in conflict it is common for the group with more power to reach out to the group with less power. But when not structured and facilitated by professionals who have an understanding of intergroup power relations, "dialogue" more often than not only reinforces the very power inequalities fueling intergroup strife in the first place. (Oftentimes students are unaware that they are not experienced in intergroup education and should probably not engage in such activities. There is a general trend among such students that facilitating intergroup work does not necessitate professional training.) For this reason, disempowered groups commonly choose not to engage in "dialogue" activities at all, which is usually misinterpreted as animosity and hostility. Further, the Jews who reach out to Muslims frequently want to organize social, rather than political, events, activities that do not incorporate discussions of how power manifests between the two groups, despite the fact that it is precisely political, and not social, issues that are dividing the two communities.

This said, despite the strength of university Jewish life—illustrated through Hillel as well as off-campus Jewish organizations involved with campus life—paradoxically, Jewish students also commonly voice feelings of disempowerment. This reflects the larger Jewish communal narrative of victimization, historically accurate when applied to the wider lens of Jewish history (and in some places in the world today), but not reflective of the current status of American Jews. Jewish students are rarely disempowered and arguably have more avenues to express their particular identity than any other American student group of the same size.

Conclusion

Over the last several years there has been a sharp increase in intercommunal violence in Israel and Palestine. Yet over the last decade this Middle Eastern conflict has firmly taken root in the United States as well, where tensions between Jews, Muslims, Israelis, and Palestinians are now as rife as ever. On some university campuses, these tensions have escalated into episodes of physical violence. Because there is a deep connection between communities in the United States and those living abroad—largely because of the role the United States has played in "East-West," America-"Muslim World," and Israeli-Palestinian relations for decades—when examining how Jewish and Muslim student groups interact with one another it is imperative to see such dynamics through the lens of global Jewish-Muslim relational trends. In other words, the interaction between student populations of American Jews and American Muslims is not only a microcosm of the Israeli-Palestinian conflict itself,[71] but also reflects how these two communities relate to one another throughout the United States. In the Israeli-Palestinian conflict, Israel is widely recognized as a functioning country, whereas Palestine is not. In this sense alone, Israelis have more power than Palestinians. (There are multiple other signs of disparity in power.) This imbalance of power also plays out on American university campuses, where Jews have much more power[72] than Muslims, evidenced ideologically and structurally.

Perceptions American Jews have of American Muslims and vice versa play a fundamental role in how these groups interact with one another. In other words, the truth these two communities have of one another is not necessarily reflective of facts. Rather, it emanates from each group's dominant narrative—of itself, of others in general, and of the American Jewish community or American Muslim community specifically. Whether an on-campus event is seen as a violent act of aggression, replete with anti-intellectual and antidemocratic values, or as just a demonstration of nonviolent resistance in line with those taken by students against American-sponsored military actions during the Vietnam era is largely the result of one's communal narrative. Macro-communal narratives assist in scripting how micro-communal acts are interpreted.

In short, the best way to move things forward between these two campus groups is by taking into account both the broader context of global

Jewish-Muslim dynamics and the wider scope of Jewish-Muslim relations throughout the United States, including the disparate histories and experiences these two communities have had, and continue to have, in "the land of the free and home of the brave." With this understanding, campus events can be better understood and dealt with, and, ideally, campuses that see intercommunal conflicts can be transformed into learning environments where students can expand, deepen, and recreate their notions of themselves and the "other."

Notes

1. Contrary to centuries past, the postmodern perspective is founded upon the notion that identity is not static but fluid.
2. I am grateful to my professional partner and friend, Huda Abu Arqoub, for having worked with me on this idea for a number of years. Huda is the co-executive director of Abraham's Vision, a conflict transformation organization working with Jews, Muslims, Israelis, and Palestinians for which I also serve as co-executive director.
3. Two important points should be considered from the outset (an idea found throughout this book). First, the identity signifiers "Jew," "Jewish," "Muslim," and "Islamic" should be understood throughout this essay as cultural, ethnic, historical, ideological, national, political, and/ or religious identities. To see Jewish-Muslim relations as encompassing religious identities only, and thus concluding that the only way to move these communities forward is through a religious-specific framework, is reductionist at best and damaging at worst. Although many Jews and Muslims identify as Jews or Muslims religiously, there are also many within these communities who do not. Second, it is far too common in the United States for people to conflate Muslims with Arabs and vice versa. This is partially due to the following statistics: Approximately 90 percent of the world's Arabs are Muslim (though among Arab Americans only 25 percent are Muslim); conversely, 15–30 percent of the world's Muslims are Arab (while among Muslim Americans only 24 percent are Arab). Though there is a potential risk that this essay reinforces the false coupling that Muslim equals Arab/Arab equals Muslim, it is my contention that the dominant voice among students from the non-Jewish university community who are involved with on-campus demonstrations—most commonly identifying as "pro-Palestinian," "pro-Palestine," "anti-Israel," or simply being critical of Israeli policies in vocal and active ways—emerges from individuals identifying as Muslim. Moreover, a Georgetown University study notes that Muslim Americans are better educated, better off, and younger than non-Muslim Americans; thus there is a disproportionate number of Muslims on American university campuses relative to their general population in the United States [see Geneive Abdo, *Mecca and Main Street* (New York: Oxford University Press, 2006), 64]. This essay contextualizes these on-campus tensions within the larger lens of Jewish-Muslim relations, rather than Jewish-Palestinian relations or other linkages, despite the fact that there are many non-Muslims who are active in on-campus activities that criticize the Israeli government, including a significant number of Jews. [For statistics on the percentage of Arabs worldwide who are Muslim, see Halim Barakat, *The Arab World: Society, Culture, and State* (Berkeley: University of California Press, 1993), 41. For statistics on the percentage of Arab Americans who are Muslim, see Chuck McCutcheon, "Arab, Muslim Vote Still in Play for Next Year's Election," Religion News of the Pew Forum on Religion and Public Life (June 25, 2003), found at pewforum.org/news/display.php?NewsID=2354, retrieved March 11, 2009. For statistics on the percentage of Muslims who are Arab, note that according to the Council on American-Islamic Relations, or CAIR, no more than 20 percent of the world's Muslims live in "the Arabic-speaking world" (found at sun.cair.com/AboutIslam/ IslamBasics.aspx, retrieved March 11, 2009) and according to the website about.com, no more than 15 percent of Muslims worldwide are Arab (found at islam.about.com/library/weekly/aa120298.htm, retrieved March 18, 2009; based on the *Britanica America*, 1997). Other sources cite additional statistics, such as John L. Esposito and Dalia Mogahed, *Who Speaks for Islam?* (New York: Gallup Press, 2007), 1–28. For statistics on the percentage of

Muslim Americans who are Arab, see Pew Research Center, "Muslim Americans: Middle Class and Mostly Mainstream" (May 22, 2007), pewresearch.org/assets/pdf/muslim-americans.pdf, 1.]

4. To date, I know of only one study aimed at analyzing this trend as it manifests on university campuses. But the goal of this previously published work does not explore potential root causes of intra-campus tensions, but rather discusses grassroots attempts to combat such strife. Published in January 2004, this previous analysis was conducted by the Cross-National Arab Jewish Dialogue Support Network, contracted by the University of Minnesota's Center for Restorative Justice and Peacemaking in partnership with the Marquette University Law School. (Though the results of this study could previously be found on the Center's website, www.cehd. umn.edu/ssw/rjp, this is currently no longer the case.) In contrast, this essay attempts to analyze the root causes of tensions between specific on-campus groups, student communities primarily comprised of Jews and Muslims, and to offer a new way to understand these tensions—within the context of Jewish American and Muslim American statuses in the larger American milieu.

5. Student groups using the following names, or likenesses thereof, have generally been involved in such incidents: American Friends of Israel, Amnesty International, Arab Student Association, Democratic Student Union, Hillel, Jewish Student Association, Lebanese Student Association, Middle East Studies Students, Muslim Student Association, Palestinian Student Association, Persian Student Association, Republican Student Union, Students for Justice in Palestine, and Students for a Just Peace in the Middle East. And although the terms "pro-Israel" and "pro-Palestine" are reductionist, these are the general terms such student groups use to self-identify.

6. A partial list of the most well-known campuses in North America that had these particular on-campus tensions between 2000 and 2005, all of whom have received media attention, is as follows: Columbia University, Concordia University (Canada), Emory University, Rutgers University, San Francisco State University, Stanford University, the University of California, Berkeley, the University of California, Irvine, the University of California, Los Angeles, the University of California, Santa Cruz, the University of Colorado, Boulder, the University of Michigan, and York University (Canada).

7. Many of these incidents have been reported in widely circulated print-media outlets. Some examples include *Los Angeles Times* [see Stanley Allison, "The Region; A Political Yet Peaceful Graduation at UC Irvine" (June 20, 2004); Ashrah Khalil, "Mideast Debate Takes Root at UC Irvine" (May 27, 2006); Roy Rivenburg, "Cartoon Display Protested" (March 1, 2006); and Kimi Yoshino, "Fresh Muslim-Jewish Discord on Campus" (May 12, 2006)]; *New York Times* [see N. R. Kleinfield, "Mideast Tensions are Getting Personal on Campus at Columbia" (January 18, 2005) and Kate Zernike, "Campus Tensions Growing with Support for Palestinians" (April 8, 2002), A6)]; *San Francisco Chronicle* [see Tanya Schevitz, "UC Berkeley's Conflicts Mirror Mideast Pain" (April 5, 2002) and Kelly St. John, "SFSU Studies Rally Tapes for Misconduct" (May 15, 2002)]; and *Washington Post* [see William Booth, "On Campus, a Reflection of Middle East Anger; Rally at San Francisco State Leads to Slurs and an Investigation as Tensions Rise at U.S. Universities" (May 19, 2002), A3)]. Media sources with smaller circulations include *Forward* [see Daniel Treiman, "California Campuses Gain a Reputation as Hotbeds of Anti-Israeli Rhetoric" (April 5, 2007); *Jerusalem Report* [see Danielle Peled, "It's Hard to be an Anti-Zionist" (May 30, 2005), 25; Yigal Schleifer, "A Tough Semester" (January 1, 2001), 32; and Sheila Teitelbaum, "Jihad at 'Gaza U.'" (October 21, 2002), 26)]; and *Nation* [see Liza Featherstone, "The Mideast War Breaks Out on Campus" (May 30, 2002)]. More overtly partisan media outlets have also added their voice, such as CAMERA (www.camera.org), *Electronic Intifada* (electronicintifada.net), *FrontPage Magazine* (www.frontpagemag.com), Jew Watch (www.jewwatch.com), Jihad Watch (jihadwatch.org), *Middle East Forum* (www.meforum.org; see also www.campus-watch.org, affiliated with *Middle East Forum*), *Online Journal* (onlinejournal.com), and Stand With Us (www.standwithus.com).

8. These intergroup campus tensions have not been limited to North American university campuses. For example, Birmingham University, the London School of Oriental and African Studies or SOAS [see Daniella Peled, "Anti-Zionism at London School Intimidates some Jewish Students," *Jewish Telegraphic Agency* (March 21, 2005)], and Oxford University [see Daniel Calvert, "Israeli Apartheid Tensions," *Oxford Student* (February 23, 2006)] have all dealt with these same types of incidents. Further, in 2006, after years of private and public debates, the United Kingdom's National Association of Teachers in Further and Higher Education

(NATFHE) approved an academic boycott of Israeli higher education institutions that did not condemn Israel's "apartheid policy," an issue that has continued to garner media attention to this day [see Andy Beckett and Ewen Macaskill, "British Academic Boycott Gathers Pace," *Guardian* (December 12, 2002) and Talya Halkan, "UK Teachers' Union Votes to Boycott Israeli Academics," *Jerusalem Post* (May 30, 2006)].

9. In August 2007 *New York Times* ran an article about Muslim students at the University of Michigan-Dearborn who asked their administration for assistance in creating washing stations in on-campus restrooms. (Muslims traditionally pray five times per day, prayers that are preceded by a ritual washing of one's hands, arms, face, and feet. In this case, it seems that some non-Muslim students were upset to find Muslim students preparing for prayer by washing their feet in restroom sinks.) The university administration decided to counter this problem by installing several $25,000 foot-washing stations in restrooms around campus. According to the article, as the Muslim student population at this campus is estimated to be as high as 10 percent, the campus administration felt fully justified in its decision, despite challenges from on- and off-campus groups that accused the campus of becoming "Islamified." The *Times* article added that the University of Michigan-Dearborn is not entirely unique, as campus administrations have installed foot-washing stations at other campuses around the United States, including Eastern Michigan University and George Mason University [see Tamar Lewin, "Universities Install Foot-baths to Benefit Muslims, and not Everyone is Pleased," *New York Times* (August 7, 2007), A10]. This episode is also examined in another essay in this book, written by Taymiya Zaman.

10. In February 2007, a group of female Muslim students at Harvard University requested that special hours be set aside at one of the on-campus dormitory gyms so that they could exercise in an environment where students would only be allowed to wear "modest" workout clothes. Shortly thereafter, during "Islam Awareness Week," the Harvard Islamic Society recited the Islamic call to prayer (*adhan*) on the main thoroughfare. Harvard's non-Muslim students voiced concerns over both of these issues. As the Muslim chaplain on campus Taha Abdul-Basser notes, "There are some people who are not just [*sic*] comfortable that Muslims, by virtue of the change of demographics, are going to be more and more visible" [see Neil Macfarquhar, "At Harvard, Students' Muslim Traditions are a Topic of Debate," *New York Times* (March 21, 2008), A14].

11. For example, Daniel Pipes, the director of the Middle East Forum and an oft-cited pundit identifying with the conservative right, went so far as to insinuate that requests for ritual footbaths at the University of Michigan-Dearborn were the first steps toward bringing about more sweeping changes in American society, part of a movement to impose *shari'a* [Islamic law] [see Oren Dorell, "Some Say Schools Giving Muslims Special Treatment," *USA Today* (July 26, 2007) found at www.usatoday.com/news/nation/2007-07-25-muslim-special-treatment-from-schools_N.htm, retrieved July 21, 2009; see also Andrea Elliott, "Critics Cost Muslim Educator Her Dream School," *New York Times* (April 28, 2008); Gershon Goremberg, "Daniel Pipes v. Religious Tolerance," *Huffington Post* (April 30, 2008) found at www.huffington-post.com/gershom-gorenberg/daniel-pipes-v-religious_b_99432.html, retrieved July 21, 2009; Debbie Schlussel, "So Long Church/State Separation," *Frontpagemag.com* (June 6, 2007), found at www.frontpagemag.com/readArticle.aspx?ARTID=26841, retrieved July 15, 2009; and Kathy Shaidle, "'Sharia Creep' Around the World," *Frontpagemag.com* (March 3, 2008), found at www.frontpagemag.com/readArticle.aspx?ARTID=30103, retrieved July 21, 2009]. Elsewhere Pipes has said, "It is hard to see how violence, how terrorism will lead to the implementation of sharia…It is much easier to see how, working through the system—the school system, the media, the religious organizations, the government, businesses and the like—you can promote radical Islam" (Elliott, "Critics Cost Muslim Educator Her Dream School").

12. For some Jews, the issue of an individual being Muslim is sometimes enough to assume a particular bias in regard to the Israeli-Palestinian conflict. (Of course, the converse can likewise be said.) Take, e.g., the following incident: A recent article from the largest Jewish weekly in the New York Metropolitan Area, *Jewish Week*, raised the question of whether or not the engagement of Congressman Anthony Weiner, a Jewish politician representing New York City's Ninth District, to Huma Abedin, a Muslim woman who is a longtime aide to Secretary of State Hillary Clinton, would potentially affect Weiner's stance on the Israeli-Palestinian conflict [Adam Dickter, "For the Love of Huma," *Jewish Week* (July 22, 2009), found at www.thejew-ishweek.com/viewArticle/c36_a163 63/News/New_York.html, retrieved July 22, 2009).

13. www.sfsu.edu/~news/announce/101.htm, retrieved December 23, 2010.

14. Though these three student groups have different organizational missions, they have adopted similar public stances on the issue of on-campus tensions related to the Israeli-Palestinian conflict at San Francisco State University.

15. Take an example of a different kind from 2007. Following the British University and College Union's resolution to consider a "Boycott of Israeli Academic Institutions," a number of American university chief administrators, including chancellors, presidents, and others, publicly censured the British-led resolution (see www.juf.org/pdf/jcrc/UCU_Boycott.pdf, retrieved July 30, 2010). These American university personnel came out in support of freedom of expression and speech as a general ethos; they did not express a particular stance related to the Israeli-Palestinian conflict per se. Yet because the specific issue involving freedom of speech was related to whether or not Israeli academics should be blacklisted due to their government's policies toward Palestinians, the position taken by these American administrators was seen by some as having been biased in favor of Israeli governmental policy.

16. See, e.g., Martin Mcquillan, ed., *Narrative Reader* (London: Routledge, 2000).

17. pewresearch.org/assets/pdf/muslim-americans.pdf, 10. In February 2008 the Pew Forum on Religion and Public Life published a survey estimating that Muslim Americans make up 0.6 percent of adult U.S. citizens, or 1.4 million adult Muslim Americans. Those such as Daniel Pipes seem to use the 0.6 percent figure as the total population of Muslim Americans rather than adult Muslim Americans, thereby reducing the Muslim population from 2.35 million to 1.8 million when using the figure 300 million as the total number of the American population [see Daniel Pipes, "How Many Muslims in the United States," *www.danielpipes.com* (April 22, 2003), found at www.danielpipes.org/blog/1, retrieved July 21, 2009]. Other figures for the Muslim American population, dating back as far as 1960, can be found at pewresearch.org/assets/pdf/muslim-americans.pdf, 11.

18. According to *Being Muslim in America*, produced by the Bureau of International Information Programs of the U.S. Department of State, "Because the United States does not track population by religion, there is no authoritative count of its Muslim population. Estimates range widely, from 2 million to 7 million or more" (www.america.gov/media/pdf/books/being-muslim-in-america.pdf, 11 and 48, retrieved July 6, 2010).

19 Tim W. Smith, "Estimating the Muslim Population in the United States" The American Jewish Committee (2001), found at www.ajc.org/site/apps/nlnet/content2.aspx?c=ijITI2PHKoG&b=838459&ct=1044159, retrieved July 22, 2009. As stated, this would not be noteworthy if the AJC conducted similar studies on other non-Jewish American groups.

20. Barksy is the director of AJC's Division of Middle East and International Terrorism. Some of her most recent claims about Muslim American organizations include the statement that most Muslim Student Association groups on university campuses today are run by individuals who are "followers of the Muslim Brotherhood" [Daniel Treiman, "California Campuses Gain a Reputation as Hotbeds of Anti-Israel Rhetoric," *Forward* (April 5, 2007) www.forward.com/articles/10471/, retrieved July 19, 2010].

21. Daniel Pipes, "How Many U.S. Muslims," *New York Post* (October 29, 2001), found at www.danielpipes.org/article/76, retrieved July 22, 2009. See also Pipes, "How Many Muslims in the United States."

22. Some argue that the AJC's intentions for conducting their study were also based on concerns that the political influence of American Muslims is growing [Rachel Zoll, "Group: Muslim Population Overstated," *Associated Press* (October 22, 2001)]. A *Los Angeles Times* article supports this claim, stating that around the time that the AJC's 2001 population survey was released, AJC "Executive Director David A. Harris urged American Jewry to unite with Israel to battle against the growing Arab and Muslim lobbies here [in the United States] and the challenge they present to long-standing U.S. support for Israel. Harris cited the 'myth' of high Muslim population figures as one tactic Muslims are using to advance their position" [Teresa Watanabe, "Private Studies Fuel Debate Over Size of U.S. Muslim Population," *Los Angeles Times* (October 21, 2001), citing a May 2001 issue of *Jerusalem Report*]. As can be expected, American Muslim leaders have been troubled by groups critiquing the population studies done on the American Muslim population *by* the American Muslim population. When the AJC came out with their study, the executive director of CAIR Nihad Awad said that the AJC-sponsored study was "part of an effort by the Jewish community to 'marginalize' Islam in the United States…Why are they worried about our numbers? What's it triggering?" Awad asked.

"We have never misrepresented our figures and have never been interested in competing with any other faith or ethnic community" [Bill Broadway, "Number of U.S. Muslims Depends on Who's Counting," *Washington Post* (November 24, 2001)].

23. Out of the United States' 2.35 million Muslim Americans, more than 65 percent are foreign-born, pointing to a much larger immigrant segment of the Muslim American population than those born in the United States. Of this group, 850,000 are under the age of eighteen (approximately 36 percent of the total Muslim American population), 1.4–1.5 million are over eighteen, and of this adult population only 39 percent have only been in the United States since 1990. In addition, more than one-third (37 percent) of foreign-born Muslim Americans have come from Arab-majority countries, including the Middle East and North Africa; an additional 27 percent emigrated from South Asia, including Pakistan, India, Bangladesh, and Afghanistan; another 8 percent have come from Europe; and 6 percent from other parts of Africa aside from the Northern Africa. As for the remaining 20 percent, they are African American (pewresearch.org/assets/pdf/muslim-americans.pdf, 1, 10, and 15). Another recent study conducted on Muslim Americans, carried out by researchers at Georgetown University, concluded almost identical results, stating that approximately 66 percent of all Muslim Americans were born outside the United States, 25 percent are African American, and of the portion of Muslims born outside the United States, 34 percent come from South Asia, 26 percent from Arab-majority countries in the Middle East, and 7 percent from sub-Saharan Africa. More important than these figures is the fact that when compared to most non-Muslim Americans, the Muslim American population is statistically better educated, better off socioeconomically, and younger, with 75 percent of Muslim Americans being less than fifty years old (Abdo, *Mecca and Main Street*, 63–64).

24. pewresearch.org/assets/pdf/muslim-americans.pdf, 11.

25. Ibid., 17.

26. For example, according to the PRC study, Muslim Americans have strong ideas on a range of issues confronting both Americans generally and the Muslim American community specifically. In the beginning of the study it says that this was the "first ever nationwide survey to attempt to measure rigorously the demographics, attitudes and experiences of Muslim Americans," among other reasons because "the U.S. Census is forbidden by law from asking questions about religious belief and affiliation, and, as a result, we know very little about the basic demographic characteristics of Muslim Americans…Muslim Americans comprise such a small percentage of the U.S. population that general population surveys do not interview a sufficient number of them to allow for meaningful analysis" ("Foreword," pewresearch.org/assets/pdf/muslim-americans.pdf). This is important because it reflects the newness of issues involving Muslim Americans. At best such studies provide a detailed description of a given community's dominant narrative; at worst they reflect only minor elements of a community's narrative, fringe ideas that subsequently are understood as dominant ideas by people outside the community. It is also important to point out that in the Pew Research Center's study many of the statistics are compared with Muslim populations in Western Europe and/or the Middle East as opposed to the way it is being presented in this essay, which compares it to a single non-Muslim American population, Jewish Americans.

27. Additional relevant statistics are as follows: (1) U.S.-born Muslim African Americans are the most disillusioned segment of the U.S. Muslim population. When compared with other Muslims in the U.S., they are more skeptical of the view that hard work pays off, and more of them believe that Muslim immigrants in the U.S. should try to remain distinct from society. Just 13 percent of this group expresses satisfaction with national conditions, compared with 29 percent of other American-born Muslims and 45 percent of Muslim immigrants. (2) Younger Muslim Americans—those under thirty—are more religiously observant and more accepting of Islamic extremism than older Muslim Americans. For example, younger Muslim Americans report attending services at a mosque more frequently than do older Muslims; a greater percentage of younger Muslims in the United States (60 percent) think of themselves as Muslims first and Americans second, whereas this drops to 41 percent among Muslim Americans ages thirty and older; and when compared with older Muslims, more than twice as many Muslim Americans under the age of thirty believe that suicide bombings can be or sometimes are justified in the defense of Islam (15 versus 6 percent). This said, very few Muslim Americans—just 1 percent—say that suicide bombings against civilian targets are often justified to defend Islam, an additional 7 percent say suicide bombings are sometimes justified in these circumstances,

and about two-thirds (69 percent) say that such tactics are never justified. Among Muslims who are thirty or older, by contrast, just 6 percent say suicide bombings can be often or sometimes justified, while 82 percent say such attacks are never warranted. (3) A quarter of Muslim Americans say they have been the victim of discrimination in the United States, while 73 percent say they have never experienced discrimination while living in this country. Far more American-born Muslims than Muslim immigrants say they have been a victim of discrimination (41 versus 18 percent). (4) Consistent with the views of Muslims in other countries, fewer than half of Muslim Americans—regardless of their age—accept the fact that groups of Arabs carried out the 9/11 attacks; just 40 percent say that groups of Arabs engineered the attacks. (5) Most Muslims in the United States express optimism that a balanced solution to the Israeli-Palestinian conflict can be found. Indeed, 61 percent of Muslim Americans say that "a way can be found for Israel to exist so that the rights and needs of the Palestinian people can be taken care of [as well]," compared with 16 percent who say that the rights and needs of Palestinians cannot be taken care of as long as Israel exists. In this regard, the opinions of U.S. Muslims closely resemble those expressed by the U.S. public as a whole (pewresearch.org/assets/pdf/muslim-americans.pdf, 3–7, 53–55).

28. Bukhari raised this point in an interview where he encourages the Muslim American community to become more involved in American society (Muslim American Society, "Muslims in American Politics" (October 14, 2004), found at masnet.org/contempissue.asp?id=1763, retrieved July 22, 2009).
29. Also called Muslim Student Unions, among other names.
30. Abdo, *Mecca and Main Street*, 101 and 197.
31. Ibid., 194.
32. Neil Farquhar, "For Muslim Students, a Debate on Inclusion," *New York Times* (February 21, 2008).
33. Abdo, *Mecca and Main Street*, 191.
34. This is a statement that was made in an Op-Ed found in the March 1968 edition of the MSAs' journal, *Al Ittihad* (ibid., 197).
35. Ibid., 191.
36. There are a number of university-based MSAs (and MSUs) that do not officially affiliate with the national MSA.
37. Sometimes this liberal versus conservative struggle plays out over issues such as gender roles. Other times it plays out between American-born and non-American-born Muslim students.
38. One major reason for this fact is that Muslim Americans, generally speaking, are one of the newest American communities. Second, in the same way that younger Muslim Americans are both more religiously observant and more accepting of Islamic extremism than older Muslim Americans, younger Muslims are likewise more outspoken in their religious and political opinions, especially with regard to the treatment of Muslim communities outside the United States. This commonly plays out on university campuses through student-led demonstrations.
39. See note 27, statistic number 4.
40. Another important statistic to underscore, stated previously, is that a majority of Muslim students maintain that the U.S. government can create a more balanced approach to the Israeli-Palestinian conflict, finding a way for Israel to exist while also satisfying the national ambitions of Palestinians. This reflects an openness toward intercommunal discussions, despite the fact that these same students have deep reservations of the benefits of such activities.
41. According to a study conducted on the American Jewish population carried out between 2000 and 2001, there are approximately 5.1 million Jews living in the United States, 4.1 million of whom are adults and 1.1 million children [United Jewish Communities, "National Jewish Population Survey," viii (2000–01), www.ujc.org/local_includes/downloads/3905.pdf]. In contrast, as previously stated, the Muslim American community is incredibly diverse, having immigrated to the United States from tens of different countries. In addition, the Muslim American population does not even make up 10 percent of the world's Muslim community, in contrast to Jews.
42. Some estimate that 80 percent of the world's 15 million Jews are Ashkenazi (Daniel J. Elazar, "Can Sephardic Judaism be Reconstructed?" *Jerusalem Center for Public Affairs*, www.jcpa.org/dje/articles3/ sephardic.htm). As for the ethnicities and races of the other one-fifth of Jewish Americans, according to Gary Tobin "perhaps 20 percent of Jewish Americans have Sephardi (strictly speaking, Jews whose ancestors lived in Spain or Portugal prior to the Inquisition),

Mizrahi (Jews from Middle Eastern countries), African, African-American, Hispanic, East Asian or mixed-race backgrounds" [Ira Rifkin, "Out of Egypt," *Jerusalem Report* (January 23, 2006) and Diane Tobin, Gary A. Tobin, and Scott Rubin, *In Every Tongue: The Racial & Ethnic Diversity of the Jewish People* (San Francisco: Institute for Jewish and Community Research, 2005)].

43. Many Jewish Americans trace their family history back to the late 1800s and early 1900s; beginning in the 1880s, mass emigration to the United States brought in large populations of Jews from Eastern Europe [Hasia R. Diner, *The Jews of the United States: 1654 to 2000* (Berkeley: University of California, Berkeley, 2004)]. This is in sharp contrast to Muslim Americans, most of whom are first generation Americans. In fact, it was not until the mid-1960s, when President Lyndon Johnson repealed immigration quotas, that large numbers of Muslims began moving to the United States. As for the 20 percent of the Muslim American community that are African American, a majority of this population grew out of the Nation of Islam movement, whose former leader Warith Deen Mumammed publicly moved toward Sunni Islam, the most popular Muslim denomination in the world, in the 1980s. Further, aside from synagogue affiliation, which is statistically higher for Jewish Americans than mosque affiliation is for Muslim Americans (as opposed to synagogue attendance versus mosque attendance), Jews commonly affiliate with other Jewish organizations, many of which have been around for decades. For example, the Jewish Federation, the first of which was established in Boston, was founded in 1895 (previously found at www.ujc.org/page.html?ArticleID=1 039&page=2). This Jewish organization has local chapters throughout the United States and, arguably, has been the most important Jewish communal structure in all of American Jewish history. In contrast, three of the most important Muslim American organizations—CAIR, ISNA (Islamic Society of North America), and MPAC (Muslim Public Affairs Council)—were all established over the last thirty years. CAIR was established in 1994 (www.cair.com/AboutUs/VisionMissionCorePrinciples.aspx, retrieved July 30, 2010), ISNA in 1982 (Abdo, *Mecca and Main Street*, 198), and MPAC in 1988 (www.mpac.org). Interestingly, on ISNA's website they state that they have been running activities for over four decades (www.isna.net/ISNAHQ/pages/About-ISNA-HQ.aspx, retrieved July 30, 2010); perhaps this is because ISNA was originally founded by members of the United States' first MSA chapter. Abdo, however, dates ISNA's inception not from the establishment of the first MSA, but rather from the time ISNA formally separated from the MSA. In short, the American Jewish community is much more homogenous—culturally, ideologically, religiously, and structurally—than the Muslim American community. Or, at a minimum, the Jewish American community is much more homogenous in how they identify ethnically—as Ashkenazi—as opposed to their actual pre-American ancestries; even Jews with mixed backgrounds outside of the Ashkenazi community sometimes identify as Ashkenazi.

44. Though there are general trends across the Jewish American community irrespective of age, there are also deviations from these norms across generational lines, with older Jewish Americans voicing less ideological heterogeneity than those who are younger.

45. The following additional information is particularly relevant when comparing trends between the Jewish American and Muslim American communities: (1) The median age of the Jewish population is older than it was ten years ago and is older than the median age of the total U.S. population. It is estimated that 20 percent of the Jewish population is under the age of eighteen, and 19 percent over the age of sixty-five. (2) Relative to the total U.S. population, Jews tend to marry at later ages. (3) Jewish women have somewhat lower fertility rates than all U.S. women, and Jewish fertility rates are below population replacement levels. (4) More Jews live in the northeast than any other region, but many American-born Jews have migrated to the south and west over the course of their lifetimes. (5) Relative to the total U.S. population, Jews are more highly educated, have more prestigious jobs, and earn higher household incomes. (6) The intermarriage rate for Jews who have married since 1996 is 47 percent. (7) Intermarriage is more common among young adults, Jews in the West, Jews with no or less intensive forms of Jewish education, those with lower levels of secular education, and the adult children of intermarried parents. Among adult Jews with intermarried parents, those raised Jewish are less likely to be intermarried than those not raised Jewish [United Jewish Communities, "National Jewish Population Survey," viii (2000–01), www.ujc.org/local_includes/downloads/3905.pdf].

46. Partially due to the fact that Muslims comprise 20–25 percent of the planet's population, in contrast to the incredibly small number of Jews worldwide, the Muslim community is not nearly as concerned with survival as are Jews.

47. Steven M. Cohen and Ari Y. Kelman, "Beyond Distancing: Young Adult Jewish American and Distancing from Israel" (August 2007), 9–10, www.acbp.net/About/PDF/Beyond%20 Distancing.pdf, retrieved August 4, 2009. Please note that the authors of this study present much of their statistical data in the form of a bar graph. As such, the precise numerical values listed in this essay are estimates. What is most pertinent from their data is that there is a clear correlation between the age of the interviewees and how they answer particular questions, with the youngest cohort, those under thirty-five, expressing the least connection to the state of Israel.

48. For our purposes, the more important statistics from this study are as follows: (1) When asked about how much one maintains that "caring about Israel is an important part of being a Jew," 83 percent of those above sixty-five, 77 percent of those between fifty and sixty-four, 62 percent of those between thirty-five and forty-nine, and 60 percent of those under thirty-five agreed. (2) When asked if one was "worried that the U.S. will not be an ally of Israel," 62 percent of those above sixty-five, 60 percent of those between fifty and sixty-four, 45 percent of those between thirty-five and forty-nine, and 41 percent of those under thirty-five agreed. (3) When asked if "Israel's destruction would be a personal tragedy," 78 percent of those above sixty-five, 64 percent of those between fifty and sixty-four, 58 percent of those between thirty-five and forty-nine, and 45 percent of those under thirty-five agreed. (4) When asked if one "talks about Israel to one's Jewish friends," 60 percent of those above sixty-five, 45 percent of those between fifty and sixty-four, 37 percent of those between thirty-five and forty-nine, and 30 percent of those under thirty-five agreed. (5) When asked if one "talks about Israel to one's non-Jewish friends," 38 percent of those above sixty-five, 31 percent of those between fifty and sixty-four, 22 percent of those between thirty-five and forty-nine, and 26 percent of those under thirty-five agreed. (6) When asked if one "is drawn to stories about Israel," 80 percent of those above sixty-five, 70 percent of those between fifty and sixty-four, 58 percent of those between thirty-five and forty-nine, and 57 percent of those under thirty-five agreed (ibid.).

49. Elsewhere in this same study Cohen and Kelman note, "Thus, members of the oldest generation of Jewish Americans, born before World War II, may be highly attached to Israel in part because Jewish American have long maintained a remarkable relationship with Israel. Over the years, their fervent attachment has produced billions of dollars in ongoing philanthropic assistance, a powerful and effective pro-Israel lobby, tens of thousands of visits annually, a steady stream of *aliyah* (settlement in Israel), and myriad other examples of contact and support, ranging from Israeli film festivals to a growing American Jewish competency in Hebrew. All these expressions of support and engagement rest upon a passionate love of Israel by some Jews, and feelings of warmth, attachment and closeness by most…Members of the oldest generation of Jewish Americans, born before World War II, may be highly attached to Israel in part because they can remember the Holocaust and the subsequent founding of the State. Their children, the Baby Boomers, have also experienced events that have, for many, forged a strong sense of Israel connection. For them, memories of the Six Day War and the ensuing period of pro-Israel mobilization have created strong feelings of attachment. Many members of these two generations see Israel as socially progressive, tolerant, peace-seeking, efficient, democratic and proudly Jewish, a society that has successfully withstood mortal threats from malevolent, hostile and fanatical enemies…If it turns out that age-related variations in Israel attitudes are tied to the family life cycle, then we can presume that many young people will come to adopt their elders' warmer attitudes toward Israel as they mature. However, if these gaps between old and young regarding Israel attachment are due primarily to birth cohort effects, then we may presume that the declines are more permanent and that the gaps today will influence the stance of American Jewry toward Israel for years to come" (ibid, 2–5).

50. Ibid., 11.

51. See, e.g., Daniel Boyarin and Jonathan Boyarin, "Diaspora: Generation and the Ground of Jewish Identity," *Critical Inquiry*, Vol. 19, No. 4 (Summer 1993), 716; Naomi Weiner Cohen, *American Jews and the Zionist Idea* (New York: Ktav Publishing, 1975); Samuel C. Heilman, *Portrait of American Jews: The Last Half of the 20th Century* (Seattle: University of Washington Press, 1995); Simon Herman, *Israelis and Jews, the Continuity of an Identity* (New York: Random House, 1970); Henry Holt, *Homelands: Portraits in the New Jewish Diaspora* (New York: Henry Holt, 2001); and Tony Kusher and Alisa Solomon, eds., *Wrestling with Zion* (New York: Grove Press, 2003).

52. www.hillel.org/about/facts/history/default, retrieved July 30, 2010. See also Jeffrey Rubin, "The Road to Renaissance, 1923–2002," Hillel, 2002, www.hillel.org/NR/rdonlyres/ C5146418-3638-435A-8BB9-24592F55 00F9/0/hillel_history.pdf, retrieved July 30, 2010.

53. www.hillel.org/about/facts/who_what/default.htm, retrieved July 30, 2010. Please note that the national organization of the MSA does not publicize how many chapters they have, nor do they publicize their organizational budget.

54. The exact number was $26,143,301 (see their 2007 990 form, found at www.guidestar.org/ FinDocuments //2008/521/ 844/2008-521844823-051153c8-9.pdf, retrieved July 30, 2010). This represents the budget for Hillel International, the Hillel headquarters in Washington, DC, and does not represent the individual budgets of each separate Hillel chapter. As stated earlier, the annual budget of the MSA is not readily available.

55. See William Marra, "Muslim Student Groups Turn to Jewish Organizations for Inspiration: Cash-strapped Muslim Student Groups Learning about Organizing from Hillel," ABC News (August 8, 2007), abcnews.go.com/US/story?id=3459548&page=1, retrieved July 8, 2010. According to this report, the international budget for Hillel is sixty-six million dollars. I am grateful to Taymiya Zaman for bringing my attention to this source.

56. These include such organizations as the American Jewish Committee, the Anti-Defamation League, the David Project, the Jewish Federation, the Jewish Community Relations Council, Stand With Us, and the Zionist Organization of America, among others.

57. This is reflective of the generational differences between older and younger Muslim Americans in regard to taking public stances on political issues; younger Muslim Americans are much more outspoken. And although MSAs often receive monetary support from off-campus Muslim organizations, and members of some off-campus Muslim communities offer their guidance and support to campus-based Muslim students, many issues on campuses are not issues off-campus Muslim communities chose to address publicly, something also reflected in the PRC's study.

58. There has been controversy surrounding the building of Muslim community centers and mosques in a number of cities across the US, such as Boston [see Raja Mishra, "Muslim, Jewish Leaders See Fresh Start," Boston Globe (May 31, 2007)] and New York City [Laurie Goodstein, "Across Nation, Mosque Projects Meet Opposition," New York Times (August 7, 2010), www.nytimes.com/2010/08/08/us/08mosque.html?_r=1&scp=12&sq=Ground Zero mosque&st=cse, retrieved February 7, 2011.].

59. During my interviews, a number of American Jews expressed dismay that Muslim Americans voiced general feelings of disempowerment, surprised that a community that made up 20–25 percent of the world's population could feel marginalized.

60. Deepa Bharath, "Muslim Student Union Members Shocked by Suspension," *Orange County Register* (June 14, 2010), www.ocregister.com/articles/university-253265-union-student.html, retrieved July 8, 2010. See also Lisa Armony, "UC Irvine Suspends Muslim Group," *Jewish Journal* (June 15, 2010), www.jewishjournal.com/community/article/uc_irvine_suspends_ muslim_group_20100615/, retrieved July 8, 2010 and Omar Kurdi, "UC Irvine's message: Criticize Israel, get suspended," *Los Angeles Times* (June 21, 2010), www.latimes.com/news/ opinion/opinionla/la-oew-0622-kurdi-uci-muslim-20100622,0,1942963.story, retrieved July 8, 2010.

61. "Anti-American values" as defined by those such as Bill O'Reilly (see note 65).

62. See Randy Lewis, "Time to Stand Back, Take a Deep Breath," *Daily Pilot* (June 27, 2004).

63. "ADL Statement on the Muslim Student Union at UC-Irvine" (June 18, 2004), www.adl.org/ PresRele/Mise_00/4520_00.htm, retrieved July 30, 2010.

64. The ADL's retraction read as follows: "The Anti-Defamation League is respectful of the Shahada, the Muslim Declaration of Faith, which is expressed by millions of Muslims around the world. ADL's statement referring to the Shahada addressed our concerns about the abuse of this religious expression by radical Islamic groups and individuals in connection with suicide bombings and other forms of terrorism. At [our local university] some members of the Muslim Student Union engage in this abuse by wearing the Shahada on armbands at the same time that they rationalize terrorism and express support for the terrorist groups, Hezbollah and Hamas. It was never our intent to offend anyone and we apologize to those who took offense" ("ADL Statement on the Muslim Student Union at UC-Irvine, UPDATED," June 22, 2004; ibid.).

65. "Campus Controversy at U.C. Irvine: Factor Follow-up," Fox News Channel (June 19, 2004), www.foxnews.com/story/0,2933,123274,00.html, retrieved July 30, 2010.

66. One such group was the Orange County Independent Task Force on Anti-Semitism, origi-
    nally founded by Jeffrey Ripps, the executive director of the Hillel Foundation of Orange
    County [Associated Press, "Jewish Group Forming Task Force on Anti-Semitism at UC
    Irvine" (February 15, 2007)]. However, after Ripps decided to officially disaffiliate Hillel
    from the investigation, in October 2007, the Task Force renamed themselves with the newly
    inserted word, "Independent," and continued their investigation. See, e.g., "Orange County
    Independent Task Force on Anti-Semitism at UCI Report," octaskforce.wordpress.com/
    (February 15, 2008); Zionist Organization of America, "Press Release" (October 22, 2007),
    previously found at www.zoa.org/2007/10/zoa_disappointe_11.htm.

67. Brad A. Greenberg, "Quiet War on Campus: Israel Remains under Attack Despite Fewer Public
    Protests," *Jewish Journal* (August 20, 2008), www.jewishjournal.com/education/article/quiet_
    war_on_campus_israel_remains_under_attack_despite_fewer_public_protes/, retrieved July
    30, 2010.

68. anteatersforisrael.org/2008/03/uci-jewish-student-leaders-stronglysupport-chancellor-
    drake/, retrieved July 30, 2010.

69. Marla Jo Fisher, "Jewish Students Say UC Irvine is Safe," *Orange County Register* (March 28,
    2008).

70. The term "dialogue" has taken on a stigma by numerous disempowered groups because in con-
    texts when there are two groups at play the group with less power leaves such meetings feeling
    disempowered. Meetings of this kind commonly create environments where the empowered
    group dominates the conversation and/or the logistical planning for the meeting (where it is
    held, when it is held, etc.), creating experiences that actually further disempower the already
    disempowered group. Some intergroup education organizations, such as Abraham's Vision, do
    not use the term "dialogue" for this precise reason.

71. As stated earlier, though "Arabs" and "Muslims" are not synonyms, and therefore neither are
    the identities of "Palestinian Arabs" and "Muslims," a majority of Palestinians are Muslim
    and the primary way the Israeli-Palestinian conflict plays out on American campuses is in and
    through student groups identifying as Jewish or Muslim (see note 3).

72. By no means does this statement support such notions that "Jews are in control" of x, y, and
    z; power is quite different than control. Rather, it is a fact that Jewish Americans are dispro-
    portionately represented in U.S. government positions, the film industry, and the media, three
    important spheres of power and influence in America. For additional readings on power in
    general, see Peter Ackerman and Jack Duvall, *A Force More Powerful: A Century of Nonviolent
    Conflict* (New York: Palgrave, 2000); Hannah Arendt, *On Violence* (New York: Harcourt Brace
    & Company, 1970); Walter Benjamin, "Critique of Violence," in *Reflections*, Peter Demetz, ed.
    (New York: Schocken Books, 1978); Jacques Derrida, "Force of Law: The Mystical Foundation
    of Authority," in *Acts of Religion*, Gil Anidjar, ed. (New York: Routledge, 2002); Paulo Freire,
    Pedagogy of the Oppressed (New York: Continuum, 2006); Fred Halliday, *The Middle East in
    International Relations: Power, Politics, and Ideology* (New York: Cambridge University Press,
    2005); Nadim N. Rouhana and Susan T. Fiske, "Perception of Power, Threat, and Conflict
    Intensity in Asymmetric Intergroup Conflict: Arab and Jewish Citizens of Israel," *The Journal
    of Conflict Resolution*, Vol. 39, No. 1 (March 1995), 49–81; Carl Schmitt, *The Concept of the
    Political*, George D. Schwab, trans. (Chicago: University of Chicago Press, 1996); Gene Sharp,
    The Politics of Nonviolent Action: Parts One, Two, and Three (Boston: Porter Sargent Publishers,
    1973). See also Ami Eden, "Playing the Holocaust Card," *New York Times* (January 29, 2005),
    www.nytimes.com/2005/01/29/opinion/29eden.html, retrieved July 30, 2010.

CHAPTER SEVEN

Muslims, Jews, and Religious Visibility on American College Campuses

Taymiya R. Zaman

Introduction

The institutional accommodation of Muslim religious practice has posed a challenge to American college campuses. The installation of footbaths (used by Muslims to wash their feet before prayer) at the University of Michigan, Dearborn, in 2007 drew heated protest, as did Harvard University's decision to grant Muslim women's request for women-only gymnasium hours in 2008. At the same time, the presence of spaces in which Jewish students can practice religious rituals has not raised similar questions about the separation of church and state on these same campuses. This is because historical differences in the immigration experiences of Jewish and Muslim communities in the United States have meant that Muslims and Jews negotiate group identity differently on campuses. The overt nature of anti-Semitism on American campuses in the early twentieth century meant that Jews in higher education found ways to protect religious observance and promote group advocacy without relying solely on university funds. Today, privately funded Jewish groups such as Hillel are able to create spaces for Jewish religious observance without needing to use university funds to do so. Conversely, the relatively new presence of Muslims in institutions of higher education and the steep rise in anti-Muslim sentiment since the attacks of 9/11 have meant that Muslim student groups formulate methods of advocacy on campuses that appeal to the protection of institutional structures. This leads to conflicts between institutional commitments to secular education, and commitments to diversity and tolerance. (Regarding the two episodes mentioned earlier, e.g., critics asserted that both Harvard and the University of Michigan, Dearborn, privileged Islam over other religions by integrating Muslim religious adherences into the arranging of public space.)

This essay examines the challenge posed to American campuses by visible Muslim practices, and historicizes these challenges by examining the divergences and similarities in Jewish and Muslim immigration experiences in the United States. It also analyzes moments of collaboration between Jewish and Muslim student groups—the Muslim Students Association in Dearborn, for instance, actively turned to Hillel for guidance—and puts forth suggestions of ways that the presence of religious ritual can lead to dynamic instances of interfaith learning and civic engagement on American campuses. Through this piece, my goal is to illustrate how visible instances of religious observance, far from interfering with the goals of liberal arts education, can actually enhance them.

Accommodating the Unfamiliar

The rituals associated with Muslim prayer occupy an abiding and familiar presence in the Muslim world. If one were to trace the path of sunrise across the Muslim world, beginning in Jakarta, moving northwest toward Dhaka, across the Indian subcontinent to Kabul, further west through Isfahan and Damascus, and finally across northern Africa, from Cairo to Rabat, the day would begin with the *azan*, or call to prayer. It is not unusual in these cities to walk through a crowded bazaar and see shopkeepers praying in the backs of their shops. Nor is it unusual to see prayer in public parks, on university campuses, or on sheets spread hurriedly on the ground at the side of a long road.

Similarly, washing for prayer is a familiar ritual. I can personally attest to having watched Muslims washing for prayers sitting in parked cars, kneeling beside rivers and streams, and perching comfortably at washing stations for prayers in airports. The public enactment of these rituals is familiar even to those who do not participate in them in the same way that the rituals of Christmas and Thanksgiving are familiar to me, after having lived in the United States for over a decade.[1] If the landscape of a new country should be unfamiliar to an immigrant, then it stands to reason that a landscape lacking a space for Muslim prayer—beyond the obvious physical presence of mosques—should be alienating to Muslim immigrants. It also stands to reason that Muslim attempts to change the landscape by asking that the rituals associated with prayer be institutionally protected would be perceived as a glaring indication of something fundamental to Muslim communities that puts them at odds with America.

In October 2007, the University of Michigan, Dearborn, made one such institutional commitment by deciding to spend twenty-five thousand dollars to install footbaths for Muslim students to wash their feet for prayers. The decision came after reports of puddles on bathroom floors; with no sound alternative, Muslim students had been using sinks to wash their feet. The controversy over the university's decision centered upon the conflict between the nonsectarian commitments of the administration and their alleged preference for one religion over others through their accommodation of its practices. Kary Moss, the director of the American Civil Liberties Union in Michigan, stated that the footbaths could be perceived as having been necessary because of safety concerns, and were not inherently religious because they could be used by anyone and were not limited to one group of students only.[2]

Angry editorials and blog entries on both sides of the argument ensued. Those in favor of the footbaths argued that commitments to diversity should include religious diversity, and that were footbaths a part of Christian prayer their presence on American campuses would not be questioned.[3] Those against the school's decision emphasized the secular commitments of public universities, maintaining that they were not singling out Islam but were rather focusing on a specific Muslim practice to make a larger point about the need for separating church and state. Many editorials were tinged with the fear and distrust of Muslims, which has become a part of the American landscape following the attacks of 9/11.[4]

Why do Muslims on college campuses come into contact with administrative commitments designed to repeat a circular discursive pattern? Eruptions of this pattern are endemic on college campuses, and are almost formulaic in their unfolding. A Muslim student group makes a request for a particular accommodation, as in the case of Harvard University, where Muslim women requested and were granted gym hours restricted only to women in 2008, or the presence of Muslim students leads to an accommodation, as in the case of Dearborn.[5] Regardless of the decision of the institution, reports of the accommodation—denied or granted—circulate in a virtual world composed of personal blogs, online newspapers, and websites, many of which are dedicated to collecting information about the threat that Muslims pose to American institutions. Muslim advocacy sites respond to such hate speech by emphasizing the urgency of institutional accommodations of Muslim practice, and the cycle gains momentum once again when sparked by another event. Such a cyclical, formulaic method of disseminating information lends fixity to irreconcilable positions rather than leading to innovative ways of questioning why such positions are the only way to understand the presence of a minority perceived as being a threat.

I believe that an historical narrative of Muslims on American campuses can further our understanding of the causes of this cycle. In doing so, we can aid in breaking the pattern altogether. While the question is one clearly rooted in diversity and accommodation, it is also a question that has arisen because of history and experiences of Muslim immigrants as reflected in the microcosm of the American college campus. The question can be answered more fully when comparing Muslim students with Jewish ones who come from a community of immigrants whose religious adherences and practices bear a striking similarity to Muslim ones, but whose claims on space do not present a challenge on college campuses today.

Jewish and Muslim Immigrant Communities and
American Campuses

At first glance, an ahistorical perspective of Muslims and Jews as religious communities reveals certain similarities. As emphasized in interfaith dialogue or instances of intercultural collaboration on college campuses, both communities share a belief in God's covenant with Abraham. Both follow similar dietary laws and pray in a comparable manner. Both communities are also relatively recent immigrants to North America, compared to Christian immigrants of Western European origin. Aside from isolated instances, Jews began to immigrate to the United States in larger numbers in the late nineteenth century, and there is evidence that immigrants from the Arabic-speaking Middle East (both Muslims and non-Muslims) began to immigrate to the United States at about the same time.[6]

However, two major differences between Jews and Muslims who immigrated to the United States determine the politics of Islam and public space that affect American college campuses today. First, while Jewish immigrants lost certain aspects of their ethnicity when creating a new Jewish American identity, until as late as the 1970s Muslim immigrants continued to privilege their non-American ethnic and national identity over their religious identity. This was partially because of the international attention given to the nations from which Muslim immigrants came.[7] Second, Jewish immigrants arrived as an ethno-religious minority that promoted its own advancement though cultural assimilation, which eventually manifested in their reliance on private funds to support Jewish students on university campuses. In terms of divergent privileging of ethnic identities over religious identities, Muslims were not able to come together in this manner, nor were they able to create a unifying financial platform for their religious needs. Because of this comparative disadvantage, Muslims continue, even outside of college campuses, to work through universities' institutional support for their causes rather than relying on private funds. Campus politics regarding religious accommodation have subsequently become a by-product of broader historical patterns of immigration and assimilation.

The history of Jewish students on American campuses has been well-documented, as has the anti-Semitism Jews faced in the United States in the nineteenth and early twentieth centuries. In the 1920s, elite universities such as Harvard, Princeton, and Yale adopted policies that restricted the number of Jewish students allowed to enroll, imposing similar restrictions on other marginalized minorities, such as African Americans. The "Jewish problem" meant that elite colleges faced a lack of support from their (non-Jewish) donors, which was compensated for by demonstrating their commitment to maintaining a campus where Jews could enroll only in limited numbers.[8] At the same time, the emphasis placed on education by Jewish immigrants meant that Jews came to constitute a highly educated minority. Indeed they even created a number of their own private universities: Hebrew Union College-Jewish Institute of Religion was founded in 1875; Yeshiva University was established as a school for religious learning in 1886, as was the Jewish Theological Seminary; and Brandeis University was established as a "nonsectarian, Jewish-sponsored institution" in 1926.[9] More than a century after the establishment of the country's first Jewish universities, there is no equivalent for Muslim education in the United States. In fact, it is only in the past decade that American Muslims have begun to pioneer efforts toward creating institutions of higher learning for Muslims. The Islamic University of Minnesota was founded in 2007, and Zaytuna College in California is currently seeking applications for its first freshman class, to begin in fall 2010.

The creation of Jewish institutions of higher learning led in turn to the creation of spaces for Jewish life on campus. This need arose as a result of Jewish exclusion from Christian fraternities and student clubs that for the most part catered solely to Christian students. Hillel, currently the largest organization for Jewish life on American universities, was created at the University of Illinois, Urbana-Champaign, in 1923, and by 1939 had established chapters on thirty campuses.[10] The founding of Hillel marked a key historical moment in the Jewish American experience, something that arguably set the tone for Jewish campus life for the next century. Before the founding of Hillel, local Jewish community leaders had discussed the importance of having a synagogue near campus to meet the needs of Jewish students. In 1918, Sinai Temple in downtown Champaign was built using funds procured from Jewish philanthropists and members of other Jewish congregations. Rabbi Benjamin Frankel, ordained by Hebrew Union College, served as the institution's founding leader. After growing acquainted with a number of Jewish students, Frankel impressed upon the Chicago Board of Rabbis the need for funds to support Jewish life on campus.[11]

By creating Hillel through funds generated from the American Jewish community, Frankel was able to forge links between students and the larger national community to which they belonged. The early recognition that access to private funds was integral to protecting group identity proved to be a defining decision of the community in the years ahead. Hillel grew to become a national Jewish student organization that met the religious, educational, and social needs of Jewish university students while emphasizing the Judeo-Christian heritage professed by many, if not most, American college students.[12] In this, Hillel not only protected Jewish identity, but also played an active role in shaping the identities and allegiances of Jews across campuses. Currently, Hillel operates internationally with an estimated budget of sixty-six million dollars.[13] As in the case of Jewish universities, there is no national campus organization for Muslims that parallels Hillel.

In turning to Muslim history in the United States it is germane to address the term "Muslim" itself. While "Muslim" is a category that seems to be all-encompassing for most Americans, the diversity within the Muslim

world is one that must be understood if we are to accurately contextual-
ize the relative newness of organizations that cater to a student's Muslim
identity alone. I began this essay by discussing how the act of prayer is
common to Muslims across the world. Not common to Muslims across
the world are the local frameworks through which they practice their
religion. By this I mean that aspects of culture—such as food, language,
and devotional practice—that are dear to individual Muslims are far from
identical across the vast territory that constitutes Muslim-majority countries. The Muslim in Jakarta may pray in Arabic the way the Muslim in
India does, but the cultural world to which he belongs and the language
in which his parents speak to him are different. In the same way, a Muslim
from Sri Lanka may have more in common culturally with a Buddhist
from Sri Lanka than she would with a Muslim from Saudi Arabia. As
such, on a university campus, such a Muslim student may choose to join an
on-campus group that focuses on her Tamil cultural heritage rather than
one that focuses solely on her Muslim beliefs.[14] This is why it is unsurpris-
ing that the wave of middle-class professionals from Arab countries who
arrived in the United States in the 1960s often chose to join organizations
that catered to a shared Arab heritage inclusive of Christians and Muslims
rather than joining organizations exclusive to Muslims.

This said, the rapid growth in the population of Muslim students on
college campuses, the emergence of demands for the protection of civil
liberties, and the prominence given to religion as a form of identity in
newly emergent postcolonial Muslim-majority nations have made the formation of the Muslim Student Association (MSA) well in keeping with
the climate of the times. As such, the MSA of North America and Canada
was founded in 1963 (interestingly also at the University of Illinois at
Urbana-Champaign). While Hillel was founded by a rabbi and funded
through outside sources, the MSA at Urbana-Champaign was founded by
students and relied primarily on university funds.

But it wasn't until 1983 that the first national organization for Muslims,
the Islamic Society of North America (ISNA), was founded, established
by members of the MSA.[15] Today, though the MSA has many chapters,
individual Muslim groups on campus need not affiliate with them. The
MSA remains loosely tied to ISNA, but the degree to which any chapter
of the MSA attends ISNA conferences varies across campuses and depends
on the nature of student leadership at any given time. Although the website for the MSA does not document the history of the organization in
any great detail, it provides instructions for students to create "Muslim-
friendly" campuses. This includes appealing to a school administration
for prayer rooms, and settling for interfaith spaces should the request for
a room not be granted.[16] The MSA also has guidelines for requesting a
college to provide food that is in keeping with Muslim dietary guidelines.
In these cases, the MSA relies on college space, funds, and accommodations in a way that Hillel does not. Meanwhile, ISNA sponsors programs
of outreach and education for Muslims, and appears to recognize that

the crux of mobilization is funding. For example, at ISNA's first Annual Muslim Chaplain Conference, Dr. Ingrid Mattson, ISNA's current president, acknowledged that just as Hillel is able to fund their own campus clergy, so too should ISNA follow such a model.[17] And, as mentioned in the case of the footbaths installed at the University of Michigan, Dearborn, Muslim students actively turned to Hillel for advice on how to organize in order to finance religious activities.[18]

It is also worth noting that Muslim immigrants who came to the United States in the 1960s often came from countries where they did not constitute a minority. Unlike Jews, they lacked a history of community organizing on the basis of having a minority identity. They also did not come from a background marked by persecution equivalent to the anti-Semitism historically faced by European Jewish minorities. I would speculate that the relative privilege that such Muslim immigrants brought with them and the America to which they came meant that they have been more likely drawn to institutional structures rather than challenge or bypass them altogether. (Interestingly, African American Muslims, who in fact have a longer history with the movement for civil rights in the United States than any other American Muslim group, did not play a large role in the formation of early Muslim student groups.[19])

Furthermore, given American constitutional commitments to the protection of religious diversity, appealing to institutional structures on college campuses has been fairly successful for Muslims. In the case of the footbaths in Dearborn, for instance, local Muslim leaders decided not to raise private money to pay for footbaths following the ACLU's declaration that the footbaths did not raise constitutional problems.[20] Although Muslim attempts to seek institutional accommodation are used by critics to point to the fundamental otherness of Muslims, the diffuse, localized presence of Muslim groups in America is indicative of the many cultures within the American Muslim community rather than any singular difference that places all of them at odds with non-Muslim America.

Inventing the American Muslim

The American Muslim—where "Muslim" and "American" occupy two inviolate identities to be privileged over others—is a relatively new phenomenon. This might explain the absence of urban spaces catering to individuals seeking to identify as such. The events of 9/11 acted as a catalyst for the urgency that is currently linked to the emergence of this identity, simultaneously making Muslims more visible as a group based solely on religious classification. In the fall of 2001, numerous Muslim community leaders appeared on American television, earnest about proving their allegiances both to Islam and to America. The years that followed saw a burgeoning of academic positions in the history, religions, and politics of the "Muslim world." Muslims also began to raise awareness about

Islam in a performative manner that was distinctly American; Islam, as such, appears now on billboard campaigns, bumper stickers, t-shirts, and magnets.[21] These purchasable forms of public expression are American in form, but Muslim in content.[22] They are also part of a process through which Islam has become stripped of ethnicity and narrowed down to its religious texts and teachings.[23]

While Muslim statements about the need to learn from Hillel may be seen on the surface as an encouraging sign of interfaith collaboration, the implicit premise that if Jewish people could prosper in America despite blatant anti-Semitism so can Muslims is one that should be interrogated further, especially because it calls for a downplaying of ethnicity in favor of religion.[24] This raises the following points of inquiry: Is it useful or meaningful to reduce the mosaic of Muslim ethnicities and cultures down to an amalgam of religious teachings and allegiances to America? Can there be more imaginative methods of civic engagement among Jews and Muslims on college campuses? And finally, are the nonsectarian commitments of universities inherently valuable, and are such commitments necessarily the best safeguard for the diversity of religious and cultural expression?

My answer to the first question, as both an historian and a Muslim, is a resounding no. I have taught classes on the Ottoman, Mughal, and Safavid Empires, and have found my students enthralled with the diversity that is to be found in the vast scope of the Muslim world. In the centuries that saw the expansion of Islam, lived practices and local laws carried as much, if not more, weight than religious texts. Since the goal of Muslim empires was the expansion of power rather than conversion, it was simply more pragmatic to allow local practices to continue, and to patronize local craft guilds, ruling families, and ethnic communities as a means of vitalizing the economic and social life of the empire.[25] It was only under the legal codes created by colonial rule that Muslims, Christians, and Jews came to be defined and differentiated from one another on the basis of their religious texts alone; these definitions have created more bloodshed than can possibly be accounted for. The seeking of a Muslim identity easily packaged into "1-877" numbers and billboards, while well-intentioned, marks a break with the past, and a move toward homogenization that is counter to the expressions of diversity that have characterized most of Muslim history.[26]

By emulating such a model on contemporary American campuses, and by hoping to create a Muslim equivalent to Hillel, students are unconsciously reaffirming the very category to which they are reduced by those who seek to emphasize their otherness. Furthermore, the nonsectarian commitments of universities lend themselves to this process by placing religion in a category whose access to institutional funds is problematic. In this, religion, and especially religion that has not yet found a way to become "American," implicitly becomes suspect. The more suspect it becomes, the more protection it requires through appeals to the very institutional structures that do not possess the ability to accommodate its complexity and color.

I am reminded here of a poignant and haunting essay by Matthew Goodman in *The American Scholar*.[27] The essay, titled "Falling in Love with Yiddish," chronicles the author's foray into the world of Yiddish and his sadness at the loss of a language that captured a Jewish world no longer welcome in campaigns of assimilation where Hebrew emerged as the dominant language of a new American Jewish identity. Goodman describes Yiddish as a language existing in a world of hats, coats, and elderly people, and its fading as an inevitable consequence of the cruel twentieth century. I would say this reflects losses that are likely to come about as Muslims forge an American Muslim identity. Will American Muslims study Arabic to learn about the Qur'an at the expense of the textures of Urdu, or the resonance of Persian, or even the particular nuances of commentaries on the Qur'an in languages other than English?

I believe that civic engagement between Muslims and Jews should not center only on a model of winning at being American that is embodied by Hillel. Rather, it should involve an appreciation for the cultural diversity within both communities, as well as an openness to question the structures of power that place Jews and Muslims at odds with one another by making them competitors in a model of assimilation that damages even as it grants privilege.[28] Finally, I do not believe that there is anything *inherently* valuable about the nonsectarian commitments of educational institutions in the United States. There is no evidence that institutional accommodations of religious practice affect the quality of liberal arts education or interfere with the atmosphere that nonsectarian institutional commitments seek to provide. While the view that an ahistorical entity called "religion" causes strife and warfare is fashionable, there is no historical evidence that religiously affiliated educational institutions are any more or less damaging to diversity than those that identify as secular.

Writing as a Muslim professor who teaches at a Jesuit Catholic University, I have found that the religious commitments of the University of San Francisco, for example, provide for an atmosphere more tolerant of the practice of my faith than I have found at secular institutions. When I have expressed to Muslim colleagues elsewhere that my leaving class to break my Ramadan fast is considered by the administration to be a valuable way for my students to learn about Islam, they have expressed surprise at this degree of institutional support. My students have found that watching the otherwise rigid hours of classroom time change to hours marked by the setting of the sun has contributed to their understanding of worship in the Muslim world. Allowing students to see the link between worship and the changing of the light has been a tangible way of bringing Islam to the classroom through my own lived practice rather than through textual description alone.

I would speculate that in an atmosphere where faith is part of an admissible institutional vocabulary, the multiplicity of religious expression does not cause the ruptures that it does elsewhere. Instead, the presence of a diverse body of Muslims teaching Islam at Jesuit Catholic universities is a promising area in which institutional commitments to religious practice enhance religious dialogue and education.[29] This is not to say that I believe religious affiliations on the part of educational institutions always create dynamic spaces for religious diversity. Rather, the ability that such schools have to do this is one that has not been given the attention it deserves precisely because it is the conflicts between Muslims and secular institutions that make national news. Such incidents feed into the cyclical and formulaic rhetoric that surrounds the presence of Muslims in the United States. Without the interventions of historical understanding, such rhetoric is unlikely to yield meaningful change.

Concluding Thoughts: History for the Future

I have spoken with several Muslim students who chose to study Arabic in college instead of the native language of their parents, and who frequently engage in interfaith dialogue with Jewish students regarding similarities between the Torah and the Qur'an. However, Jews are not the Torah, and Muslims are not the Qur'an; nor for that matter are Hebrew and Arabic the only languages through which Jews and Muslims have historically chosen to represent themselves. There is no college campus that would not benefit from accommodating the many ways that people express their Jewish or Muslim identities or from adding historical context to interfaith dialogue. For instance, dialogue between Muslim and Jewish students could include the study of immigration and identity, and dialogue among Muslims could include a willingness to see diversity within Muslim communities as a strength rather than an obstacle on the way to becoming American. Such topics are often left to professors like myself to teach in upper-division courses; however, they are of enormous consequence to a different kind of dialogue between Muslim and Jewish students, one that should take place.

What would collaboration between Muslims and Jews look like if, along with comparing the Torah and the Qur'an, they were to read the poetry of Said Sarmad, a seventeenth-century Indian poet and mystic who identified as both a Jew and a Muslim, and gained the honor of being buried next to Delhi's grandest mosque, commissioned by Shah Jahan, the Muslim king who built the Taj Mahal?[30] What would happen to the otherness of Muslims—as typified by footbaths—if Jewish students were to insist on using the footbaths in an act of solidarity, or if Muslims and Jews were to pray together on a campus lawn? These instances of collaboration might allow Muslim and Jewish students to challenge the idea that their communities have a history of timeless conflict, and to view Jewish and Muslim identity from an angle that moves beyond religious texts. Just as I believe the lessons of history should move beyond the classroom, I believe that religious observance should spill out of the boxes (privately funded or funded through institutional means) to which it has been allocated. For many Americans, including myself, the college campus is a charged, vibrant, and often unforgettable space in which individual growth happens through encounters across religious and cultural divides. If students are exposed to *lived* aspects of Muslim or Jewish religious practice, it would only contribute to such growth, while also creating transformative opportunities for college communities in which Jews and Muslims are often placed at odds with one another, or made to engage in dialogue in which history is absent.

Notes

1. I was born in the United States, grew up in Pakistan, and returned to the United States for college and graduate school.
2. See, for instance, Marzia Chowdhury, "The Fight for Footbaths at UM-D," Muslim Media News Network, October 11, 2007, muslimmedianetwork.com/mmn/?p=1395, retrieved October 10, 2009. See also Tamar Lewin, "Universities Install Footbaths to Benefit Muslims, and Not Everyone is Pleased," *New York Times* (August 7, 2007), www.nytimes.com/2007/08/07/education/07muslim.html?_r=1, retrieved November 8, 2009.
3. This parallel has been drawn by Becky Miller in "What's the Big Deal over Footbaths?" [Weblog entry], Preemptive Karma (May 2, 2007), www.preemptivekarma.com/archives/2007/05/whats_the_big_d.html, retrieved October 10, 2009.
4. See, for instance, Debbie Schlussel, "So Long Church/State Separation: University of Michigan to Fund Muslim Footbaths" (May 30, 2007), www.debbieschlussel.com/1347/exclusive-so-long-churchstate-separation-university-of-michigan-to-fund-muslim-footbaths/, retrieved May 7, 2010.
5. For an analysis in popular media about Harvard University's women-only gymnasium hours, see Bob Considine, "Harvard Gym Restriction Stirs Controversy: To Accommodate Muslim Women, University Sets Aside 'No Men' Time," MSNBC (March 10, 2008), www.msnbc.msn.com/id/23556551/, retrieved November 8, 2009.
6. There is also a body of literature that historicizes the presence of Muslim practices among black communities. See, for instance, Clifton E. Marsh, *From Black Muslims to Muslims: The Transition from Separatism to Islam, 1930–1980* (Metuchen, N.J.: Scarecrow Press, 1984). See also Harold Cruse, *Plural but Equal: A Critical Study of Blacks and Minorities and America's Plural Society* (New York: William Morrow and Company, Inc., 1987), 232–236. Like Cruse, I view the Nation of Islam as a local movement that emerged against racist practices in America. This is why I have chosen not to include it in my analysis of Muslim immigration practices and campus politics in the early twentieth century.
7. For an analysis of Jewish immigration to the United States, see Calvin Goldscheider, "Immigration and the Transformation of American Jews: Assimilation, Distinctiveness, and Community," *Immigration and Religion in America: Comparative and Historical Perspectives*, Richard Alba, Albert J. Raboteau, and Josh DeWind, eds. (New York and London: NYU Press, 2009), 198–223. For an analysis of Muslim immigration to the United States, see, in the same volume, Yvonne Yazbeck Haddad, "The Shaping of Arab and Muslim Identity in the United States," 246–276. I rely on the work of both of these authors for the argument I make regarding the difference between Jewish and Muslim negotiations of ethnic and religious identity.
8. For a thorough analysis of Jewish students and anti-Semitism at elite American Universities, see Jerome Karabel, "Status-Group Struggle, Organizational Interests, and the Limits of Institutional Autonomy: The Transformation of Harvard, Yale, and Princeton, 1918–1940," *Theory and Society* Vol. 13, No. 1 (January 1984), 1–40.
9. www.brandeis.edu/about/defining.html, retrieved June 28, 2010.
10. Hillel's website contains online links to historical documents related to the organization. See Hillel, "Paging Through Hillel History" Hillel website, www.hillel.org/about/facts/hillel_historical_docs.htm, retrieved December 25, 2009.

11. See Winton U. Solberg, "The Early Years of Jewish Presence at the University of Illinois," *Religion and American Culture: A Journal of Interpretation* Vol. 2, No. 2 (Summer 1992), 215–249.
12. For the formulation of a Judeo-Christian heritage as Cold War rhetoric, see Michelle Mart, "The 'Christianization' of Israel and Jews in 1950s America," *Religion and American Culture: A Journal of Interpretation* Vol. 14, No. 1 (Winter 2004), 109–146.
13. See William Marra, "Muslim Student Groups Turn to Jewish Organizations for Inspiration: Cash-strapped Muslim Student Groups Learning about Organizing from Hillel," ABC News (August 8, 2007), abcnews.go.com/US/story?id=3459548&page=1, retrieved July 8, 2010. According to this report, the international budget for Hillel is sixty-six million dollars.
14. For an analysis of ethnicity among Muslim groups, see Karen Leonard, "South Asian Leadership of American Muslims," *Muslims in the West: From Sojourners to Citizens*, Yvonne Yazbeck Haddad, ed. (New York: Oxford University Press, 2002), 233–249.
15. ISNA has created a documentary in two parts that chronicles the founding of the MSA and the founding of ISNA. Islamic Society of North America, "History of ISNA," ISNA website, www.isna.net/ISNAHQ/pages/Documentary.aspx, retrieved December 25, 2009.
16. Muslim Students Association, "Make Your Campus More Muslim-Friendly," MSA website, www.msanational.org/resources/, retrieved December 25, 2009.
17. For a summary of the conference, see Mumina Kowalski, "Muslim Chaplains: Challenges, Opportunities, and the Road Ahead," September 1, 2005, www.isna.net/Leadership/pages/First-Annual-Muslim-Chaplain-Conference.aspx, retrieved November 25, 2009.
18. See Marra, "Muslim Student Groups Turn to Jewish Organizations for Inspiration." This report also recognizes the key role played by private financing in avoiding the inevitable debate about the use of public funds to finance religious activities.
19. Sherman Jackson argues that the wave of Muslim immigrants into America in the late 1970s meant that it was their voices rather than those of black American Muslims that came to dominate public discourse and representations of Islam in America. See "Preliminary Reflections on Islam and Black Religion," *Muslims' Place in the American Public Square: Hopes, Fears, and Aspirations*, Zahid H. Bukhari, Sulayman S. Nyang, Mumtaz Ahmed, and John L. Esposito, eds. (Walnut Creek, CA: AltaMira Press, 2004), 201–221. While a full discussion of campus politics between black Muslims and Muslim immigrants is outside the scope of this essay, I would venture that the involvement of African Americans in the Civil Rights Movement was based on shared experiences of racial discrimination. This would mean that Muslim identity would play a secondary role in the affiliations of black Muslims. Furthermore, the role played by racial prejudices among immigrants to America toward African Americans cannot be discounted. See Bruce Lawrence, *New Faiths, Old Fears: Muslim and Other Asian Immigrants in American Religious Life* (New York: Columbia University Press, 2002), 20–21, 80–84.
20. See Karen Bouffard, "Muslims Won't Fund Footbaths," *Detroit News* (June 18, 2007), pluralism.org/news/view/16707, retrieved November 25, 2009.
21. This is not to say that bumper stickers are foreign to the Muslim world. Rather, the politics of being a minority in America impact how identity is expressed to a public perceived to be in need of familiarization with, and acceptance of, such identities.
22. For a popular website selling Muslim products to be used in public announcements of identity, see www.hijabman.com. The website represents a grassroots Muslim PR campaign that seeks, through t-shirts and bumper stickers, to make Islam palatable to an American mainstream.
23. The phenomenon of an ethnicity-free Islam has been discussed at length. See Mohamed Nimer, "Muslims in American Public Life," in *Muslims in the West*, 169–186. See also Yvonne Yazbeck Haddad, "The Dynamics of Islamic Identity in North America," *Muslims on the Americanization Path?*, Yvonne Yazbeck Haddad and John Esposito, eds. (New York: Oxford University Press, 2000), 19–46.
24. At the same time, alliances with Jewish organizations exist in an uneasy space between collaboration and conflict. See Karen B. Leonard, "American Muslim Mobilize: Campus Conflicts in Context," Centre for Minority Studies, History Department, Royal Holloway University of London, November 29, 2007, eprints.rhul.ac.uk/622/1/Karen_Leonard.AMERICAN_MUSLIMS_MOBILIZE.pdf, retrieved December 20, 2009. Leonard provides an analysis of Muslim mobilization on college campuses and relations with Jewish groups.
25. This argument is one shared by most scholars of the premodern Muslim world. It has been put forth in an elegant and informative manner by Marshall Hodgson, and I would recommend his

work to anyone interested in gaining a sense of the breathtaking diversity of the Muslim world. See his *The Venture of Islam, Vols. 1–3* (Chicago: University of Chicago Press, 1974).

26. The Islamic Circle of North America has sponsored a billboard campaign that advertises a "1-877" number through which one can contact a Muslim to answer questions about Islam. The website for the "Why Islam" campaign can be accessed at www.whyislam.org.

27. Matthew Goodman, "Falling in Love with Yiddish," *The American Scholar* Vol. 69, Issue 3 (Summer 2000), 37–47. The disappearance of Yiddish has been documented by Hasia Diner in *The Jews of the United States, 1654–2000* (Berkeley: University of California Press, 2004), 241–243. I am grateful to Tony Fels for this reference.

28. Questions of collaboration across minority groups have been examined by Cheryl Greenberg in the context of Jewish and African American civil rights individuals and agencies, and I am grateful for her willingness to correspond with me as I thought through these questions. I am also grateful to Daniel Horowitz, my former professor at Smith College, for putting us in touch. See Cheryl Greenberg, *Troubling the Waters: Black Jewish Relations in the American Century* (Princeton, NJ: Princeton University Press, 2006). Greenberg addresses the common obstacles that brought Jewish and black Americans together and how racial and class differences— obscured by a dialogue of shared suffering—eventually led to a parting of ways. It is precisely this obscuring of context that hampers constructive collaboration between Muslims and Jewish students on campus. Their religious practices may be similar, but their positions within broader structures of privilege are markedly different, as are the historical processes by which their communities have engaged with such structures.

29. For an article about Muslim academics at Jesuit institutions, see Thomas Michel, "An Unusual Partnership: Islamic Academics at Jesuit Universities," *America: The National Catholic Weekly* (September 15, 2008), www.americamagazine.org/content/article.cfm?article_id=11038, retrieved December 21, 2009.

30. For a brief account of Sarmad, see Nathan Katz, "The Identity of a Mystic: The Case of Sa'id Sarmad, a Jewish-Yogi-Sufi Courtier of the Mughals," *NUMEN: International Review for the History of Religions* Vol. 47, No. 2 (2000), 142–160.

CHAPTER EIGHT

J Street and Current Directions in American Muslim-Jewish Dialogue

HANNAH ELLENSON AND
RABBI DAVID ELLENSON

Introduction

There are those in the American Jewish community who argue that the issue of Israel and Palestine drives such an intractable wedge between American Jews and American Muslims that dialogue between the two groups is at best undesirable and at worst impossible. We disagree with this position. We begin this essay with the assertion that such dialogue is necessary on both practical and moral grounds. Thereafter, in light of the necessity for such dialogue, we address how the emergence of J Street as a political force within the American Jewish community, however controversial it may be regarded in some Jewish quarters, is ultimately a positive development for facilitating such dialogue. This essay is predicated on the notion that the American Jewish community needs to recognize that such a development does more than foster a much-needed Jewish-Muslim conversation in the United States. It also promotes a connection and allegiance to Israel on the part of a significant number of younger Jews, whom recent polls have shown are growing increasingly hostile or indifferent to the Jewish state.

Pragmatic and Moral Grounds for Jewish-Muslim Dialogue

In his classic 1955 essay "Protestant-Catholic-Jew," Will Herberg writes that America had become a "triple melting pot." Indeed, Herberg states, "not to be either a Protestant, Catholic, or a Jew" was "somehow not to be an American."[1] In a 1992 article that explores this idea, Jonathan Sarna notes that Herberg should have acknowledged that the religious diversity that marked 1950s America disproved his triple melting pot theory as "an adequate depiction of America's religious landscape."[2]

If the Herberg assessment was problematic more than fifty years ago, it is simply inaccurate in the multicultural and religious reality that marks contemporary America. Demographic estimates today indicate that the American Muslim population stands at least at four million and may reach as high as eight million in the near future.[3] This reality, in which the Jewish population of America is rivaled or exceeded by Muslim numbers, arguably means that there are simply too many adherents of Islam in the United States for Jews to avoid interreligious dialogue with Muslims. This provides an important and pragmatic context for insisting upon the necessity of Muslim-Jewish conversation in the United States, even though the contentious issue of Israel and Palestine seems to consistently drive a divisive and controversial wedge between these two groups.

Yet it is precisely because of the potentially volatile nature of the issue of Israel and Palestine that we maintain there is a moral necessity for discourse between Muslims and Jews. The value of such interreligious encounters is inestimable. As the Jewish philosopher and theologian Michael Wyschogrod has observed,

> There is a value in talking to one another in and by itself, apart from any "result" achieved... To be with fellow [human beings] is to become aware of [their] mode of being in the world, of the reality of [their] being... Let us realize that the alternative to speaking is violence. There really is no such thing as ignoring a fellow human being. Not to speak with my neighbors is a mode of relating to [them], and even if the mode does not immediately express itself in violence, it points onward because the alternative to speech is communication by deed, violent deed.[4]

When an individual fails or refuses to speak with the "other," a stereotyping—even a dehumanization—can easily arise. Demonization all too often results in bloodshed. As committed Jews, terrorist bombings in Israel and events like the 1994 slaughter of Muslims engaged in prayer in Hebron all too painfully remind us of the tragedy that can ensue when the path of dialogue is not taken; dialogue is thereby a moral imperative.

J Street, Israel, and Muslim-Jewish Conversation in America

In April of 2008, J Street—a new political action committee—emerged on the American Jewish scene. Since that time, a number of liberal organizations committed to social justice (such as Americans for Peace Now) have banded together to support J Street in its efforts to redirect the political conversation in the United States regarding Israel.[5] Defining itself as "pro-Israel, pro-peace," J Street seeks to position itself, in the words of political and social writer and commentator Jeffrey Goldberg, as "a left wing alternative" to the American Israel Public Affairs Committee, also known as AIPAC, which seems to have monolithically charted American Jewish opinion in regard to U.S.-Israel relations for close to three decades.[6] As Jeremy Ben-Ami, executive director of J Street, says, "We believe it is an urgent matter of life and death for the State of Israel, as a Jewish democratic state, to reach a resolution on the conflict it has with its neighbors and with the Palestinians in the very near future."[7]

Keenly aware of population projections that lead prognosticators to assert that Palestinian population growth will outstrip Jewish growth in Israel, the West Bank, and Gaza in the decades to come,[8] J Street has advanced an argument that insists upon a two-state solution to the Israeli-Palestinian conflict. In the words of Ben-Ami, this is as "essential to Israel's survival as the national home of the Jewish people and as a vibrant democracy." J Street also advocates for American diplomatic leadership to play a catalytic role in attaining a comprehensive peace, even when such leadership sometimes leads to judgments that run contrary to the avowed policies of the Israeli government.

J Street has departed from the AIPAC posture of defending and promoting the policies of the Israeli government regardless of what those policies are. At the present, this means that AIPAC supports the policies largely shaped by the current Israeli prime minister, Benjamin Netanyahu, which are wary of negotiating with the Palestinian leadership and supportive of Israeli expansion of settlements in East Jerusalem and the Palestinian territories of the West Bank.

In contrast, according to Ben-Ami, J Street maintains that while "the State of Israel is near and dear to us and we are concerned about its security," the J Street commitment to "a two state solution" is "not [merely] a nice idea, but an existential necessity for Israel."[9] This stance has subsequently led J Street to support the administration of President Barack Obama even when the administration runs in opposition to Israeli governmental policy, such as in the recent row between the two countries over freezing all settlement activity, including in East Jerusalem, and dismantling existing "outposts" (i.e., settlements not officially sanctioned by the Israeli government). In short, J Street's rasion d'etre has been to redress what it considers to be "the failure of AIPAC" to take such stances because of their policy of unqualified support for the Israeli government and refusal to criticize any Israeli governmental actions.

J Street's occasional opposition to Israeli governmental policy, its critique of American actions that it feels are not in Israel's best interest (such as the United States' initial threats to establish sanctions against Iran), its initial decision not to reject the Goldstone Report,[10] and its explicit attacks against groups such as AIPAC, Christians United for Israel (CUFI), and the Israel Project have elicited a great deal of criticism against them from some in the American Jewish community. As CUFI spokesman Ari Morgenstern says, "J Street seems to employ a strategy of publicity through controversy without considering the harm that policy does to the pro-Israel community."[11] In October 2009, the Israeli ambassador to the United States Michael Oren even refused to attend the J Street Conference in Washington, D.C., claiming two months later, in a speech given at the Biennial Convention of the Conservative Movement, that J Street is "significantly out of the mainstream" and poses "a unique problem [to those] who are 'pro-Israel.' "[12]

Some of the actions J Street has taken during the first few months of 2010—perhaps in response to these criticisms—seem to have slightly softened such negative criticism. For example, J Street has now opted to support Congressional sanctions against Iran, they recently held a celebration for Israel's Independence Day, and they actively argued against divestment from Israel in the recent University of California, Berkeley, student government's debate on this issue. In spring 2010 J Street even held a delegation trip to Israel that met with Israeli president Shimon Peres and a senior advisor to Prime Minister Netanyahu, Ron Dermer. (The group also held meetings in Ramallah with top Palestinian leaders as well as with King Abdullah II of Jordan.) Consequently, Ambassador Oren has now met with Ben-Ami, and has even gone on record saying that J Street has moved "more into the mainstream."[13] Indeed, such actions have led some on the Left to accuse J Street of becoming "AIPAC-lite."[14] Richard Silverstein, a prominent leftist blogger, has complained "that there is less and less daylight between J Street and AIPAC."[15]

Nevertheless, J Street remains firmly ensconced on the left-end of the contemporary Jewish political spectrum with regard to Israel. Perhaps most notably, J Street continues to target younger Jews, those whom Ben-Ami has called the "post-Holocaust" generation.[16] As Jewish demographers and cultural observers Steven M. Cohen and Ari Y. Kelman assert, "A mounting body of evidence has pointed to a growing distancing from Israel of American Jews, and the distancing seems to be most pronounced among younger Jews."[17] Unlike older American Jews who recall the Holocaust and the heroic, virtually "mythical" founding of the state of Israel, and Baby Boomers, who remember the fear, excitement, and relief of the overwhelming victory Israel enjoyed during the Six Day War and who, as a result, tend to view Israel as the bearer of democratic and progressive values in the Middle East, "younger adult Jews born after 1974 draw upon memories and impressions less likely to cast Israel in a positive light."[18]

While Cohen and Kelman report that liberal and conservative political viewpoints regarding the attitudes younger Jewish individuals possess about Israel do not seem to have as determinative an impact as one might assume, they do not dismiss the theory that those who identify as more liberal are also likely to feel more disenchanted with the tone of the dominant Jewish political conversation that takes place in the United Sates vis-à-vis Israel. By offering a different voice, one that supports Israel while simultaneously being more critical of Israeli governmental actions than other pro-Israel groups, J Street has the potential of combating the indifference and hostility that these Jews may feel toward Israel. Thus, J Street can appeal to both Jews who do not identify with AIPAC and those who find openly anti-Zionist Jewish groups disturbing.

J Street's ability to attract such Jews can be seen in the success it has enjoyed in absorbing the now defunct Union of Progressive Zionists (UPZ) into its organizational structure through the creation of J Street U, their new university programming platform. UPZ was originally established in 2004 by members of Meretz USA, Ameinu, and alumni of Habonim Dror North America and Hashomer Hatzair North America, all of whom identified with the old Zionist Left. Prior to combining with J Street, UPZ had chapters in more than a dozen American campuses, carrying out such activities as a "Peace, Pluralism, and Social Justice" trip to Israel through Taglit-Birthright Israel.

Yet these groups did not have an official political channel to represent their political views. They were characterized by a posture that was both explicitly Zionist and critical of Israeli governmental policy on issues such as settlements and negotiations with Palestinians, and were proactive in promoting Israeli-Palestinian and Jewish-Muslim dialogue. J Street's decision to have a university centered programming wing has extended its capacity to promote Muslim-Jewish dialogue in the United States, particularly as it manifests against the backdrop of the Israeli-Palestinian conflict. In so doing, they have promoted a conversation about Israel and Palestine among a younger generation of American Jews whose attitudes regarding the Middle East, and whose experiences of cultural, racial, and religious diversity, are markedly different than those of older generations of American Jews.

Though distinct from Jewish-Muslim dialogue, J Street is also playing a seminal role in promoting U.S.-based Arab-Jewish dialogue. For example, in October 2009 the Arab American Institute and J Street convened a joint meeting at the J Street conference that was addressed by Tina Tchen, the director of the Office of Public Engagement for the White House. As explicitly mentioned at the time, the main purpose of this session was to build support in both the American Jewish community and the American Arab community for the initiatives President Obama had then put forth to restart Palestinian-Israeli peace talks. As Tchen said, "There are hearts and minds in the United States that need to be changed."[19] Dr. James Zogby, president of the Arab American Institute, described both the meeting and the entire three-day J Street conference in the following manner: "Without exaggeration, this is a revolution. The three days, beginning with the joint Arab American-American Jewish meeting, to the banquet at its conclusion, marks the birth of a movement and, one hopes, a transformation not only within the Jewish community's internal debate, but in Arab American-American Jewish cooperation."[20]

Clearly, such joint events with the Arab American community and the stances adopted by J Street are strengthening the foundation for the development of Jewish dialogue with the Muslim community as well; additional lines of communication between Jewish and Muslim spokespeople have been opened as a result. As Rafia Zakaria, the director of the Muslim Women's Legal Defense Fund for the Muslim Alliance of Indiana, explained in February 2010,

> In the eyes of most Muslims...the actions of AIPAC has [sic] over the decades been instrumental in constructing US foreign policy's uncritical stance on Israel...[Yet] the year 2009 saw the emergence of another Jewish lobbying group called J Street that has since garnered the support of many liberal and progressive Jewish Americans. One of J Street's foremost political platforms is the advocacy of a two-state solution and "the right of Palestinians to a state of their own." The organization overtly opposes the construction of new settlements on Palestinian land.[21]

Zakaria maintains that the emergence of J Street possesses the potential to promote positive dialogue between Jews and Muslims in America.

Such dialogue was further realized on April 14, 2010, when Ben-Ami and Salam Al-Marayati, the executive director of the Muslim Public Affairs Council, met in Washington, D.C. at a public roundtable event to discuss how Jewish and Muslim Americans can work together to promote peace in the Middle East.[22] This event brought the two communities together to discuss a political solution to the Israeli-Palestinian conflict against the backdrop of Muslim-Jewish dialogue. During the course of their conversation, the two men discussed how they will promote conversations on these topics between their two American communities to the mutual advantage of both groups. As Al-Marayati said, "I am here to promote understanding between Muslims and Jews so we can have an effective constituency for a peace process."[23] Ben-Ami claimed that they were attempting to activate the "moderate majority" of Jews and Muslims in the United States who want a broader discussion of Israeli-Palestinian politics to include Palestinian views of the conflict.[24] While Ben-Ami asserted that he does not necessarily affirm the correctness of those views, he noted that he believes providing the space to discuss such views both within and beyond the Jewish community is essential for Israel's security.

Conclusion

It is far too early to predict how successful J Street will be in its mission. Nor can one accurately affirm that its impact on the American Jewish scene will be sustainable; numerous critics of J Street still exist within the Jewish community. However, what is clear beyond a shadow of a doubt is that these critics have been unsuccessful in stifling J Street's powerful voice. J Street's evolving positions have become increasingly integrated into Jewish, Muslim, and governmental circles in the United States.

We are among those who see such growth as a positive development on the American Jewish scene. On moral and pragmatic grounds, we maintain that J Street can attract younger and more liberal Jews to reengage with Israel. Likewise, we believe that J Street offers hope for the enhancement of Jewish-Muslim relations in the United States by opening new paths to Jewish-Muslim dialogue against the backdrop of the political thicket in which the Israeli-Palestinian conflict is mired. While the path of dialogue is surely fraught with difficulty, reality demonstrates that the alternatives—ongoing conflict and inexorable violence—are not healthy options. Dialogue between Muslims and Jews is surely an imperative for the American Jewish community, for the state of Israel, and for the future of the Palestinian people.

Notes

1. Will Herberg, *Protestant-Catholic-Jew: An Essay in American Religious Sociology* (New York: Doubleday and Company, 1955), 257.
2. Jonathan D. Sarna, "The American Jewish Experience and the Emergence of the Muslim Community in America," *The American Journal of Islamic Social Sciences* Vol. 9, No. 3 (Fall 1992), 370–374.
3. Carla Power, "The New Islam," *Newsweek* (March 16, 1998), 34; and "Religious Adherents in the United States of America" in *Encyclopedia Britannica Book of the Year* (2004), www.britannica.com/EBchecked /topic/1244719/religion-Year-In-Review-2006, retrieved April 15, 2010.
4. Michael Wyscogrod, *The Body of Faith: Judaism as Corporeal Election* (San Francisco: Harper and Row, 1983), 242.
5. James Traub, "The New Israel Lobby: Can J Street and the Obama Administration Change Washington's Middle East Policy?" *New York Times Magazine* (September 13, 2009), 39.
6. Jeffrey Goldberg, "J Street Blows It," *Atlantic* (January 5, 2009), www.theatlantic.com/international/ archive/2009/01/j-street-blows-it/9282/, retrieved April 14, 2010.
7. Steve Kornacki, "The Other Pro-Israel Lobby Senses its Moment," *New York Observer* (May 6, 2009), www.observer.com/3410/other-pro-israel-lobby-senses-its-moment, retrieved April 25, 2010.
8. In his article "If Israel Ceased to Exist," *Commentary* (June 2007), author Hillel Halkin warns that the "demise" of Israel as a Jewish State "could…take place…by means of demographic swamping alone." He supports this position by arguing that the "demographic future" of Israel is "precarious" because "in the absence of large-scale Jewish immigration, and even assuming a steady drop in Israeli Arab birthrates as the Arab standard of living rises, Israel's Jewish majority, whose ratio to its Arab minority was 10-to-1 in the 1950's and now stands at 4-to-1, will continue to shrink, almost certainly to 3-to-1 and possibly well beyond that before some sort of stasis is achieved." Similarly, writing in *Time* (May 8, 2008), Hebrew University of Jerusalem demographer Sergio DellaPergola writes, "Whether Israel at 120 will be a Jewish and democratic state will largely depend on demographic trends and their interface with policy decisions…Population projections assume continuing faster [population] growth [among] Palestinians in Israel, the West Bank, and Gaza—with [Jewish] immigration to Israel nearing its lowest levels ever. Different family sizes and strikingly diverse composition by age groups make the percentage of Jews among the whole population [living between the Jordan River and the Mediterranean] likely to shrink in 2068 back to where it was in 1948, on the eve of Israel's independence—about 35%. On the other hand, Israel within its pre-1967 borders might have a Jewish share above 70%—a majority but not a culturally homogeneous society. Swaps of some small areas densely settled by Arabs in Israel and by Jews in the West Bank, and redeployment of Israelis from the West Bank into Israel might keep Israel's Jewishness above 80%."

9. Haviv Rettig Gur, "Jerusalem Sees J Street Inch to Consensus," *Jerusalem Post* (April 30, 2010), www.jpost.com/Israel/Article.aspx?id=174367, retrieved April 30, 2010.

10. Josh Nathan-Kzais, "In Shift, Oren Calls J Street a 'Unique Problem,'" *Forward* (December 8, 2009), forward.com/articles/120600/, retrieved April 15, 2010.

11. Ron Kampeas, "J Street, Oren Mending Fences—But Wariness Lingers," *Jerusalem Post* (February 17, 2010), www.jpost.com/JewishWorld/JewishNews/Article.aspx?id=168932, retrieved April 15, 2010.

12. Nathan-Kzais, "In Shift, Oren Calls J Street a 'Unique Problem.'"

13. Jewish Telegraphic Agency, "Oren: J Street Conflict Near Resolution," *Jewish Journal* (February 10, 2010), www.jewishjournal.com/nation/article/oren_j_street_conflict_near_resolution_20100210/, retrieved April 15, 2010.

14. See Philip Giraldi "My Problem with J Street" (October 29, 2009), original.antiwar.com/giraldi/2009/10/28/my-problem-with-j-street/, retrieved July 30, 2010; and Alex Kane, "Which Side Are You On, J Street?" (May 2, 2010), kanan48.wordpress.com/2010/05/02/which-side-are-you-on-j-street-by-alex-kane/, retrieved July 30, 2010.

15. See Richard Silverstein, "J Street Official Praises AIPAC," *Tikun Olam* (April 26, 2010), www.richardsilverstein.com/tikun_olam/2010/04/26/j-street-official-praises-aipac-touts-groups-moderate-positions/, retrieved July 30, 2010.

16. Traub, "The New Israel Lobby."

17. "Young US Jews 'Detached' from Israel," *Jerusalem Post* (September 6, 2007), www.jpost.com/JewishWorld/JewishNews/Article.aspx?id=74410, retrieved April 12, 2010. Also see Steven M. Cohen and Ari Y. Kelman, "Beyond Distancing: Young Adult American Jews and Their Alienation from Israel" (The Jewish Identity Project of Reboot, Andrea and Charles Bronfman Philanthropies, 2007), 2.

18. Cohen and Kelman, "Beyond Distancing," 3.

19. Ron Kampas, "Tina Tchen to J Street: Have Our Back (and We Have Yours)," *Jewish Telegraphic Agency* (October 26, 2009), blogs.jta.org/politics/article/2009/10/26/1008746/tina-tchen-to-j-street-have-our-back-and-we-have-yours, retrieved April 14, 2010.

20. James Zogby, "J Street Again," *Huffington Post* (November 2, 2009), www.huffingtonpost.com/ james-zogby/j-street-again_b_342115.html, retrieved April 17, 2010.

21. Rafia Zakaria, "J Street: The Other Jewish Lobby," *Muslim Voices* (February 10, 2010), muslim-voices.org/j-street/, retrieved April 16, 2010.

22. J Street's Twitter feed (April 14, 2010).

23. Ibid.

24. Ibid.

PART III

Challenges and Opportunities in Reaching across the Divide

Introduction to Speeches by Rabbi Eric Yoffie and Dr. Ingrid Mattson

Sayyid M. Syeed

Long before 9/11, Muslim-Christian dialogues and partnerships were flourishing at the local and national levels. The Islamic Society of North America (ISNA) developed a close relationship with the National Council of Churches (NCC). The two organizations cooperated like twins, one as the umbrella organization of thousands of mainstream Protestant-affiliated churches and the other as the umbrella organization of hundreds of mosques across the United States. Similarly, ISNA and the United States Conference of Catholic Bishops (USCCB) were working together both at the local and national levels. I was personally invited to speak to the NCC and USCCB executive boards, while ISNA invited the secretary general of the NCC and a number of bishops from USCCB to address our national conventions and our regional conferences. After the 9/11 tragedy, relations between ISNA and these Christian organizations only grew stronger and more visible.

From ISNA's perspective, what was missing in this landscape of formal interfaith dialogue was the presence of Jewish organizations. ISNA's American Muslim members were already interacting with Jewish individuals as colleagues, teachers, neighbors, and religious leaders. But the absence of a formal and public interaction on the organizational level was conspicuous. Although ISNA's interfaith committee routinely invited officials from national Jewish organizations, along with a long list of Christian leaders, to address their national events in Chicago, the invited officials declined the offers numerous times and, indeed, even voiced suspicion of our organization.

In December 2005, as secretary general of ISNA, I was invited to give a keynote address at the annual conference of the Religions for Peace in Chicago. At the end of the presentation, people from the audience approached me to shake my hands, some even hugging me as they expressed their heartfelt respect and appreciation for what I had said. As is common in such situations, a number of people were taking pictures of our embraces, trying to capture the joyful moments of interfaith celebration of love and happiness. While hugging me, one of the attendees saw another person about to take our picture. He immediately jumped at the photographer, stopping him from taking the photo, shouting that he would lose his job if the picture with me—a Muslim leader—went out to his organization. Upon inquiry, I found out that he was a representative of a national Jewish organization. He then admitted to me that among certain Jews there was a tangible fear of being seen socializing with Muslim leaders.

This was a serious challenge to our ability to engage the Jewish community as a formal partner. A few years later, in an effort to break down the barriers of mutual suspicion between us, I approached the largest single denomination of American Jews, the Union of Reform Judaism (URJ). ISNA had worked with the leaders of URJ in other settings, particularly in trying to advance efforts for peace in the Middle East. It seemed natural, therefore, to pursue a formal dialogue between these two organizations. After a few admittedly intense meetings with URJ leaders in New York City and Washington, D.C., it became clear that we Muslims were as religiously committed to opening a dialogue with Jews as we were with Christians.

ISNA had already made countless formal statements against acts of terrorism carried out in the name of Islam, deploring such actions as those of suicide bombers who have murdered innocent civilians. But it was our common and passionate advocacy for peace in the Middle East and a respectable resolution to the Israeli-Palestinian conflict that brought us together with the URJ. The URJ leadership realized that we were genuinely seeking to build bridges of understanding with Jewish Americans, something that was particularly critical in light of the deteriorating conditions in the Middle East. Both ISNA and the URJ felt that we could build trust and goodwill between each other, ultimately using this positive cooperation to address injustices committed abroad. We both understood that our choice was either to do nothing and be confronted with the same tensions and mutual hatred being imported to the United States from overseas, or open up our communities to each other to promote mutual respect, understanding, and intercommunal partnership.

Since this was the summer of 2007 and the annual ISNA convention was to be held shortly thereafter, we decided to invite the president of the URJ Rabbi Eric Yoffie to address our forty-fourth annual convention in Chicago. His speech was delivered at the inaugural session of the convention, on August 31 of the same year. Contrary to the misgivings of many, the audience was respectful; at the end of his speech, Rabbi Yoffie even received a standing ovation. Though the coming together of nearly forty thousand American Muslims for ISNA conventions always makes the news, with Rabbi Yoffie's inaugural speech the conference sparked headlines across the globe. It was truly an historic event. In December of the same year we reciprocated this gesture of friendship when the URJ invited ISNA's president Dr. Ingrid Mattson to address their Biennial Convention in San Diego, the first time a Muslim woman, let alone the head of America's largest Muslim organization, had ever addressed a URJ gathering. The extraordinary hospitality, love, and attention that the ISNA delegation received at the conference were overwhelming.

These two historic speeches were later followed by other projects and programs meant to foster interfaith dialogue between the American Jewish and American Muslim communities. Other Jewish organizations equally interested in having formal organizational partnerships and collaborating on joint projects began to approach ISNA. We brought together imams and rabbis to condemn Islamophobia and anti-Semitism, and established a program between synagogues and mosques throughout the United States to promote a better understanding of one another's traditions and beliefs. Through the two speeches given by Rabbi Yoffie and Dr. Mattson many new doors have opened, leading to increased intercommunal cooperation, and creating a new atmosphere of respect and trust. As challenges between American Jews and American Muslims seem to be growing more and more difficult, it is our hope that the relationship between our two communities will only grow stronger. Let these two important speeches remind us of our intercommunal collaboration's potential.

CHAPTER NINE

Inaugural Address at the Forty-fourth Annual Convention of the Islamic Society of North America

Rabbi Eric H. Yoffie

I am deeply honored by your invitation to be present at this convention.

I am here as the leader of the Union for Reform Judaism, the largest Jewish religious movement in North America, consisting of more than 900 congregations and 1.5 million Jews.

My organization is currently discussing with your leadership a joint dialogue and education program that we hope to launch in the very near future, involving our congregations and your mosques. This project is a matter of the utmost importance to my movement and to me personally. With my time today I would like to share with you why that is so.

There exists in this country, among all Americans—whether Jews, Christians, or nonbelievers—a huge and profound ignorance about Islam. It is not that stories about Islam are missing from our media. There is no shortage of voices prepared to tell us that fanaticism and intolerance are fundamental to Islamic tradition, that violence and even suicide bombing have deep Qur'anic roots. There is no lack of so-called experts who are eager to seize on any troubling statement made by a Muslim thinker and pin it on Islam as a whole. It has been far too easy to spread the image of Islam as America's enemy, a religion made up of terrorists, the frightening unknown.

How did this happen? How did it happen that Christian fundamentalists, such as Pat Robertson and Franklin Graham, have been able to make vicious and public attacks against your religion? How did it happen that when a Muslim Congressman took his oath of office while holding a Qur'an, a Jewish pundit, Dennis Prager, was able to suggest that the Congressman is more dangerous to America than the terrorists of 9/11? How did it happen that Tom Tancredo, a Republican member of Congress who ran for president, has been able to call for the bombing of Mecca and

Medina? Perhaps even more importantly, how did it happen that law-abiding Muslims in this country can find themselves condemned for dual loyalty, blamed for the crimes of terrorists they abhor? How did it happen that in the name of security, Muslim detainees and inmates are exposed to abusive and discriminatory treatment that violates the most fundamental principles of the American Constitution?

One reason that all of this has happened is profound ignorance. Most Americans know nothing about Islam. That is why we Jews must educate our members. For this we will need your help. We hope that in this process we will set an example for all Americans. The time has come to put aside what the media says is wrong with Islam and to hear from Muslims themselves about what is right with Islam. The time has come to listen to our Muslim neighbors speak about the spiritual power of Islam and their love for their religion, from their heart and in their own words.

The time has come for Americans to learn how far removed Islam is from the perverse distortions of the terrorists who too often dominate the media, subverting Islam's image by professing to speak in its name. The time has come to stand up to the opportunists in our midst—the media figures, religious leaders, and politicians who demonize Muslims and bash Islam, exploiting the fears of their fellow citizens for their own purposes. And finally this—the time has come to end racial profiling and legal discrimination of any kind against Muslim Americans. Yes, we must assure the security of our country. This is absolutely our government's first obligation. But let's not breach the Constitution in ways we will later regret. After all, civil liberties are America's strength, not our weakness.

We hope to accomplish all this and more with our dialogue program. This unprecedented program will give synagogues and mosques the tools they need for constructive conversation with their neighbors. This dialogue will not be easy. It will work only if we approach it with humility. We should remember the words of President Abraham Lincoln at his second inaugural address. He spoke about a transcendent God whose will we cannot hope to entirely know. Surely, this God is big enough to accommodate a range of thinking and an inescapably pluralistic religious reality. Because God is God and we are not God, surely we can recognize that other religions have much to teach us.

The dialogue will not be one way, of course. You will teach us about Islam and we will teach you about Judaism. You will help us overcome stereotyping of Muslims, and we will help you overcome stereotyping of Jews. We Jews are especially worried now about anti-Semitism and Holocaust denial. Anti-Semitism is not native to the Islamic tradition. But a virulent form of it is found today in a number of Islamic societies. We urgently require your assistance in mobilizing Muslims here and abroad to delegitimize and combat it.

A measure of our success will be our ability to discuss and confront extremism in our own communities. As a Jew I know that our sacred texts, including the Hebrew Bible, are filled with contradictory propositions; these include passages that appear to promote violence and thus offend ethical sensibilities. Such texts are to be found in all religions, including Christianity and Islam.

Though the overwhelming majority of Jews reject violence by interpreting these texts in a constructive way, a tiny, extremist minority chooses destructive interpretations instead, finding in the sacred words a vengeful, hateful God. Especially disturbing is the fact that the moderate Jewish majority sometimes cowers in the face of this fanatical minority—perhaps because they seem more authentic or appear to have greater faith and greater commitment. When this happens, my task as a rabbi is to rally that reasonable, often-silent majority and encourage them to assert the moderate principles that define their beliefs and Judaism's highest ideals.

My Christian and Muslim friends tell me that precisely the same dynamic operates in their respective traditions. From what I can see, this is manifestly so. Surely, as we know from the headlines, you have what I know must be for you as well as for us an alarming number of extremists of your own—those who kill in the name of God, hijacking Islam in the process. It is therefore our collective task to strengthen and inspire one another as we fight the fanatics within our communities, working together to promote the values of justice and love that are common to both our faiths.

I am optimistic that we can do this. After all, there is much that we share. As small minorities in the United States, we both worry about how we will fare and if we will survive in the great American melting pot. As committed God-seekers in an age of moral relativism, we are distressed by the trends that pollute our children's lives: incredibly trashy television, high divorce rates, and media images that demean and objectify women. At the same time, and without contradiction, we are both beneficiaries of the blessings bestowed on our communities by this great and wonderful country. For all of its problems, America provides us with a sanctuary that safeguards our right to be different. Despite the prejudice that we still confront, America offers a measure of diversity and tolerance unmatched in any place or time in human history.

Compare this with the situation in Christian Europe. For centuries we Jews and Muslims were the European "other." Some Europeans have little ability to deal with difference, showing suspicion or outright contempt for people of faith. As you are well aware, there are places in Europe where wearing a headscarf in a public school is a criminal offense. What an outrage this is! What an abomination! In a global media culture that fawns over Britney Spears and Lindsay Lohan, why should anyone criticize the voluntary act of a woman who chooses to wear a headscarf or a veil? Surely the choice these women make deserves our respect, not to mention the full protection of the law.

America, fortunately, is different in this regard. What distinguishes America is our religiosity and our pluralism. More than 150 million

Americans worship on a regular basis in an astonishing number of different denominations. Americans respect religion and believe in God, having learned to respect religions different from their own. If we add to this the great principle of the separation of church and state, we can be certain that our religious autonomy is assured. We can conduct our dialogue not in despair but in hope, knowing that we will ultimately find a secure place in the American religious mosaic.

Permit me to conclude with a few words about the situation in the Middle East—because this, too, must also be included in our dialogue. American Jews have a deep, profound, and unshakable commitment to the state of Israel. We Jews see assuring the security of Israel as one of our community's most important accomplishments, and we see maintaining her security as one of our most important priorities. At the same time, we understand the ties of American Muslims and Arab Americans to the Palestinian people. The challenge that we face is this: Will we, Jews and Muslims, import the conflicts of the Middle East into America, or will we join together and send a message of peace to that troubled land? Let us choose peace. Let us work toward the day when a democratic Palestinian state will live side by side, in peace and security, with the democratic state of Israel.

The basic outline of such a peace has been clear for a long time. For peace to be achieved, territorial compromise will be required of Israel. Unconditional acceptance of Israel as a Jewish state will be required of the Palestinians. Jews will need to accept the reality of Palestinian suffering, and understand that without dignity for Palestinians there can be no dignity for Israel. Palestinians will need to accept the reality of Israel's vulnerability, including the vulnerability of that tiny nation's ever-threatened borders.

And what can we do, American Muslims and Jews? Three things.

First, while the terms of a settlement must be negotiated by the two immediate parties, an American role in achieving such a settlement will be essential. We must urge our government to commit itself to active, high-level engagement, in order to move the parties toward peace.

Second, if the conflict between Israel and the Palestinians is seen in religious rather than political terms, resolving it becomes impossible. If Israel is portrayed as "a dagger pushed into the heart of Islam," rather than a nation-state disputing matters of land and water with the Palestinian people, we are lost. As religious Jews and religious Muslims, let us do everything in our power to prevent a political battle from being transformed into a holy war.

And finally, to all those who desecrate God's name by using religion to justify killing and terror, let us say together, "Enough!" No cause in the world, and surely no religious cause, can ever justify murdering the innocent or targeting the uninvolved. One cannot honor a religion of peace through violence. One cannot honor God if one does not honor the image of God in every human being. One cannot get to heaven by creating hell on earth. If we can agree on nothing else, let us agree on this. Let us remain united on this point, come what may. We Jews have expressed these views, and so have you, with your clear statements condemning terrorist attacks. But let us agree that this task will not be done until the message is heard, and others in the Muslim world join with ISNA in ringing denunciations of terror that will be heard throughout the globe.

Our agenda is long and difficult. There is nothing simple or easy about the project that we are about to undertake. But, interconnected since the time of Abraham, thrust into each other's lives by history and fate, and living in a global world, what choice do we really have? Surely here, in this land, we cannot permit fanaticism to grow or prejudice to harden. Surely here, in America, as Muslims and Jews, we have a unique opportunity to reclaim our common heritage and to find a new way and a common path. Brothers and sisters, let us begin.

Thank you very much. May God bless the work of this assembly.

Note

This address was originally delivered in Chicago, IL, on August 31, 2007. This version of the speech has been slightly modified from the original.

CHAPTER TEN

Address at the Sixty-ninth Conference of the General Assembly of the Union for Reform Judaism

INGRID MATTSON

Good morning and greetings of peace from the Islamic Society of North America. It is a great honor to have this opportunity to speak to the members of the Union for Reform Judaism at this wonderful convention.

Almost four months ago, Rabbi Eric Yoffie, leader of the URJ [Union of Reform Judaism], stood in front of a general audience of attendees at the forty-fourth annual convention of the Islamic Society of North America (ISNA), the organization that I have been president of since 2006. ISNA's membership is diverse. It includes Muslims from all parts of the world, men and women who adhere to different schools of thought within the Islamic tradition. We are an umbrella organization for Muslim individuals and organizations who wish to identify with and contribute to a larger vision of what it means to be a Muslim in North America, and who cooperate to develop strategies for achieving that vision. In the forty-four years since we held our first convention, our umbrella has expanded, even as our membership has diversified to include more women, more scholars representing different practices and schools of thought—both modern and traditionalist—and leaders from other religious traditions. Indeed, one significant feature of the American Muslim community is that it is dynamic, open to learning new ideas, and interested in expanding its understanding of what it takes to be an ethical and balanced Muslim in contemporary America.

There are two major factors that have contributed to the positive and dynamic transformation of the immigrant Muslim community in the United States. First, religion plays an important role in American history and culture. Muslims in the United States, unlike many Muslims in Europe, have found that religious affiliation and practice is valued in America. True, it was not and is not always easy to find ways to accommodate the specific religious practices of Muslims in an overwhelmingly Christian society. But, at a minimum, religion itself is not derided and marginalized in the United States. Muslims, therefore, are indebted to those who have championed the two twin pillars of religious vitality in American society: freedom of religion and the separation of church and state.

The second major factor that has contributed to the transformation of the American Muslim community over the past few decades is the diversity of our community. As Muslims from different parts of the world came together in America to worship and fulfill the tenets of their faith, they did not always find themselves in agreement about the true Islamic position on many issues. Sometimes the conversations became rather heated—and those disagreements have not yet ended in many places. Still, engaging in such conversations has yielded two positive results. First, Muslims were forced to confront the reality that many cultural practices and beliefs contrary to our faith have been integrated into traditional understandings of Islam. Through confronting the differences, we became aware that sometimes the Islam that was taught in traditional Muslim societies was not in harmony with the ethical teachings of the Qur'an and the Prophet Muhammad, but were, in fact, misogynistic, authoritarian, and/ or extremist views antithetical to the true meaning of Islam. Second, the very act of discussing these differences in a free society without a state-enforced religion has encouraged more respect for diversity within Islam, decreased support for authoritarian tendencies, and fostered a greater feeling of responsibility on the part of ordinary Muslims to learn more about their religion.

I have to emphasize that not all American Muslims have embraced this perspective. In particular new immigrants from other countries, some of whom are still deeply attached to their customs, and those who are simply ideologically opposed to dialogue and change, have had trouble embracing this worldview. Yet because many members of the Islamic Society of North America have gone through the process of transformation, and embraced pluralism, our community is now ready to engage in a meaningful way with Jewish communities through the "Children of Abraham Dialogue Project." I suppose I should not have been surprised when the Muslims assembled in the hall at our recent annual convention gave Rabbi Yoffie a standing ovation after his speech. Indeed, in the weeks following the convention I was approached by many people who were excited by our engagement with the Union for Reform Judaism. Many of our members have already established some connection between their local congregation and a nearby Jewish community. Others are interested in reaching out, but do not know where to start. Most of our communities are severely limited in resources to develop such programs.

Muslims are not new to America—a significant number of the Africans brought to the Americas as slaves were Muslim. But, of course, they were neither allowed to practice their religion nor permitted to transmit it to their children. It is only in the last few decades that our community has been able to establish institutions that support our religious life, allowing us to teach our children our practices and values. We are still in the early stages of our development. Many Muslim communities are still building mosques, while others have moved on to build other basic facilities such as community centers and schools. Our human resources are even less developed. We are blessed to have many wonderful people who volunteer to serve our communities, but, of course, they are limited in their time as well as in the expertise needed to minister to and support American Muslim communities.

Although this lack of development might seem to be a drawback, as it limits the capacity of many of our communities to fully engage with neighboring Jewish congregations, the fact is that the very existence of this gap in development provides a wonderful opportunity for constructive engagement. Jewish communities can offer practical advice, from their own American history, at this formative stage of the development of Islam in America. In many cases, Muslims have instinctively turned to the example of American Jews to understand how to deal with the challenges we face as a religious minority in the United States—whether these challenges involve securing the right to religious accommodation in public institutions or dealing with workplace discrimination. At the same time, I believe that the Jewish community will also benefit from having Muslim partners in the struggle to uphold the constitutional separation of church and state, to promote civil liberties, to extend religious accommodation to minorities, and to counter prejudice and hatred.

In his speech at our convention, Rabbi Yoffie discussed the increased hatred and intolerance toward Muslims that is being expressed throughout the country in public forums, in the media, and even by politicians. When Keith Ellison, the first Muslim elected to congress, chose to have his ceremonial swearing in to office using Thomas Jefferson's personal copy of the Qur'an, he was denounced as un-American and a terrorist sympathizer. During the 2008 presidential primaries, we witnessed candidates being asked to prove that they comply with an ever-narrowing definition of what it means to be Christian—forget about being a Muslim or a Jew. Alarmingly, many Americans are, implicitly or explicitly, using a religious test for who should be president of the United States. This and other issues involving the separation of church and state and religious freedoms are important areas of cooperation between American Jews and American Muslims.

Since 9/11, there has been a great deal of false information disseminated by religious and political ideologues about Islam in general and the American Muslim community in particular. Many Americans know little or nothing about Islam and naturally extrapolate from the nasty figures they see in the news to all Muslims. It is we Muslims who have the responsibility to reclaim Islam from the terrorists and extremists. That is why American Muslims have been public in expressing their views on terrorism and extremism in the name of religion. American Muslim leaders

have published numerous *fatwas* [religious edicts] clearly stating that suicide bombing, vigilante operations, terrorism, and hate-mongering are all
prohibited acts in Islam. We have issued press releases. We have published
articles and books. We have delivered sermons. We have given lectures
to Muslims of all ages. We have held workshops and seminars. We have
met with government officials in the United States and abroad. We have
engaged in each of these acts with the goal of spreading the message that
mainstream Muslims oppose violent extremists. We are continuously putting our efforts, individually and institutionally, into marginalizing those
who misuse our religion for nefarious purposes.

But the sad reality is that no matter what we do, there are some who
choose to continue to characterize us and our religion as essentially evil.
There is a long tradition of anti-Muslim discourse in European history
and culture—from Dante to Don Quixote to basic Orientalist scholarship.
I will never forget my visit to Spain's Cathedral of Zaragoza a few years
ago, where I was confronted with an image of a Muslim literally being
crushed under the feet of Santiago, Spain's patron saint. On the other side
of the Cathedral was a statue of Saint Dominguito—the patron saint of
choir boys, who, according to our tour guide, "the Jews of Zaragoza con-
spired to murder." All of the alleged conspirators—all falsely accused—
were executed. We all know, of course, what happened to the Muslims
and Jews of medieval Spain after the *Reconquista*.

In modern times, other forms of communication—newspapers, car-
toons, films—have continued to produce hateful images of Muslims, as
was previously done with Jews. (Sometimes it seems that the caricatures
are almost identical.) As you know, in medieval and modern Europe
Jews were dehumanized, depicted as deceptive creatures, odd in manner
and dress, conspiring to overthrow Christian rule, a phenomenon that
softened the ground for the atrocities of the Holocaust. In the twentieth century, six million Jews in the heart of Europe were brutalized and
murdered in the most despicable manner. How could this have happened
if not for the successful campaign of propaganda as well as a ruthless but
efficiently rational system of identifying, classifying, collecting, moving,
and exterminating Jewish men, women, and children? This is one of the
greatest tragedies of modern history and ISNA will bear witness to this
truth at anytime and to anyone in the Muslim world or otherwise who
chooses to deny it.

Today, I do not fear that such a crime could happen to the American
Muslim community. Yet I am anxious about the degree to which my
community is also being dehumanized. I am worried that it is politically
correct to mock and insult Muslims in the media and in public. It concerns me that when I spoke in a church recently, one man in the congregation likened the Muslims of the world to ants in a colony, who while
seeming to work separately are in fact working together for a common
purpose. To compare my community to insects is deeply disturbing, to
say the least. But to imply that we are conspiring toward some nefarious

goal is even more upsetting. Such beliefs can quite easily justify violence against Muslims and, in fact, has already laid the groundwork for general American apathy regarding the waterboarding, sensory deprivation, and other forms of torture inflicted upon Muslim detainees, some of whom have even been American citizens.

I believe that hatred and intolerance is easily transferable. I am not surprised that some young men who recently responded "Happy Hannukah" to a "Merry Christmas" greeting were attacked on a New York City subway. I am happy that it was a Muslim who jumped in to defend these (mostly) Jewish victims. This small incident highlights our common threat just as it highlights our common interests and shared humanity. This is why I am delighted that ISNA and the URJ are embarking on this dialogue project, allowing our communities to learn about each other to rid ourselves of the ignorance we have of the other, and to move on, God willing, to work together for the greater good.

I am not naïve about the challenges we face as we undertake this project. Certainly, when discussing the Jewish community, my community will need to draw upon the skills we have developed to distinguish true Islam from cultural biases and medieval accretions to our religion. Muslim anti-Semitism was never like European Christian anti-Semitism, but it existed. And, unfortunately, there are ambitious political rulers in the Muslim world who currently manipulate religious sentiment against Jews in an effort to extend their authoritarian rule. At the same time, American Jews need to recognize that the concerns of American Muslims regarding the suffering of the Palestinian people is both genuine and justified. We need you to refrain from assuming that such concern originates from a hatred of the Jewish people. I have seen the tears of elderly Palestinian men as they spoke about being forced to leave the homes of their fathers and their fathers' fathers during the founding of the state of Israel. I have been moved by those tears just as I was moved by the sight of numbers tattooed on the forearms of elderly men who survived the Holocaust. If religion is about anything, it should be about the ability to extend empathy beyond our own family or tribe or community to humanity at large.

Certainly our *children* know this. Our Jewish and Muslim children meet each other in school and compete alongside each other in sports; they care about each other. The question we need to address is whether or not the religious teachings that we impart to our children will serve to expand their empathy and encourage solidarity with others at the same time that these teachings give them a deep sense of attachment to their specific communities and traditions. Polls show that in the last decade fewer numbers of Americans identify with any religious tradition at all, and that an increasing number of Americans view religion as a negative force in society. If our religious traditions are going to survive, they have to demonstrate not only that they are good in themselves, but also that we are good together; that religious differences do not necessarily lead to conflict and disorder in society, but rather serve to enrich our collective understanding of the Creator, the One who is beyond the comprehension of any created being. The Qur'an states, "To each among you have we prescribed a law and an open way. If God had so willed, He would have made you a single people, but (His plan is) to test you in what He has given you: so strive as in a race in all virtues. The goal of you all is to God. It is He who will show you the truth of the matters in which you now dispute" (5:48). Let us strive for good in order to improve each one of us, and thus improve all of us.

May God help us in this effort.

Note

This address was originally delivered in San Diego, CA, on December 16, 2007. This version of the speech has been slightly modified from the original.

CHAPTER ELEVEN

Integration or Separation: The Relationship between Iranian Jewish and Iranian Muslim Communities in Los Angeles

SABA SOOMEKH

Los Angeles is home to the largest concentration of Iranians outside of Iran.[1] After the 1979 Iranian Revolution and the fall of Mohammad Reza Shah (1941–1979), Iran's long-serving monarch, some seventy thousand Iranian Jews fled the newly formed Islamic Republic of Iran and flocked to the United States. There are now approximately one hundred thousand Iranians in the Los Angeles metropolitan area, and it is estimated that forty-five thousand of them are Jewish.[2] Under the reign of Mohammad Reza Shah, Iranian Jews were able to move out of the Jewish ghettos, hold jobs that were once restricted to them, and assimilate and acculturate fully into Iranian society, where they socialized with Iranian Muslims. However, upon moving to Los Angeles, Iranian Jews became much more insular, socializing almost exclusively with other Iranian Jews.

The Iranian-American Jewish mentality of exclusiveness is not common among other Jews living in Los Angeles (or the United States), with the exception of the ultra-orthodox and Hasidic communities. Jews and Muslims living in America both face discrimination, whether overt or subtle. While Jewish history and Muslim history in the United States are quite different, the two groups share a common challenge of living as minorities in a country in which roughly four-fifths of the citizens are Christian.[3] Dialogue between Jewish and Muslim religious leaders and scholars in the United States has been promoted through a range of different conferences and institutes. In Los Angeles in particular, it is generally within the Reform[4] and Conservative[5] synagogues that we find interfaith dialogue programs. For example, over the last few years Sinai Temple, a well-known Conservative Ashkenazi synagogue[6] in West Los Angeles, had a scholar from the Islamic Center of Southern California speak to their congregants and answer questions; the religious school's seventh-grade class visited the Islamic Center's mosque and observed a Friday prayer session; and most recently, on April 20, 2010, Sinai Temple invited Christian and Muslim religious leaders to an interfaith dialogue and concert, wherein Jewish, Muslim, and Christian prayers were offered by the attendees to kick off the event.[7]

This same type of dialogue is not embraced by Iranian synagogues. For example, a congregant of Nessah Temple, an Iranian synagogue located in Beverly Hills, jokingly told me that interfaith dialogue for the Iranian Jewish community means having discussions with Ashkenazi[8] Jews. While this statement was said in jest, it reflects the reality of an Iranian Jewish community that rarely socializes, and indeed seems uninterested in engaging, with non-Iranian Jews, let alone Iranian Muslims. Arguably, what sets the Iranian Jewish community apart from other immigrant communities in Los Angeles is its financial and human capital, which, along with its exilic mentality, enables an insularity that has led to rising tensions with the Iranian Muslim community in Los Angeles. The purpose of this essay is to explore the roots of this tension and to discuss why it is that Iranian Jews in Los Angeles tend to identify more with their ethnoreligious background than with their Iranian national identity.

Methodology

This research is based on fieldwork conducted between 2008 and 2009 with twenty Jewish and Muslim women currently residing in West Los Angeles, all of whom are originally from the Iranian cities of Hamadan and Tehran.[9] These women all grew up—and became mothers—during the reign of Mohammad Reza Shah, and immigrated to Los Angeles either in the final years of his reign or shortly after the Iranian Revolution. I chose to interview Jewish and Muslim women from Hamadan and Tehran because of the significance these cities have in Judeo-Persian history and culture, and because of the cities' contrasting natures. Hamadan holds great importance in Judeo-Persian history because Iranian Jews believe it to be their community's place of origin. In fact, according to Iranian Jewish tradition, this city is the site where the story from *Megillat Esther* [a sacred text read on the Jewish holiday Purim] took place.[10] Jews in Hamadan were more integrated into the Muslim-majority community than in other Iranian cities.[11] Because of the Alliance schools[12] and the numerous Christian missionaries who settled in Hamadan, Hamadanian Jews had a deep connection to and knowledge of their own traditions while also being exposed to other religions. In contrast, Tehrani Jews were ghettoized and less integrated into Iranian society. It was not until the early 1960s that the majority of Iran's Jewish population was integrated into the greater Muslim majority society.[13] Nevertheless, because most Tehrani Jews were forced to remain in the ghetto until the 1960s, they were less assimilated—and typically more religious—than Jews from other parts of Iran.

I am a younger-generation Iranian-American Jew. My mother's family is from Tehran whereas my father's is from Hamadan. Though I was born in Tehran, my family immigrated to the United States immediately before the 1979 Iranian Revolution, and I was raised in Los Angeles. Several of the matriarchs in my family provided me with the names and contact information of Jewish women who were able to reflect on their transitions from life in Iran to life in the United States, particularly in terms of interaction and assimilation with Iranian Muslims. In turn, many of these women provided me with the names of other women who agreed to be interviewed. I also found interviewees by attending the aforementioned Nessah and Sinai Temples. As for interviewing Muslim Iranian women, I was able to collect names and contact information through other, non-Iranian women in the Muslim community.

I met my subjects at their homes and spent a few hours talking with each one, drinking tea and eating fruit and pastries. I recorded, transcribed, and translated the interviews, all of which were conducted entirely in Persian. I did not use a formal questionnaire in my interviews, but I did ask specific questions about the interaction between their community and the "other" group. I structured my interviews around key topics, such as the social interaction between the two religious communities in Iran and Los Angeles and the criticism that Iranian Jews in Los Angeles have received regarding their insularity.

All of my interviewees recalled life in Iran with both romanticism and trepidation. Early in the interview process, they were hesitant to truly open up to me about Jewish-Muslim relations, worrying about being impolite or not wanting to say anything negative about the other community. But after persistent questioning, the women felt more relaxed and gave me a less idealized opinion of the relations between these two Iranian communities, both back in Iran and in the United States.

Iranian Jews during Modernization

The generation of women raised under the reign of Mohammad Reza Shah was heavily influenced by the Shah's forced policy of "modernization," which was explicitly associated with Westernization.[14] During this time, specifically between the end of World War II and the 1979 Revolution, the Iranian Jewish community transformed from an oppressed and poor community into one that was both affluent and well integrated.[15] The emergence of upper-class Jews in the 1960s was a new phenomenon, developing largely because Jews benefited from the financial boom caused by the oil industry. Almost overnight, Jews became prosperous, achieving prestigious positions and becoming an increasingly integral part of Iranian society.[16] A majority of my Jewish interviewees who came from affluent backgrounds discussed how their families appropriated the lifestyle the Shah promoted—modern, secular, and European—and thus, many became less religious, while still maintaining their Jewish identity.

When describing Jewish practices and identity in Iran, Leah Baer, a Jewish sociologist, writes that Iranian Jews did not have categories or labels such as Reform, Conservative, Orthodox, or Unaffiliated—terms that have been a central part of the American Jewish experience. They did not have the rules—the "dos and don'ts"—that certain movements impose on their members. Instead, such Iranian Jews were at ease with the practices of their religion. Their Jewishness was defined in terms of identity and not based solely on ritual or practice. Some families had to conceal their Jewishness, but even these individuals never denied it entirely. They valued and protected their Jewish heritage and identity even when in secret. They taught their children that they were Jews, and even though many did not go to Jewish schools or attend the *knisa*[17] on a regular basis, they still felt their Jewishness. Baer writes that Jewish observance was learned in the home with a deep familial closeness, warmth, and love that accompanied such instruction.[18]

Many Jewish women attended elite European, Jewish,[19] or public schools where the Shah's European "secular" mentality was taught. Thus they were habitually socializing not only with coreligionists but also with Iranians of other faiths—particularly Iranian Muslims. Sima,[20] a fifty-one-year-old Tehrani woman, recalled that when she was growing up everyone wanted to be Europeanized. She said,

> Under the Shah, my father's business became successful, and we lived in a neighborhood with upper-middle-class Jews, Muslims, and Armenian Christians. No one discussed religion anymore. You didn't want to identify yourself through your religious tradition. However, we always knew that no matter how much we assimilated, we were still Jews and would always be seen by Muslims as Jews.

While assimilation became important for many "modernized" Jews, such Jews were not distributed across the whole range of middle-class professions and occupations. They married among themselves and remained exclusively bound to their own community.[21] Though Iranian Jews under the Pahlavi regime were expected and encouraged to appropriate Muslim culture, no matter how affluent and "modernized" they became, the Jews of Iran never truly assimilated into Iranian society. There were limits placed on how successful they could become in their professions, and they remained exclusively bound to their own community and their Jewish identity.

Regardless of how much a family shed itself of ritual observance, intermarriage was still taboo. When I asked Sima if her family approved of intermarriage, she said, "Absolutely not. No matter what, no matter how secular we were, we still held on to our Jewish ethnicity, and I would never bring that stigma and embarrassment to my family. No matter how educated, nonreligious, and assimilated a family was, you still didn't marry a non-Jew. It was considered to be a curse on the family."

Attempting to assimilate into the Iranian Muslim-majority culture was important for Jews. One way of showing one's assimilation was by having Muslim friends and acquaintances. For example, Giti, a fifty-three-year-old psychotherapist, told me, "Everybody was proud of saying, 'Oh, I have a lot of Muslim friends.' Why? Because it meant that you were accepted into Iranian society. You had a sense of pride in having Muslim friends." The more religious Jews at this time tended to come from lower socioeconomic backgrounds; by saying one had many Muslim friends, it was a way of connoting affluence and a "modernized" mentality.

Religion was stigmatized under the Pahlavi regime. "Anyone who was too religious," recalled Mehri, another interviewee, "was considered to be old-fashioned and out of date. This was the trend of life in Iran. The whole country and population was embracing modernity and assimilation. People didn't want to be different from each other." Many of the Jewish women I interviewed said they were raised with Muslim friends and grew up in assimilated neighborhoods. When asked about the differences between Muslim and Jewish women, many said that secular Muslim families did not emphasize being *najeeb*, a Persian term for sexual modesty. Muslim girls were allowed to date and socialize with boys outside of their family. Iranian Jewish women believed that because Muslims were the majority in Iran, Muslim women did not have to worry about being part of an insular community in which there was a lot of gossip and the ever-present fear of ruining one's family name. Thus, many of the women I interviewed said that Muslim women had more freedom outside of their homes than Jews, and were more comfortable with their sexuality.

Iranian Muslims during Modernization

When I discussed the issue of having more freedom than Jews with my Muslim interviewees, specifically as it relates to sexuality, they were infuriated by the claim. Azadeh, a fifty-three-year-old Muslim hairstylist, said,

> It is ridiculous to assume that Jewish women had to be more *najeeb* than Muslim women. I grew up in a strict household; my parents had the same rules in regard to sexuality and dating that Jewish parents had. Jewish women assumed we had all lax rules, but it was something they made up in their heads. It wasn't reality.

Farah, a sixty-one-year-old Muslim grandmother, added, "Sex was not something that was discussed amongst friends in Iranian culture. Thus, do you really think Jewish women knew what was going on in the bedrooms of other women's lives if all of society remained quiet on such a taboo topic?"[22]

Despite the difference in opinion regarding Muslims and freedom of sexuality, it is clear that Muslim women had more freedoms due to career opportunities provided by the Shah. In contrast, Jewish women were not encouraged to work, and the community assumed that if a woman worked, she was neglecting her familial duties and her family must have been experiencing economic difficulties.[23] While Jewish culture discouraged women from having careers, Muslim culture did not attach the same stigma to working women. Many of my Muslim interviewees agreed that they had more opportunities than Jewish women to establish careers outside of the home.

Muslim women were also less involved in domestic chores and did not have the same domestic pressures placed on them as Jews.[24] As a result, they were able to embrace their careers and had the privilege of focusing more time and energy on themselves.[25] However, not all the Jewish women I interviewed agreed that Muslim women had more freedom and rights. Ladan, a forty-eight-year-old Tehrani woman, recalled her experience at a boarding school in Geneva where she studied alongside Iranian Muslims. She remembered that there were not many differences between her and Iranian Muslim girls from her same socioeconomic background. Ladan said,

> It was the incredibly wealthy Muslim girls, those that came from the Shah's family or from families that worked for him, that were the ones who had all the freedom in the world. They were very open about their sexual activities, abortions, dating. [Yet a]ll the Muslim girls I went to school with who had a similar background to mine also had to [publicly] maintain their *najeebness* and were expected to come home after boarding school and get married.

Delaram, an Iranian Jewish woman, had only Muslim friends at the nonreligious elementary school, high school, and university she attended. She believes that because few Jewish women had close Muslim friends, most did not have an accurate concept of what Muslim women's lives were like. "All of my friends were Muslim, and they too had to be *najeeb* and live a morally strict lifestyle," she said. "Muslim women had the same values as Jewish girls. I don't see a difference in values between my Muslim friends and me. I don't think Jewish women had the social interaction with Muslim women to know what their values are."

This said, Delaram admits that there was a difference between Muslim and Jewish women in regard to educational and career ambitions.

> Most of my classmates, if they were Jewish, were very behind academically. They all got married at a very early age, and if they finished high school they went into home economic classes. I studied literature, and there were other Jewish girls who were very progressive and took science courses. But usually the Jewish girls were trained from the beginning to get married by the age of eighteen.

They didn't believe there was a need for them to study or think about a career. I was told numerous times as I was pursuing my academic degree, "What are you doing this for? If you go to university, the men will not marry you."

Delaram recalled that after her divorce, it was her Muslim girlfriends who encouraged her to go back to school to pursue her master's degree. While the Jewish community felt pity for her, it was her Muslim "sisters" who reminded her of her academic ambitions and urged her not to let the divorce stop her from achieving them. Delaram believes that Muslim women placed a higher value on education and careers than Jewish women, but that this was the only difference between the two groups.

Nina, a fifty-five-year-old Iranian Muslim woman who converted to Christianity after moving to Los Angeles, disagrees with the way in which Muslim women were perceived by my Jewish interviewees. Like many Iranian Jewish women, Nina grew up in a "progressive" family that was not religious. She was sent to a British school where she had many Jewish friends, and like them, her family stressed the importance of being *najeeb* and getting married. She admitted that because the Jewish community was a minority community and very insular, her Jewish girlfriends had to worry more about people gossiping and focus on maintaining a reputable image. But she did not have any of the sexual freedoms and openness that many of my Jewish interviewees believe were afforded to Muslim women.

According to Nina, a woman's ethno-religious community did not determine the amount of freedom she had. She recalled, "I always thought that I was discriminated against because I am a woman. I never looked at it within a religious context but within a gendered one. Boys had more freedom than girls did; I don't think religion made a difference. Even if you came from the most secular Jewish or Muslim family, girls had to follow many restrictions." Nina also divorced her husband in her mid-twenties. Although she had no children, her family did not approve of the divorce and tried to force her to stay in a bad marriage. She said, "It is completely untrue that Muslim women can get a divorce and face no repercussions. I was in a loveless marriage with someone who was not good to me and everyone treated me like I was crazy for leaving him. My family dealt with the same stigma that a Jewish family would [have]."

Iranian Jews and Muslims in Los Angeles

What became of Iranian Jewish-Muslim relations after the mass migration to Los Angeles? Based on what my interviewees said, and on my own experience growing up in Los Angeles, I maintain that although there is amicable interaction between the two communities, there is also an overt lack of closeness. Even though the Shah allowed Iranian Jews to assimilate and acculturate into Iranian society, they still faced prejudice and discrimination in Iran, which caused them to identify more with their ethno-religious background than with their national identity. Ethno-religious background was further emphasized by Iranian Jews in the United States around the time of the "Iranian hostage crisis,"²⁶ during which time tensions between Iran and the United States ran high. In an effort to avoid prejudice and discrimination from Americans, Iranian Jews stressed their Jewishness over their Iranianness.

Part and parcel to this insularity, while the Iranian Muslim immigrant community is spread out all across the United States and Europe, Iranian Jews mostly settled in Los Angeles,²⁷ specifically in West Los Angeles and the San Fernando Valley. Their financial capital and large numbers allowed them to be less dependent on people outside of their community. This translated to a lack of desire to get involved with people outside of their own group, whether they were Iranian Muslims or Ashkenazi Jews. As one Iranian Jewish interviewee discussed in regard to raising her children in Beverly Hills,

> My kids go to a public school system where most of their classmates are Iranian Jews. They will then go to Beverly Hills High School, where a majority of their peers will also be Iranian Jews, and then probably go to UCLA or USC—again, where there is a large Iranian Jewish community. They can easily go through their whole lives and only socialize and be among Iranian Jews.

While financial capital, self-sufficiency, and a large population allow Iranian Jews to be insular, others believe that religious identity and the Israeli-Palestinian conflict also play a large part in this process. Many of my Jewish interviewees said that while they always supported Israel in Iran, living in a city with a large Jewish community like Los Angeles, and in a country that overwhelmingly supports Israel politically, has allowed them to be more vocal about their Zionist viewpoint as well as their religious identity. "That is one of the reasons there is an unspoken separation among the two communities," said Shahnaz, another Jewish interviewee.

> In Iran, we never felt comfortable enough to talk about Israel or our Jewish identity publicly. But now in Los Angeles, with its large Jewish population, we are the majority and take great pride in being involved in Jewish organizations. Even if we never discuss religion or politics among our [Iranian] Muslim friends, it is always something that is there.

Another Jewish interviewee said that during the Israel-Gaza violence of 2008–2009, she felt a rift with her Muslim girlfriends, whom she has known since grade school. She said,

> Even though none of us ladies are political or religious, I truly felt separated from them during this time because of how we felt about

what was going on in the Middle East. My relationship with them
has not been the same since. There [were] a couple of things that they
said in regard to Jews and Israel that I definitely found offensive.

In contrast to these opinions, very few of my Muslim interviewees believe
that religion or politics plays a role in Iranian Jewish insularity. One Muslim
interviewee said, "Religion was never important for me. I never grew up in
Iran caring if someone was Jewish, Christian, or Baha'i. Religion had nothing to do with our household. I feel the religious rift more in America than
in Iran." My Muslim interviewees posit that this insularity comes from the
extensive social networking among the Jewish community, which serves
both business and social purposes. Most Jewish women socialize with their
extended families and with other women in *dorehs* (a Persian term for social
gatherings), most of which consist of women from the same socioeconomic
background. Many of my Jewish interviewees confirmed this, telling me
that women attend *dorehs* not only to socialize with each other, but also in
the hopes that their children might befriend each other, setting the stage for
future marriage prospects. In other words, Jewish women spend a great deal
of time with their families and socializing with other Jewish women. "Very
rarely do you see a[n Iranian] Muslim family invited to a Sabbath dinner or a[n Iranian] Muslim woman invited to a *doreh* with [Iranian]Jewish
women," said one of my Muslim interviewees.

Many Muslim women said that Jews' insular social networking makes
the Iranian Jewish community seem extremely exclusive. Some said that
Iranian Jewish families do not bother befriending or maintaining friendships with Muslims because they do not want their children to marry
outside of their faith and subculture. However, five of my Jewish interviewees do attend *dorehs* with their Muslim friends. And while they do
admit to seeing their Jewish friends more frequently, they all said that
maintaining relationships with their Muslim childhood friends is still very
important to them.

When I addressed the issue of exclusivity with my Jewish interviewees,
none of them denied that the Jewish community is exclusive. Many said
that the reason they have maintained their insularity in Los Angeles is that,
due to the Islamic Revolution and the negative orientation toward Jews at
that time, they were forced to flee Iran and become an exiled community.
This experience caused them to reexamine their Jewishness. Thereafter they
choose to define themselves as Jews, perhaps above anything else. This has
also allowed them to develop and maintain their Iranian Jewish culture.

As an Iranian Jew who grew up and currently lives in Los Angeles, I
have noticed that few Iranian Jewish families that came to Los Angeles
in the 1960s and early 1970s have many non-Iranian Jewish friends. One
interviewee, Jacqueline, who moved to Los Angeles with her husband in
1971, said,

We made a conscious choice to leave Tehran and move our family
to Los Angeles. We had and still have many Muslim friends that we

are close to. There were very few Iranian Jews in Los Angeles at that time; thus we had very few people from the community to socialize with. We were lucky—we sold our house, our properties, and I was able to pack everything and bring it with us. We didn't have to leave Iran in a matter of days like many Jews did right before or after the Revolution. I still don't think the community has recovered from that pain.

This exilic mentality, with its desire to maintain the Iranian Jewish culture and community after immigration, has connected Iranian Jews to each other. In addition, the social structure, financial capital, and sheer numbers of Iranian Jews have allowed them to be a very insular and cohesive community—despite the fact that all of my interviewees made sure to point out that there are many instances in which the Iranian Jewish and Iranian Muslim communities come together, particularly at cultural events such as Persian concerts, poetry readings, and plays. As the first and second generations of Iranian Jews are born and raised in Los Angeles, where Iran is an idealized memory of their parents' past, it remains to be seen whether the Iranian Jewish community will continue its history of separation or embrace integration.

Notes

1. Mehdi Bozorgmehr, *Internal Ethnicity: Armenian, Baha'i, Jewish, and Muslim Iranians in Los Angeles*, doctoral dissertation (University of California, Los Angeles, 1992).
2. Mehdi Bozorgmehr and Gap Min Pyong, "Immigrant Entrepreneurship and Business Patterns: A Comparison of Korean and Iranians in Los Angeles," *International Migration Review* Vol. 34, No. 3 (Autumn 2000), 717.
3. Douglas A. Hicks, "Fragile Alliances," *The Christian Century* Vol. 126, No. 5 (March 2009), 31.
4. Reform Judaism refers to various beliefs, practices, and organizations associated with the Reform Jewish movement in North America, the United Kingdom, and elsewhere. In general, it maintains that Judaism and Jewish traditions should be modernized and should be compatible with participation in the surrounding culture. Many branches of Reform Judaism hold that Jewish law should be interpreted as a set of general guidelines rather than as a list of restrictions whose literal observance is required of all Jews.
5. Conservative Judaism is a modern stream of Judaism that arose out of intellectual currents in Germany in the mid-nineteenth century, taking on new institutional forms in the United States in the early 1900s. The principles of Conservative Judaism include a deliberately nonfundamentalist teaching of Jewish principles of faith, a positive attitude toward modern culture, an acceptance of both traditional rabbinic modes of study and modern scholarship and critical text study when considering Jewish religious texts, and a commitment to the authority and practice of Jewish law.
6. While many of the congregants at Sinai Temple are Iranians, the synagogue practices Ashkenazi customs. Many Iranians choose to attend this synagogue because they like the head rabbi David Wolpe. Sinai Temple also has a very popular Conservative Jewish day school, Akiba Academy, which has a large Iranian student body. Enrollment in the day school also includes Temple membership.
7. Jessica Pauline Ogilvie, "Religious Leaders Meet for Interfaith Dialogue at Sinai Temple," *Jewish Journal*, April 22, 2010.
8. Ashkenazi Jews are descendants of the medieval Jewish communities who lived along the Rhine in Germany, from Alsace in the south to the Rhineland in the north.

9. I chose to interview only women because, as a woman, I had an easier time getting access to other women than to men. I also found that when I started interviewing men from both religious communities, they were more hesitant to give me honest answers, whereas the women eventually became open and honest with their opinions.

10. According to Iranian Jewish tradition, this city is the same one referred to as Shushan in the biblical book of Esther.

11. Although Hamadanian Jews did experience hostility, persecution, and forced conversions, they were still more integrated into the community than Jews in other Iranian cities.

12. The most popular schools both in Tehran and Hamadan were the Alliance Israelite Universelle schools, which opened in 1898. The Alliance schools taught the students French, Hebrew, and Persian. Their official aims were to work everywhere for the emancipation and moral progress of world Jewry and offer effective assistance to Jews subjected to anti-Semitism; their written publications also promoted these goals.

13. Sarshar Houman, "Mahalleh," *Esther's Children: A Portrait of Iranian Jews*, Sarshar Houman, ed. (Philadelphia: The Jewish Publication Society, 2002), 105.

14. Western countries, particularly the United States, considered Iran an ally. Thus, there was an effort by the modernizing state to transform "backward" Muslim society into the image of the modern West [Paidar Parvin, *Women and the Political Process in Twentieth-Century Iran* (Cambridge: Cambridge University Press, 1995), 8]. Modernization theory maintained that the state was expected to introduce Western institutions in the Middle East, reversing "backwardness" and creating a "civilized" Westernized society in its place. Modernity entailed the secularization of the state, industrialization, urbanization, the nuclearization of the family, education, and paid employment. In short, during this time, traditional sources of identity such as ethnicity and religion were replaced by secularism and modern institutions (ibid., 9). Mohammad Reza Shah continued the policies of reform and development initiated by his father, Reza Shah, by focusing on the country's infrastructure. In 1961, he launched a program of land reform, followed by a series of reforms focused on rural development, health, and education. These changes, which he referred to as the White Revolution, had limited success. During the ten years that followed the White Revolution, government propaganda portrayed revolutions as generally positive social phenomena. By 1973, oil prices had skyrocketed, and the government launched a new propaganda campaign. This campaign, called the Great Civilization, promised Iranians that within a few years, Iran would reach a level of industrialization equal to that of Japan, if not greater [Amanat Mehrdad, "Nationalism and Social Change in Contemporary Iran," *Irangeles: Iranians in Los Angeles*, Ron Kelly, ed. (Los Angeles: University of California Press, 1993), 17–20]. The Shah ignored his advisors' recommendations for slower growth and a more thoughtful spending policy that would take into account the country's limited resources and infrastructure. As a result, the Great Civilization campaign led to rampant inflation, high rates of urbanization, and extreme socioeconomic inequality. Class distinctions and national identity became even more important in Iranian society, with aristocratic, religious, and ethnic privileges being replaced with new measures of social status, such as educational level and influence in state agencies. A new class was formed comprising professionals, army officers, bureaucrats, and entrepreneurs (ibid.). In his attempt to transform Iran from a dependent society into a modern independent nation state, the Shah made certain changes regarding women's societal status. In the domain of the family, the Shah gave women more of a say in issues surrounding divorce, custody, and polygamy; changed the minimum age of marriage to twenty for men and eighteen for women; and even legalized abortion in certain circumstances (ibid.). In 1963, the Shah gave women the legal right to vote. Yet although the state's policies on education and employment improved the position of women, they did not affect the balance of power between genders. For example, although the overall proportion of educated and employed women increased during this time—by 1976, the rate of literacy among women was 35.7 percent, and 11.3 percent of urban women had entered the workforce— women's opportunities to enter higher education were much more limited than men's. In 1976, only 30 percent of students in higher education were women. Women were even encouraged by state policies to take up "feminine" professions and faced discrimination and lower pay if they attempted to enter traditionally male-dominated professions. Women were also absent from top decision-making jobs. Although the Shah attempted to involve women more extensively in his modern state, he was not able to effectively bring about male-female equality, and modernization failed to fully integrate women into the process of national development

[Yeganeh Nahid, "Women, Nationalism and Islam in Contemporary Political Discourse in Iran," *Feminist Review* Vol. 44 (Summer 1993), 6].

15. D. Mladinov, "Iranian Jewish Organization: The Integration of an Émigré Group into the American Jewish Community," *Journal of Jewish Communal Service* (Spring 1981), 245–248.

16. Michael Reichel, *Persian American Jewry at a Crossroads: Will the Traditions Continue?* (New York: LV Press, 2004), 64.

17. A Persian term for synagogue.

18. Leah Baer, "The Challenge of America," *Padyavand*, Amnon Netzer, ed. (Los Angeles: Mazda Publishing, 1996), 98.

19. Jewish day schools, such as *Etefaqh* in Tehran, were very popular, renowned for their high quality of education; thus, many Muslim students also enrolled in such educational institutions.

20. All names have been changed.

21. Jacob Katz, "German Culture and the Jews," *The Jewish Response to German Culture: From the Enlightenment to the Second World War*," Jehuda Reinharz and Walther Schatzberg, eds. (Hanover: University Press of New England, 1985), 85–86.

22. When I asked my Jewish interviewees if they knew for a fact that Muslim women were more sexually lax or if they just assumed they were, many quickly acknowledged that they would never personally discuss the issue with their Muslim friends and thus had never had an actual conversation about it.

23. Tohidi writes that women's employment outside of the home conflicts with the cult of domesticity and the traditional ideal of femininity among the Iranian urban upper class. During the 1970s—the peak years of the Shah's modernization of Iran—women made up only 12 percent of the labor force. Many women who worked outside the home did so out of economic necessity, as opposed to the desire for self-actualization or to ascend in one's career. [Nayareh Tohidi, "Iranian Women and Gender Relations in Los Angeles," *Irangeles: Iranians in Los Angeles*, 190].

24. According to my Jewish interviewees.

25. A majority of my Jewish interviewees also claimed that Muslim women focus too much on themselves and not enough on their families. Many also claimed that, unlike Jewish women, Muslim women are quick to get divorced.

26. November 4, 1979, to January 20, 1981.

27. Great Neck, New York, has the second largest Iranian Jewish community in the United States.

CHAPTER TWELVE

Challenges and Opportunities for Muslim-Jewish Peacemaking in America

SALAM AL-MARAYATI

My Personal Introduction to Jewish-Muslim Relations: The National Commission on Terrorism

"Gephardt Bows to Jews' Anger" was the headline in the *New York Times* on July 9, 1999. The article was about my rescinded appointment to the National Commission on Terrorism, a panel created by the U.S. Congress earlier that year to review U.S. counterterrorism policy and make appropriate recommendations. At that time, my organization, the Muslim Public Affairs Council (MPAC), was the only American Muslim organization that had issued a counterterrorism policy paper, which was recognized by several members of Congress as authentic and invaluable to the U.S. government.

I was appointed by Congressman Richard Gephardt (D-MO), who was then the house minority leader. My experiences leading to the congressional appointment, and its reversal, illustrate the complexities in Muslim-Jewish relations in the United States. On the one hand, those who opposed my nomination represented somewhat stereotypical "pro-Israel" hardliners. Their objection to my nomination was that I was and continue to be a critic of the Israeli government's policies toward Palestinians.[1] On the other hand, those who supported me represented a wide spectrum of progressive Jews, whether Orthodox, Conservative, or Reform in their religious observance. Similarly, the *New York Times* article covering the episode—which was much more sympathetic to me than the piece that appeared in the *Los Angeles Times*, a paper whose reporters I had worked with for over a decade—was written by a Jewish journalist, Laurie Goodstein, who used the term "Jewish anger" when describing the pushback my appointment received from some in the Jewish community.[2] Either she was simply demonstrating her journalistic integrity, or she was sympathetic to my situation because of the sensitivity that centuries of persecution have embedded in many Jews, or both. Regardless of what led to the *New York Times* article, this experience partially taught me that if there are natural allies for American Muslims in confronting Islamophobia, the Jewish community should make the list.

Though several American Jews apologized to me on behalf of those who were ashamed or embarrassed that various Jewish organizations pushed to exclude me from this appointment, my nomination was nonetheless rescinded. Four organizations led the campaign against me: the American Jewish Committee, the Anti-Defamation League, the Conference of Presidents of Major American Jewish Organizations, and the Zionist Organization of America. Their leaders—David Harris, Abe Foxman, Malcolm Hoenlin, and Morton Klein, respectively—all pressed Gephardt to find a reason to take me off the commission. Perhaps because the Congressman could not officially rescind my nomination, he instead found a technical loop hole: my security clearance would take longer to process than the life of the commission itself, six months. This was, of course, something that could have been said about any nominee.

Upon hearing the unsettling news, I called a friend Ron Iden, who was then the assistant director in charge of the Los Angeles office of the Federal Bureau of Investigation. While he had no jurisdiction over the matter, Iden sent an official letter of commendation to MPAC for its work in keeping the United States safe from terrorism and free from extremism.[3] In the days that followed, about fifty newspapers, including the *Washington Post*, published editorials denouncing Gephardt's reversal, supporting my right to serve on the Commission.[4] The story picked up further momentum when it reached the Middle East-based media, making it an international controversy.

One Los Angeles leader who stood out from all the rest during this debacle was Rabbi Leonard Beerman.[5] At a press conference organized in my defense, Beerman described me as a passionate spokesperson for the Muslim community, and argued that people should not expect Muslims to be speaking from any other perspective than one that reflects the Muslim community. Because Beerman is both a traditional supporter of Israel and a critic of the Israeli government's occupation of the West Bank and Gaza, his solidarity with the Muslim community was extremely moving and significant to fostering positive Jewish–Muslim relations. By example, he taught me that mutual respect between Muslims and Jews necessitates that we stop trying to convert one another, not theologically but ideologically. I applied this lesson to my professional and personal relationship with another member of the Jewish American community, Daniel Sokatch.[6] He and I have the same understanding: he does not attempt to convert me to his Zionist-based perspective and I do not attempt to convert him to my Islamic one. This makes our partnership healthy and productive, rather than one based on and filled with false expectations. Another great Jewish leader who has stood with the Muslim community, out of his understanding of fairness, is Stanley Sheinbaum.[7] He taught me something very important as well—dialogue is about bringing differing parties together; it is not meant to bring together those who already agree with you. Beerman, Sokatch, and Sheinbaum have helped to shape my thinking as a Muslim American leader.[8]

The Buggs Human Relations Award

In many ways, I have a typical American story—I am married to a physician and we have three kids. I work hard, and I like to watch football. (Perhaps my greatest fault is that I am a fan of the Green Bay Packers, which means I waited thirty years between their Super Bowl appearances and have been through roller-coaster rides due to their on again/off again relationship with Quarterback Brett Favre.) The only difference between me and the average American is that I'm a Muslim. Born in Baghdad, Iraq, I left with my family around the age of four, in 1964, when my parents were forced to relocate because of political persecution. I returned for a visit to Baghdad in 1972, but have never returned due to the ongoing turmoil in the Persian Gulf.

The organization I lead, MPAC, was cofounded by one of the most influential Muslim thinkers in the United States—Dr. Maher Hathout. He is considered by many to have played a pivotal role in developing the American Muslim identity, now the mantra for virtually every mosque, Muslim organization, and community in the United States. In his own words, "Home is where my grandchildren will be raised, not where my grandparents are buried." He developed this idea well before 9/11, not because of it. In fact, the first time I recall him articulating the American Muslim identity was back in 1988, the year MPAC was formed.

Unfortunately, Hathout became a target of attack by some Jewish organizations when he was selected to receive the John Allen Buggs Human Relations Award by the County of Los Angeles in 2006. Groups like the Zionist Organization of America and Stand With Us were upset that a man like Hathout could receive such an award, given his history of criticism of Israeli governmental policies. Some of them wanted the Los Angeles County board of supervisors to fire the executive director of the Human Relations Commission for even considering Hathout to be a suitable candidate. But one man, Dan Wolf, took a stand of courage and conscience against the tide of self-identified pro-Israel hardliners.

His father, the late Rabbi Alfred Wolf, was the recipient of the Buggs Award back in 1972. In addition, the elder Wolf and Hathout developed one of the first Muslim-Jewish dialogues in Southern California. As leaders of two of the most important religious institutions in Los Angeles, the Wilshire Boulevard Temple and the Islamic Center of Southern California, they joined together to create a new intercommunal partnership over thirty years ago. More than that, the two men were close friends. In a hearing that was scheduled to review the decision to honor Hathout, Wolf testified saying, "Were he alive today, my father would be here instead of me, speaking far more eloquently than I on behalf of Dr. Hathout and his life as a fellow builder of bridges. To be sure, Dad and Dr. Hathout did not agree on everything—what brothers do? But brothers they were."[9] Hathout had to confront almost the same exact groups I faced opposition from during the Gephardt controversy. In his response to their criticism of his receiving the award based on his criticism of Israeli government policies, Hathout said that he was being honored by the county of Los Angeles not the state of Israel, a point that arguably went by his detractors without understanding or notice. In the end, key Jewish allies of the Muslim community made a huge impact in the discourse surrounding this issue—and as a result, the Human Relations Commission held their ground and went forward with honoring Hathout for his tremendous role in building bridges of understanding in Los Angeles.

For Hathout and me, the issue at stake in this example and elsewhere is beyond either one of us as individuals. It has to do with violating a core right of American Muslims, the right to serve *as* an American *for* America and *in* America. It has never been about Jews and Muslims being against one another. Rather it's been about people who believe in pluralism and civil discourse standing up against those who prefer exclusion and monologue. American Muslims are regularly "tarred and feathered" by pro-Israel hardliners, who recklessly challenge the patriotism of decent Americans by creating false paradigms of "you're either with us or against us." They do not allow for dissent, even though dissent from the status quo for the sake of serving American interests and principles can be the most patriotic action that a person of conscience can undertake.

In an effort to move forward after the Gephardt episode, Hathout proposed the establishment of a "Code of Ethics" for Muslim-Jewish relations. Quoting the Qur'an and the Torah as central building blocks for understanding how our two communities should engage with one another, the document suggests such things as speaking with one voice against violence and both groups verifying rumors before making public pronunciations. It was signed by approximately eighty Muslim and Jewish leaders in Los Angeles on December 6, 1999, and was displayed in City Hall for many years.[10]

The Pro-Israel Litmus Test

Dr. Hathout and I have not been the only targets of pro-Israel hardliner group efforts to intimidate and silence people on issues related to the plight of Palestinians. In a recent meeting with an American Muslim law professor, I learned that in the 1960s several Muslim/Arab Americans were turned away from work by the U.S. State Department because of their lack of unwavering support for the policies of the state of Israel.[11] This exclusion continues to take place today. Recently, an American Muslim who was hired to work on South Asian affairs at the U.S. Commission on International

Religious Freedom was asked about her positions on political issues related to the Middle East. Because of her sympathy toward the suffering of the Palestinian people, she was asked to look for a position elsewhere.[12]

Another related common and problematic phenomenon taking place across America is the division of the Muslim community into "good Muslims" and "bad Muslims." Perhaps what is worse about this "with us or against us" mentality is that the division has nothing to do with Islam but rather with whether or not a Muslim is quiet or uncritical on issues pertaining to Israel-Palestine. Even those who seek funding from prestigious U.S. foundations cannot take public positions on the Palestinian issue. Aside from movies such as "Obsession" and "The Third Jihad," both egregiously labeling many normative American Muslim organizations as closeted hotbeds of terrorism,[13] one tactic is for pro-Israel hardliner groups to parade around individuals such as Wafa Sultan—whose preamble to her public support for Israeli governmental policies toward Palestinians was that she had renounced Islam.[14] In 2004, the American Jewish Committee launched a speaking tour for a Sufi figure who made a dangerous and reckless accusation against American Muslims, falsely claiming that 80 percent of them are extremists.[15]

This strategy only antagonizes mainstream Muslim groups. In explaining how this may eventually lead to the marginalization of both American Muslims and American Jews, Rabbi Steve Jacobs co-wrote an op-ed for the *Los Angeles Times* in which he promoted a new vision of intercommunal discussion between Jews and Muslims.[16] Along with Hathout, Jacobs spends time speaking publicly about the plurality of both the Jewish and Muslim communities.

Anti-Semitism and Islamophobia

Muslims have great respect for Judaism and, in particular, for the prophets Abraham and Moses. The story of Moses and his struggle to liberate the Children of Israel from Pharoah is found in the Qur'an.

> Verily, those who have attained to faith [in this divine writ], as well as those who follow the Jewish faith, and the Christians, and the Sabians—all who believe in God and the Last Day and do righteous deeds—shall have their reward with their Sustainer; and no fear need they have, and neither shall they grieve. (2:62)

The Qur'an tells Muslims to believe in all the Prophets of God who brought to humanity a common message: believe in One God, believe in one human family, and do good.

> Say, "We believe in God and that which was revealed to us and that which was revealed to Abraham and Ismail and Isaac and Jacob and their descendants, and that which has been given to Moses and Jesus,

and that which has been given to all the [other] prophets by their Sustainer. We make no distinction between any of them. And it is unto Him that we surrender ourselves." (2:136)

The issue of believing in one God, called *tawhid* in Arabic, is intertwined with the belief in human equality and in the protection of the Peoples of the Book (i.e., Jews and Christians). The legacy of Islam is actually an Abrahamic one. Perhaps the greatest threat to this legacy is the fundamentalist and exclusivist ideology one finds in the very religions that profess Abraham as their common forefather. The biblical prophets are Islam's prophets, too, and the protection of Jews and Christians, and their synagogues and churches, must be revered and respected by all Muslims. There are, however, Muslim and Jewish fundamentalists who deliberately distort the Abrahamic relationship.

Israeli prime minister Benjamin Netanyahu articulated such a fundamentalist view when he compared the Spanish Inquisition to the displacement of Palestinians from their land. He applauded the ethnic cleansing of Muslims from the Iberian Peninsula, saying, "What the Spaniards achieved after eight centuries, the Jews achieved after twelve—but the principle is identical."[17] The demonization of the Palestinian people by Netanyahu has cued pro-Israel hardliner groups in America to defame American Muslims who support the Palestinian cause, hence connecting Islamophobia with a seemingly pro-Israel stance.

This fundamentalist and exclusivist mentality encroaches on our democratic process in America. For example, certain pro-Israel hardliner groups demand that American Muslims accept Jerusalem as the undivided capital of the state of Israel, or that Jewish settlements should be allowed to engulf the Holy City. Some American Jews want American Muslims to accept Israel's treatment of Palestinians without criticism; indeed, such individuals and groups often equate criticism of Israel with anti-Semitism and/ or Islamic extremism. It is this attitude that explains why I have so often been a target of anti-Muslim rhetoric by pro-Israel hardliner groups.

Of course, I am not alone. Former president Jimmy Carter has been repeatedly attacked for describing Israel's treatment of Palestinians in the West Bank and Gaza as an "apartheid." Even an orthodox Jew named Daniel Kurtzer, a former U.S. ambassador to Egypt and Israel, was classified as anti-Israel for criticizing the Israeli policy of the military occupation of the West Bank and Gaza. Thus, when I am attacked for my criticism of Israeli policies, I know that I am in good company with fellow Christians and Jews.

NewGround: Muslim-Jewish Peacemaking

NewGround, a program created and cosponsored by MPAC and the Progressive Jewish Alliance, is preparing the next generation of Muslim and Jewish leaders from both communities to have a better chance of effectively engaging issues of mutual concern. NewGround provides opportunities for young Muslim and Jewish professionals of all backgrounds to build honest, authentic relationships with one another, to establish a common commitment to change, and to become a new cadre of leaders who inspire hope in a troubled world. NewGround has been praised by both Jewish and Muslim leaders for providing a space for authentic interfaith dialogue.

Rabbi Laura Geller, Senior Rabbi of Temple Emanuel in Beverly Hills, called NewGround "an extraordinary program that not only can build bridges between the Muslim and Jewish community but also can provide the common ground necessary for a younger generation of Muslims and Jews to walk together as partners in making Los Angeles a better place. It is a model that should be duplicated all over the country." Shakeel Syed, the executive director of the Islamic Shura Council of Southern California, has also lauded the efforts of NewGround: "Mending bridges and building bonds is an Abrahamic legacy, radically different from the prevailing culture of building walls and burning bridges. The NewGround project is a twenty first century version of that Abrahamic legacy!"

Before NewGround, Muslim-Jewish dialogue in Los Angeles suffered from massive setbacks whenever war, terrorism, or any political controversy erupted in the Middle East. Usually, one side would demand conditions from the other before agreeing to move forward on the dialogue, a formula for failure and, frankly, for self-destruction. The American people are growing impatient with both sides of the conflict. Muslims and Jews need to create a peacemaking constituency to support the U.S. government's Middle East peacemaking initiatives, or they will be viewed as supporting violence over peace in the region.

That peacemaking constituency is precisely what NewGround offers, as one Muslim participant discovered at a meeting that took place in the midst of Israel's invasion of Gaza in January 2009: "NewGround allowed a forum to show the human side of our community and allowed us a voice for the voiceless in Gaza and the West Bank and Jerusalem." He continued in saying,

> Even during and after the January 2009 bombardment in Gaza, many said that there was no way to speak to the Jewish community, that none of them would listen. NewGround provided a forum that aimed at doing exactly the opposite. We all got together in early 2009, both [the first and second year cohorts of] NewGround programs, and talked about the impact that the bombings in Gaza had on our community and on the Palestinians. To see a Palestinian participant cry and tell her personal story about her family living in Gaza and not knowing what the next day will bring is a lot different than reading an op-ed or a position paper on why Israel's actions were unjustified. It's a lot more impactful.

The fact that Muslims and Jews can discuss the Israeli occupation of Palestinian territories in the West Bank and Gaza strip while also addressing the perspective that Israel should remain a Jewish state, regardless of whether or not one agrees with such viewpoints, is important to creating a peacemaking constituency in America, which is a goal I share with J Street. With its mantra "pro-Israel and pro-peace," J Street is a credible force in the Jewish American mosaic. I was invited to their inaugural convention and, as expected, Zionist extremists wanted J Street executive director Jeremy Ben-Ami to cancel my talk, and applied a great deal of pressure to achieve their goal. Unlike several politicians, Jeremy did not buckle.

Prior to the conference, I wrote an op-ed for the Jewish Telegraphic Agency, entitled "U.S. Jews, Muslims must look forward, not back."[18] In this essay, I wrote about a common criticism leveled against me—a statement I made during a local Los Angeles radio talk show on 9/11. At the time, I was being interviewed about the attacks on the Twin Towers. The guest before me stated that Islam should be viewed as the primary suspect—an awful stereotype, especially considering that the interview took place well before anyone knew that Al Qaeda was the culprit for the worst terrorist attack on American soil in the history of this country. As a hypothetical rejoinder, I replied that if you want to look at suspects, we should look to who benefits the most from the attacks, namely Israel. The next day, I apologized on the same program for responding to one awful stereotype with another. The Jewish leaders who accepted my apology continue to work with MPAC. Others use this quote as an excuse to attack my work with these very same Jewish leaders.

Jewish Allies in Congress

Ironically, Jewish members of the U.S. Congress have been the most helpful for American Muslims in terms of helping create greater government engagement: The late Senator Paul Wellstone wrote the foreword to an MPAC policy paper; Congresswoman Jane Harman, a strong supporter of Israel, invited MPAC to testify at a congressional hearing on national security (she was confronted with anti-Muslim propaganda, which is now unfortunately a cottage industry, but to her credit, she did not waiver and continued with the hearing); Senator Russell Feingold was the only senator to oppose the USA PATRIOT Act, partly out of concern for its impact on American Muslims; Congressman Adam Schiff remained a good friend of the Muslim community even when his political opponent accused him of sympathizing with terrorism for merely meeting with MPAC representatives. These members of Congress do not agree with many American Muslims on the issues confronting the Middle East. But they do recognize that the experience of American Muslims mirrors the American Jewish experience. They also know that American Muslims and American Jews need to make peace in the United States before having any credibility for pushing for peace in the Middle East.

Muslim-Jewish Commonality in America

During their struggle for integration into American society, Jews worked to conform their traditions and mores to those of other Americans, even while maintaining an independent Jewish identity. Education and preservation of the Jewish legacy was the key to the success of American Jews. American Muslims now face the same challenges. American values of life, liberty, and the pursuit of happiness are already in line with the goals and values of Islamic law—the development of the rights to life, expression, faith, property, and family. Educating Muslims about the essence of Islam, as opposed to the politics of the Muslim world, is now the greatest priority for Western Muslim communities to thrive.

A great many Muslims in the United States have been either unwilling or unable to separate their ethnic and cultural identities from their religious identification. Many Jews, particularly those from the Middle East and Europe, have faced similar challenges during their experiences in the United States, where Jews have historically endured political attacks. During the McCarthy era, several American Jews were accused of communist ties. One famous example of civil liberties violations against Jews is the case of the so-called Hollywood Ten. In the mid-1940s, xenophobic accusations against Jews were commonplace, just as they now are against Muslims who are faced with the prospect of having to prove that they are not tied to terrorism and violence. Put simply, the Muslim community has become suspect. Perhaps the most alarming repercussion of this political assault is the closure of American Muslim charities.

Middle East Narratives

Because of their common religious roots and common experiences in the United States, American Muslims and American Jews have the potential to be natural allies. In many instances they are. Yet the conflicts in the Middle East have led to major clashes between Muslims and Jews in the United States. For Jews, the state of Israel has created a safe haven, a Jewish-majority country in which Jews can feel secure and free from oppression. For Muslims, the Palestinian cause is emblematic of the struggle against colonialism. But while American Jews and American Muslims may hold diametrically opposed views about the conflicts in the Middle East, they cannot fight out their differences in American courts or in American political circles without ultimately having the American people reject both narratives. Unless Muslims and Jews in the United States learn to deal with the issues surrounding the Middle East in an effective way, by, for instance, creating peacemaking constituencies within the United States, they will both become scapegoats for U.S. failures in the region.

It is a mistake to think that because Muslims are in their nascent stages of political effectiveness, they can be ignored or eliminated from U.S. policy discussions about the Middle East. With all the challenges facing MPAC, we have still met with Presidents Clinton, Bush, and Obama on several occasions. We have been in dialogue with cabinet officials. We have held forums on Capitol Hill, in federal agencies, and have made presentations to prestigious think tanks such as the Brookings Institution. The participation of American Muslims in U.S. policymaking is of vital interest to the U.S. government, and an increasing number of government officials are beginning to realize this fact. The campaign to exclude or marginalize American Muslims from U.S. politics is a failed effort, and those who sponsor such campaigns will only bring shame to themselves.

A new paradigm in U.S. Muslim-Jewish cooperation on Middle East issues is desperately needed. This is no longer a conflict confined to the "pro-Israel" and "pro-Palestinian" camps. It has become a conflict between two competing mindsets: one representing an Abrahamic approach to the Middle East and Muslim-Jewish relations in the United States; the other representing an exclusivist attitude for the region and for America. Moses, Jesus, and Muhammad all preached the same message of belief in one God, of one united human community, and of doing good works for others. The terms *tikkun olam* for Jews and *islaah* for Muslims both imply a movement of reform and transformative healing toward a better world. Unless Muslims and Jews deal with the Middle East effectively, within the authentic understanding of their respective faiths, mutual suspicion will continue to spread, not just in America but throughout the world.

Governance for Humanity

I believe that both Muslims and Jews have failed in creating good, responsible governance that can serve the needs of their people. The idea of a Jewish state that is also a democracy is structurally flawed if Palestinians cannot in principle become equal citizens. By the same token, Muslims who use slogans for supporting the idea of an Islamic state but ignore the principle of justice—the essence of Islam—are also deceiving themselves. Serving humanity and good governance are important for success in the Middle East. As the Qur'an says, "We have bestowed dignity on the Children of Adam" (17:70).

American Muslims and American Jews can celebrate their respective religious holidays together. They can share in the common values taught by their scriptures. They can discuss common challenges they face as religious minorities in the Untied States. Both groups include well-educated and affluent Americans. They share a legal code that is a central element of their respective faiths. They both consider justice to be the highest divine value. They both have much to gain and much to lose.

Those Muslims and Jews who want to remain in their adversarial orientation are stuck in the past; and those who blindly support their coreligionists in the Middle East will become irrelevant to America. However, if both communities are willing to base their relationship upon the Abrahamic framework, both will benefit, and both will take a leading role in the United States. They will be seen as saviors of their own people and peacemakers for all humanity.

We as Americans should never bow to anyone's anger. Instead we should bow in submission to God as one nation. Unfortunately, we have used the fear of God to terrorize one another. We have demanded that God serve our desires rather than demanding that we serve God. The defining issue for America's Muslims, Jews, and Christians must be how to be instruments of peace.

Many people feel angry when they are excluded from the political process or forced to answer false charges. I feel that it is my task as an American to challenge misconceptions about Islam and Muslims, whatever the personal cost. And so I am grateful to God for giving me the opportunity to build bridges with my Jewish brothers and sisters. The Qur'an teaches me to convert people from enmity to friendship: "Evil and good are not equal; so repel evil with that which is better, so that the one with whom there is enmity becomes a close friend" (41:34).

This must be the task of all peoples of faith.

Notes

1. At the time I suggested that we Americans should look into root causes of terrorism; a similar assertion was made by President George W. Bush after 9/11. Unlike the former president, I was cast as a terrorist sympathizer for making this point. I still maintain this position.
2. Laurie Goodstein, "Gephardt Bows to Jews' Anger over a Nominee," *New York Times* (July 9, 1999), also available at nytimes.com/1999/07/09/us/gephardt-bows-to-jews-anger-over-a-nominee.html, retrieved July 30, 2010.
3. Personal correspondence from former assistant director in charge of the Los Angeles Field office of the FBI, Ron Iden, found at mpac.org/docs/Ron-Iden-support-letter.pdf.
4. Benjamin Wittes, a member of the editorial staff of the *Washington Post* at the time, impressed me with his lucid style of writing to the point that I contacted him; we've been colleagues ever since.
5. Along with Reverend George Regas, Beerman was a pioneer of peace and justice groups in America, having worked with Muslims since the 1980s when the two joined together to lead the Los Angeles Interfaith Center to reverse the Nuclear Arms race. In 1990, when the U.S. government began building up its forces in the Persian Gulf, Beerman led his synagogue, Leo Baeck Temple, to ally with the Islamic Center of Southern California and All Saints Church in forming the Religious Coalition Against War in the Persian Gulf.
6. Sokatch was the founding executive director of the Progressive Jewish Alliance and is currently the chief executive officer of the New Israel Fund.
7. Sheinbaum even helped bring the United States respect globally by creating the premise for the Oslo Accords. At that time, he visited former Palestinian chairman Yasser Arafat, though other Jewish organizations derided him for this bold step.

8. Another Jewish American I want to thank is unknown to me. Thanks to information from this FBI informant, a December 2001 bomb plot devised by the Jewish Defense League against my office, the King Fahd mosque, and the office of Congressman Darryl Issa, an Arab American, was foiled. I never met that courageous person, but I thank him nonetheless. It should be noted that Muslims have also been found guilty in targeting synagogues and Jewish centers. I am proud that my organization, the Muslim Public Affairs Council, and other mainstream Muslim organizations have consistently taken a strong stand against anti-Semitism and any targeting of Jews.

9. Brad Greenberg, "Award Confirmed, Muslim to Keep Humanitarian Honor," *Jewish Journal* (September 19, 2006), also available at www.thefreelibrary.com/AWARD+CONFIRMED+ MUSLIM+TO+KEEP+HUMANITARIAN+HONOR-a0151678479, retrieved July 30, 2010.

10. "Muslim-Jewish Code of Honor" can be found at www.mpac.org/docs/Code-of-Ethics-Muslim-Jewish-Dialogue.jpg.

11. Conversation with Muslim members of the Chicago Council on Global Affairs Task Force on Muslim Civic and Political Engagement in Chicago, IL (June 2006).

12. Michelle Boorstein, "Agency that Monitors Religious Freedom Abroad Accused of Bias," *Washington Post* (February 17, 2010), also available at washingtonpost.com/wp-dyn/content/ article/2010/02/16/AR201002 1605517.html, retrieved July 30, 2010.

13. During the 2008 presidential elections, twenty-eight million DVD copies of the propaganda piece "Obsession" were inserted into Sunday copies of the *New York Times* in battleground states. The producers of the documentary were traced back to a religious seminary based in the Old City of Jerusalem called Aish HaTorah International (see www.mpac.org/docs/Exposing-Obsession.pdf). For a strong rebuttal of the film, see Rabbi Steve Jacobs' interview with one of the film's spokespersons Gregory Ross (see www.youtube.com/watch?v=Ct7sdHWk1Q8, retrieved July 30, 2010). This episode is discussed elsewhere in this volume, in Omid Safi's chapter "Who Put Hate in My Sunday Paper?"

14. Susan Crimp and Joel Richardson. *Why We Left Islam: Former Muslims Speak Out* (WND Books: 2008).

15. www.amislam.com/pincus.htm, retrieved July 30, 2010.

16. Salam Al-Marayati and Steven Jacobs, "Another Wedge Issue: Exploiting the Muslim-Jewish Divide is the Wrong Way to Win Votes," *Los Angeles Times* (June 26, 2008), also available at articles.latimes.com/2008/jun/26/opinion/oe-almarayati26, retrieved July 30, 2010.

17. Benjamin Netanyahu, *A Place among the Nations: Israel and the World* (Bantam: New York, 1993), 26.

18. Salam Al-Marayati, "U.S. Jews, Muslims Must Look Forward, Not Back," *Jewish Telegraphic Agency* (September 16, 2009), also available at jta.org/news/article/2009/09/16/1007929/op-ed-us-jews-muslims-must-look-forward-not-back, retrieved July 30, 2010.

PART IV

Toward the Future: New Models in Jewish-Muslim Relations

CHAPTER THIRTEEN

Beyond Sarah and Hagar: Jewish and Muslim Reflections on Feminist Theology

AYSHA HIDAYATULLAH AND JUDITH PLASKOW

Dear Judith,

This letter to you is a long time coming. For a decade now, there has been a fire in my belly ignited by my experiences of marginality as a Muslim woman. But, until now, it has been too difficult to trust non-Muslims with these feelings.

I am writing you now across the religious, political, and generational lines that divide us, at a time in which Muslims are dying every day as a result of U.S. military incursions in Muslim-majority countries, when not a day passes without reports of Muslims being harassed, assaulted, and treated like foreigners in the only place I have ever called home, the United States of America. It is a time of wars and violence against Muslims, much of which has been justified by long-standing prejudices against Islam, including claims that Muslims categorically oppress women. Because of this, I have long been afraid that speaking to you openly about my struggles as a woman would make the problem worse for Muslims, who have so much to lose right now. And yet I feel it is time to stop being afraid. I believe there may be far more to lose by keeping quiet. I know I can trust you to hold my words in all of their vulnerability.

Even though I am writing to you only now, I feel that I have known you for years through your work, which I have studied in the same way I learned to study people as a little, brown, Muslim girl growing up in the Bible Belt, carefully deciding who to trust, calculating how to survive in a place where I never experienced the ease of belonging. I have let go of the fear that speaking openly about injustices within my own tradition would amount to a betrayal of my community. Indeed, now I know that the real betrayal would be to remain silent and to close myself off to the possibility of contributing to change in my community by forming trusting partnerships with others.

In your work, I have heard the echoes of my own rage, shame, and ambivalence as a woman who is deeply devoted to her religion and yet deeply pained by the ways in which it has marginalized, excluded, and denied my experiences as a woman. At times hearing your voice has helped me make out the whispers of my own, when you have revealed something to me with a new clarity that has confirmed my own instincts. Since before I was even born, you have been working to shatter the long silence that has enabled the treatment of men as the normative recipients of Judaism and the imagining of God as male. You have testified to your experiences of being "other" as both a woman and a Jew. You have opened yourself up to criticism and revision of your own theological positions. You have been willing to change your own thinking time and time again, taking criticism of your work in stride, constantly adding new insights to your belief system. You have been doing this all along as a Jewish feminist. And I have been listening to you, for many years, as a Muslim feminist searching for her own voice. You have given me so much without knowing me.

But now I ask, will you know me? Can we talk both about the things that have brought us together without us even knowing it and about the things that have kept us apart for so long?

With my respect and admiration,
Aysha

Dear Aysha,

Thank you very much for your letter. I feel honored to be trusted with it. I have always hoped that my work would have resonance beyond the Jewish community, and I'm gratified to hear that it has been helpful to you. Where to begin when it feels as if there is so much we have in common as well as so much that divides us?

I was thinking recently about the Women Exploring Theology conference that took place in Grailville, OH, in 1972, and about the ways in which it was my first taste of so much that has been both problematic and wonderful about being a Jewish feminist theologian in a Christian-dominated academy and culture. The conference was an amazing event at which sixty women—all Christian except for me—came together not just to express our pain and anger at our marginalization within our various communities, but also to initiate new modes of thinking and acting as religiously committed women. It was a life-changing experience for me, a week during which I made formative friendships and witnessed the power of women working together to transform our respective traditions. But I got to be there only because a friend, Carol Christ, was unable to attend and offered me her spot. The organizers were willing for me to serve as a substitute but felt no need to think about what it would mean to have a Jewish woman present. Daily worship, for example, was a central part of the experience for almost all the participants, but I went only once and felt profoundly alienated. On one level, I was an important part of the group and contributed a great deal. Yet, on another level, I was very much an outsider.

This double consciousness has been central to my experience for the last forty years. First chairing and then being part of the Women and Religion Section of the American Academy of Religion (AAR) has been crucial to my intellectual and personal life. And yet I cannot count the number of panels on which I have had the burden of representing "*the* Jewish perspective" on a given topic of feminist concern. For the last several years, a single Muslim scholar has been added to the mix in many such sessions. Each time this has happened, I have been aware of both a strong sense of kinship and an important difference in our situations. As someone who has been involved in feminist studies in religion for four decades, I know I am often perceived as a person with the power to define the agenda for feminist work in the academy. And while I have had that power together with others, I have also consistently struggled to articulate and maintain my Jewish voice in an overwhelmingly Christian-majority environment. When I was a graduate student at Yale, a feminist student in the sociology department wrote a dissertation showing that when women make up less than one-third of a graduate program, they are more likely to drop out than men. However, when they constitute more than one-third of graduate students, they finish more quickly and do better. I have often thought of this finding when confronted with the near impossibility of getting Jewish concerns heard in settings where I am the lone outside voice. On those few occasions when I have been at feminist conferences or events at which there were several Jewish women present, I have been struck by my sense of relief at feeling the burden of representation lifted. Most of the time, I'm not aware of what I'm missing!

I have also wrestled with the question you raise in your letter about speaking critically about our traditions in contexts in which people already come in with many negative stereotypes about Judaism and Islam. "Washing dirty linen in public" is a strong taboo in the Jewish community, and I assume that the same is true for Muslims. I recognize that in a political context in which Muslims face violence, racial profiling, and denial of civil liberties, the stakes are much higher for you than for me. I have felt most acutely conflicted when I have spoken in Germany or when I teach Judaism to my Catholic undergraduates, most of whom have been raised with some version of Christian triumphalism. What I have learned over time, though, is that when I speak critically I help others come to perceive Judaism as a living and changing tradition. Many Christians take for granted that Judaism stagnated once Christianity began, and that Jewish women are oppressed. What they do *not* know is that Jewish women are speaking up and speaking back, taking upon ourselves the power to interpret Jewish tradition. My students have the same reaction of interested surprise and respect when they read about feminism within Islam. I have thus reframed for myself the way I think about speaking critically in public: I am not washing dirty linen. Instead I am modeling a critical stance that we all need to take toward our traditions.

Looking forward to continuing our conversation,
Judith

Dear Judith,

Thank you so much for your response. It is sobering to learn that when you look back over forty years of work you still have the feeling of being a lone outside voice, enduring the burden of representation, and carrying the perennial double consciousness of feeling both profoundly connected to and alienated from Christian colleagues and friends in the feminist struggle. It had never occurred to me that—despite the long legacy of Jewish struggles for belonging in this country, and despite all the respect and recognition you have personally earned—you could still experience this kind of marginality. It is even more troubling since it is a marginalization you have experienced within the very conversation that you have been so vital in creating and defining.

I find it poignant that you could be this vital and powerful force but still struggle to maintain your Jewish voice. It makes me wonder how long it will take before non-Christian voices are no longer tokenized, when the invitations extended to us to sit at the "side-table" of interreligious conversations (feminist or not) will finally give way to something that feels less like we are being "given" a voice and more like we are taking and claiming one for ourselves—making this claim at *our own* table. I marvel at what it is that makes this kind of "othering" so powerful and so enduring, how it maintains itself so stubbornly and insidiously even in the company of people who care so deeply and sincerely for us. And indeed how important it is to note that all of this happens in a field of inquiry founded on the rupturing of enduring and oppressive silences. How bitter it is that the thing that has helped us find a voice would also silence us. I wonder: if feminist theology has participated in the very thing it has been built upon resisting, what does that make it now? What is left of feminist theology, and does it still deserve this title at all, or has it lost the right to call itself that?

So yes, it is painful to reflect on this with you, especially since I thought that with Jews having been part of this discourse for so long things would be better than they are. I must also admit to the tendency in my work and in the works of many other Muslim women to make generalizations about "Jewish-Christian" feminist theology. Thank you for the reminder that Jewish and Christian feminist theologies should not be so casually grouped together.

For Muslims, it is not only that we are much newer participants in such discussions than other religious communities. It is that even when Muslim voices are present in these conversations, they often are met with a profound ignorance about Islam. Perhaps this ignorance stems from the fact that members of dominant communities have no need to study the "other" in order to survive. They see their worldview as the only worldview, and thus they are even ignorant about their ignorance regarding the "other." Without a basic knowledge of Islam, meaningful intercommunal discussions among feminists, which could yield multidirectional insights, are impossible to achieve. For example, I might understand exactly what is at stake in rereading the Adam and Eve story for Christians and Jews. But few Christians and Jews would have the slightest idea what it means for me, as a Muslim, to read the same story (it probably has never even crossed their minds); so, no one will be able to relate to what I am doing critically or creatively. I then share my piece and receive nothing in return; I don't even get a response. This kind of persistent ignorance about Islam continues to preclude meaningful exchanges between us. At this point, I question the value of continuing these exchanges unless there is something meaningful happening cross-directionally.

Moreover, I have begun to question the very premise of Jewish and Muslim (and Christian) women coming together on the basis of our mutual kinship as coreligionists in the "Abrahamic tradition"—a phrase carelessly overused since 9/11. For me, this claim to mutual kinship, while an important starting point and reminder of our shared pasts, has become an empty catch phrase, an attempt to homogenize that which is, by definition, heterogeneous. Indeed, it is even disingenuous due to the fallacies and evasions built into the paradigm of the "Abrahamic" religions. For example, hardly anyone mentions the way in which this connection to a common patriarch is based on the exclusion of all other non-Abrahamic religions. In other words, its claim to multireligious interaction is based upon the exclusion of other traditions altogether. Then there is the problem I previously mentioned: the persistent ignorance about one another's religions, such that even when we lay claim to a common lineage we do so without taking on the commitment and responsibility to develop a deep and productive knowledge of where we are all coming from. But at its most insidious I think that the Abrahamic paradigm lures us into the deceptive liberal project of "inclusion," which often functions to minimize, cover over, and ameliorate our differences and conflicts. The work of inclusion often has the dangerous effect of hastily neutralizing our differences and conflicts in a surface and short-term manner without engaging deeper persistent problems between us. In turn, such an approach often limits the potential for radical and deeply transformative change within and between our communities, change that is imperative in order for growth and progress to take place.

Finally, and perhaps most pertinent to our discussion as feminists, the claiming of a common heritage through a patriarch glosses completely over the patriarchal structures that are built into our genealogy and interactions. Abraham, after all, was a patriarch, and did in fact place his consorts, Sarah and Hagar, in untenable positions as an exercise of his patriarchal authority! In framing our responses as feminists, we have sought to recover our shared ancestry through Hagar and Sarah, looking to them as courageous and strong foremothers. It is important for us to revive their stories as a source of mutual empowerment because their stories are open to us for reclaiming, reinterpreting, and celebrating. In particular, Muslim feminists have begun turning to Hagar as a strong and exemplary symbol of female struggle in Islam, a woman who endured her trials in the wilderness with Ishmael (the patriarch to whom Muslims have traced their heritage) with unrelenting conviction and devotion to God. Some Muslim women, particularly African American Muslim women, have even looked to Hagar's story as inspiration for single mothers, women unsupported and outcast by the larger Muslim community.

And yet, the Jewish-Muslim reclaiming of Hagar and Sarah as our fore-mothers has sidestepped the enduring tensions between these figures specifically and our religions more broadly. We have failed to address the undeniably divisive elements of this story—the blame, victimhood, privilege, and power dynamics that are at the center of Sarah and Hagar's relationship—and the ways in which they, and we, continue to hurt one another.

Looking forward to hearing from you,
Aysha

Dear Aysha,

Thank you for your rich letter. You have given us a great deal to reflect on and discuss. I have often wondered what it is that, as you put it, "makes otherizing so powerful and enduring." When I first realized the pervasiveness of Christian feminist anti-Judaism, I was shocked and saddened to see feminists reproducing the exclusions that we were supposedly seeking to overcome. To me, the use of Judaism as a negative foil to demonstrate the liberatory nature of Christianity is a prime illustration of what Mary Daly calls the original sin of patriarchy, "the failure to lay claim to that part of the psyche that is then projected onto 'the Other.'"[1] But I was humbled some months after writing an article on this subject to read a piece by Alice Walker in which she described very similar dynamics in the relationship between white and black feminists and to realize that everything she said applied to me.

It doesn't in any way excuse or resolve the issue of othering to say that it is played out again and again in almost every community. How can black churches exclude women from ordination when the very same passages that they use to support such exclusion were used to defend slavery? How can Americans whose grandparents came to the United States as immigrants rant about the dangers of immigration? How can the men of some American Muslim communities consign women to the same marginal position that they find themselves thrust into in the larger society? How can Jews not treat Palestinians as we wished to be treated throughout our history and instead use our experiences of oppression as a cudgel to beat others? I agree with you 100 percent that dominant communities have the "privilege" of never having to learn about the other. But those of us in marginalized communities also have to deal with the fact that marginalization is no guarantee that we won't in turn create others ourselves.

The story of Sarah and Hagar is an incredible paradigm of this problem, isn't it? Again, I agree with you completely that claiming a common heritage—either as "daughters of Abraham" or "daughters of Sarah and Hagar"—glosses over the profound tensions in the biblical narrative. Jews read the story of the casting out of Hagar twice in the course of a year, once as part of the annual cycle of Torah readings and once on the first day of the Jewish new year, Rosh Hashanah. Every year on Rosh Hashanah, my community struggles with the fact that Sarah recapitulates her own oppression on Hagar. Why do we read this story on one of the holiest days of the year? What are we supposed to learn from it—how *not* to be in the world? It would make a fabulous session at the American Academy of Religion for Jewish feminists, Christian womanists,[2] and Muslim feminists to explore this text together, asking how we understand the story and where we locate ourselves within it.

I continue to work with Christian feminists despite the dynamics we have named because I *don't* feel that multidimensional insights are impossible. Even though Christian feminists will likely not be able to give me feedback on the Jewish substance of the issues I grapple with, I learn from them *methodologically* about how to transform our traditions. If you are on a panel with Christian and Jewish feminists who know nothing about Muslim interpretations of the creation story, you are certainly placed in a teaching position that you may not want in relation to your audience, *and*, at the same time, you may gain a great deal by hearing about the strategies that other feminists use in interpreting problematic texts. So, I agree with you that there is not the full mutuality that one might want, where scholars can engage the substance and methods of each others' proposals. But if it's full mutuality we're waiting for, we're going to be very lonely in the meantime!

I think that the session at the American Academy of Religion held a few years ago on verse 4:34 of the Qur'an was a good example of the kind of exchange that is possible in the absence of knowledge and full mutuality. The Muslim feminists on the panel talked to a packed room about the different ways in which they engage with this problematic verse, one that on its face seems to condone wife-beating. I was certainly not familiar with the strategies they discussed, and I assume that the majority of people in the room shared my ignorance. Once the panelists laid out their approaches, however, there was a rich interreligious conversation in which those present shared how they deal with difficult texts in their own traditions. I would hope that the panelists learned from the responses, even as the audience gained a great deal from the panel.

Now, admittedly and importantly, this panel was very different from one on which there are two white Christians, one Christian womanist, one Jew, and one Muslim. In this particular panel, Muslim women were framing the questions and defining the discourse, demonstrating the diversity of perspectives among themselves. I think it is critical—both for Muslim and Jewish feminists and the wider academy—that there be contexts in which the "other" gets to be at the center. In this sense, I think Muslims are in a bit of an enviable position in that, since 9/11, a lot more people are aware of their ignorance of Islam and are interested in learning about the religion. The couple of times that there have been panels in the Women and Religion Section on Jewish women, the attendance has been terrible, and there has been virtually no one in the room but Jewish women. It's actually been quite shocking.

Another reason I was excited about the session on Sura 4:34 was that the "Abrahamic religions" feminist dialogues I have participated in prior to this point were made quite difficult by what I experienced as Muslim apologetics. Before this session I had been at a number of conferences or on panels where Muslim feminists insisted that the Qur'an is perfect and completely supports the liberation of women. The implication—sometimes stated directly, sometimes not—is that we poor Jews and Christians are saddled with sexist Scriptures while Muslims are not. To my mind, on a straightforward read (in English, of course, which I realize is a problem) the Qur'an is rather similar to the New Testament in being a mixed bag for women. There are passages that seem to support women's equality and others that seem to call quite explicitly for women's subordination. As for the *Tanakh* (the term Jews commonly use for the Hebrew Bible) I see this text as the most unrelievedly patriarchal of the three. Of course, there are Christians and Jews who would argue that some parts of the Bible are perfect. Leonard Swidler's early piece, "Jesus was a Feminist," and various attempts in the early 1970s to show that Paul was a consistent supporter of women's liberation also appeal to the earliest strands of Christian tradition against later practice. But most Jewish and Christian feminists in the academy don't hold this view, so it is extremely difficult to have a real conversation when feminists come to our texts with such radically different presuppositions.

Let me name the underlying issue here. For me, as a religiously liberal Jew, the Hebrew Bible is a human text, created largely or entirely by men who placed male experience at the center of their narratives and religious interpretations. I believe that these men had genuine experiences of the presence of God. But they recorded and interpreted them in patriarchal social contexts that shaped both *what* they chose to remember and *how* they remembered it. It is left for us today—and in every present moment—to discern the divine sparks in the text in relation to our own experiences while simultaneously repudiating those aspects of it that are oppressive. I realize that many Muslims understand the Qur'an as the direct word of God in a more literal sense than even conservative Christians and Jews understand the divine origins of the Bible. It seems that acceptance of this premise is the sine qua non of Muslim legitimacy. But it is precisely for this reason I was encouraged that in the AAR session Muslim feminists, without questioning the Qur'an as God's word, were still able to find ways to approach this sacred text using critical lenses. I'd love to hear your views about the parameters of Muslim feminist interpretation and also what you see as the possibilities for conversation across different understandings of the nature of our Scriptures.

Across the fractures in the relationship of Sarah and Hagar,
Judith

Dear Judith,

I agree with you that we cannot afford to wait for "full mutuality" in speaking across religious (and racial) boundaries, however painful it is in the meantime. Thank you for reminding me of this. We must begin with whatever seeds of multidirectional insight are ready to be sown; indeed, that is what brought me to you in the first place. I suppose what I want to stress is that "otherizing" marginalized people does not amount simply to their exclusion. It is not remedied by simply including them in conversations, since "inclusion" itself often masks and even reinforces the dynamics at work within relations of power and marginality. As we are both painfully aware, we remain impoverished by relationships in which not all of us are fully open and ready to be transformed by knowing the other.

As for the renewed interest in Islam in the aftermath of 9/11, in a sense it absolutely has been productive for people to be "shocked" into a greater consciousness of Islam, to become aware of their ignorance over the last decade. At the same time though, I must also say that the spotlight on Muslims and Islam is glaring, sometimes blindingly so. I often find myself tired and resentful of the weight of the responsibility I feel for educating the ignorant, for feeling obliged to expend my time and energy doing work that somehow still keeps dominant groups at the center and keeps me preoccupied with them. In addition, I continue to fear the co-opting of Muslim feminist work by neoconservative and state actors, especially representatives of the U.S. government, in their efforts to "liberalize" Islam and forcibly promote the development of "moderate" forms of Islam throughout the world, at the expense of the self-determination of Muslims themselves, and at times even at the cost of Muslim lives. Muslim women scholars are especially vulnerable since they become treated as cultural repositories of Islam and barometers of Muslims' acclimation to broader American society and the adoption of its liberal values. Once identified as a "good" or "moderate" Muslim, a scholar then becomes especially vulnerable to being employed in the service of an agenda to create docile Muslim subjects who are less likely to engage in radical forms of protest against the given interested parties. There are many things that make me wary of this kind of attention and scrutiny. Yet your sensitivity to this predicament makes a world of difference for me and will do so for other Muslim feminists as well.

On a different note, I completely agree that Muslim women's often apologetic attitudes toward the Qur'an are extremely problematic, not only because they do not deal with very real problems within the text for Muslim women, but also because such posturing diverts the blame for sexist readings of the Islamic tradition onto Judaism and Christianity, and, as you say, implies that sexist problems are unique to the *Tanakh* and the New Testament. What complicates this further is that modernist and feminist exegetes of the Qur'an have tended to reject the use of *israiliyyat* texts (accounts attributed to Jewish and/or Christian sources) when interpreting the Qur'an as part of their contravention of traditional approaches to Qur'anic exegesis. Muslim feminist scholars have ended up trying to "purify" the Qur'an from biblical interpretations of parallel stories and statements that are problematic for women. For example, some Muslim women tend to reject interpretations of the Qur'an that draw upon biblical interpretations of the Creation story in order to distance the Qur'an from sexist meanings they claim originate from the Bible. Such maneuvers threaten the ability of Muslim women to engage in sustained intercommunal cooperation with

Jewish (and Christian) women. In merely rejecting the *israiliyyat* as a traditional source of Qur'anic interpretation, Muslim feminist scholars may find
a short-term solution to feminist problems in reading their own texts. But
they accomplish this only while simultaneously failing to fully dismantle
the appearance and force of such readings or engaging in a deeper form
of self-inquiry within the Islamic tradition, which might prove liberating
for women of all three religions. In short, such work is at best a short-term
solution, and at worst a cop-out and an act of bad faith. We need to aim for
more sophisticated solutions.

Perhaps, though, the interpretive strategy mentioned earlier has been a
product of the difficulty that Muslim women find themselves in by being
"bound" to the Qur'anic text. You are right that many Muslims consider
the Qur'an to be the intact word of God unaltered by human hands, in
contrast to the view of religiously liberal Jewish feminists like yourself,
who see the Torah as conveyed by human beings who had experiences of
the divine. While you might be able to reject parts of the biblical text that
are oppressive to women and even add to it by means of *midrash*, Muslim
feminist theologians are, for the most part, bound to the text exactly as it
is and must grapple with the interpretation of the text as is. They are able
to argue that traditional interpretations of the Qur'an were shaped by the
interests, particularities, and limitations of their male interpreters, while
remaining within the bounds of mainstream Islam.

Indeed, as I have explored in my own work, Muslim women are employ-
ing a number of critical interpretive strategies in their rereadings of the
Qur'an: they are reading the Qur'an in line with its historical context;
they are reading the whole Qur'an for its holistic, unified meanings (i.e.,
in line with the Qur'an's larger directives toward justice and mercy, rather
than reading its verses atomistically and apart from the larger ethos of the
Qur'an); and they are reading the Qur'an with special attention to *tawhid*,
or the oneness and unique sovereignty of God (in order to combat men's
inclination to make themselves God-like over women in their interpretations of the Qur'an). However, Muslim feminists' interpretations are
never viewed as "expansions" of the Qur'an; they cannot reject any portion of the Qur'an because of their commitment to the divine origins of
the *entire* text. This way, the divinity of the Qur'an itself is never at stake;
only the authority to contribute new interpretations, and the legitimacy
of them, comes under such scrutiny.

Because of their unquestioning acceptance of the entire Qur'an as
divine scripture, Muslim feminist theologians have attributed problematic meanings of the text to the interpretive errors or linguistic difficulties of human beings, never faulting the divine message itself. As a result,
Muslim feminist theologians have remained largely unable to account for
the existence of certain Qur'anic statements that appear to be irreparably
neglectful of, or even harmful to, women—including, for example, verse
4:34 (the so-called wife-beating verse).

A few new avenues have emerged recently, though. For example, Amina
Wadud, in struggling with Qur'an 4:34, has finally come to the decision

to "say 'no'" to the verse in its literal form. Wadud argues that it is the Qur'an itself that allows for human beings to say "no" to its literal pronouncements in limited cases.[3] She claims that Muslims "can promote the idea of saying 'no' to the text" while "still pointing to the text to support this...It is therefore neither un-Islamic nor heretical" to do so.[4] In this way, she is able to approach the verse unapologetically while maintaining the full divinity of the text at the same time.

In addition, Kecia Ali has advocated for a thorough revisiting of legal interpretations as a place of intervention during difficult moments in feminist interpretation of the Qur'an. For her, discussions about reform "must begin—but cannot end—with the Qur'an."[5] Ali holds that Islamic jurisprudence, which Muslim feminists have often been too quick to cast aside as irrevocably patriarchal or sexist, is a rich source of case studies for how scholars have always interpreted Qur'anic principles in flexible relation to the evolving judgments and customs of their times and places. Thus, the Islamic legal tradition may offer useful models for a more flexible, "adaptive process for Muslims today, including bypassing...even seemingly clear Qur'anic statements" in certain cases.[6]

An especially promising area of inquiry that I am particularly interested in pursuing draws upon theological discussions of the moral agency of each human being as the *khalifah* ("deputy" or "trustee") of God on earth. Regardless of one's sex, every human being, as the *khalifah* of God, is entrusted with the responsibility of representing God's will on earth—of enacting justice, upholding morality, and fighting oppression. Endowed with free will, each human being must carry out her duties as God's *khalifah* as an exercise of deep engagement with God's guidance as well as her own conscience and consciousness of justice. For this purpose, the Qur'an is an essential form of guidance upon which human beings must reflect in discerning how to fulfill their obligations to God on earth. And since the Qur'an's guidance cannot be passively translated into action, God's *khalifah* can carry out her responsibility only through an active engagement with the text in dynamic relationship to her social and historical contexts and evolving understandings of justice. It is this notion of women's (and men's) active moral agency that must be mined for its valuable insights into our faithful and dynamic interactions with the Qur'an as feminists continuing to grapple with the text.

On this note of hope for possible future directions of Muslim feminist theology, I want to thank you for embarking upon this conversation with me. It is a conversation that I hope we can regularly continue. Thank you for your insight and partnership; it is truly an honor to have your ear.

In solidarity and with hope,
Aysha

Dear Aysha,

I very much appreciate your comment that marginalized people are often "included" in conversations in ways that mask and reinforce strategies of domination and marginalization. I think the issue that we all struggle with is how to resist being tokenized: how do we use the invitations we receive to serve on panels or to attend conferences to begin to reshape the substance and assumptions of the debates? I imagine it can be very disheartening for you to hear that Jewish women still wrestle with this question forty years down the road and often feel as if we have made very little progress. Waiting for full mutuality is a bit like waiting for the Messiah!

You wrote in your first letter about the dangers of speaking out and being silent, feelings I share, but you add another dimension in this round that I have never experienced—namely the potential cooptation of feminist work by the state. This is a whole additional layer on top of the dilemma of being a feminist in our religious communities and a Jew or Muslim in the feminist world. I hear you saying that when you articulate a feminist critical perspective, in the eyes of the *state* you become a "good Muslim" who can be used against your own community—as if the state is actually interested in feminist critiques of religion! It reminds me of the incredible hypocrisy of the administration of President George W. Bush (a) in claiming that our government was liberating women in Afghanistan when the well-being of women had never been a consideration in our foreign policy, and (b) in seeking the support of right-wing Christian groups with attitudes toward women similar to the Taliban's. There is really no way out of this dilemma, is there? All you can do is speak the truth as you see it and name attempts at cooptation when they occur.

In terms of the apologetic attitudes of Muslim women, I'm very interested in what you say about the rejection of *israiliyyat* texts. I've encountered that strategy in the work of Muslim feminists, but I've never had a name for it before. Thank you. It seems rather similar to the Christian feminist tendency to blame the patriarchal elements of Christianity on Judaism, except in this case Muslim feminists deny the sexism of the Qur'an altogether.[7] I have to admit that part of me is amused when Christians are confronted with Muslim supercessionism, thereby getting a taste of what they have done to Jews for two thousand years. This said, I, of course, agree with you that this strategy undermines both interreligious conversation and the ability to confront the oppressive aspects of one's own tradition.

Some of the techniques of interpretation you describe Muslim feminists as using have been employed effectively by Jews and Christians in both feminist and queer struggles. The notion of reading particular verses in light of broader ethical imperatives can be especially powerful. My favorite example of this (which I have cited elsewhere) is a sermon given by Rabbi Lisa Edwards on the Torah portion that contains the verse against "lying with a man as with a woman." Edwards points out that the very same Torah portion contains basic ethical principles that are in direct conflict with the homophobia that Leviticus 18:22 is taken to authorize.

We are your gay and lesbian children: "You must not seek vengeance, nor bear a grudge against the children of your people" (Lev. 19:18); we are your lesbian mothers and gay fathers: "Revere your mother and your father, each of you" (19:3); we are the stranger: "You must not oppress the stranger. You shall love the stranger as yourself for you were strangers in the land of Egypt" (19:34).[8]

This technique can be taken in two different directions. It can be argued that the ethical principles expressed in these biblical verses represent the true meaning of the text and thus override particular injunctions. Or, and this is the stance I prefer as someone who sees the text as a human document, one can argue that the text contains obvious contradictions and, thus, it's up to us to decide with which voices we want to ally ourselves.

I must correct your impression of *midrash*, however, as a technique that's only available to people who deny the divinity and perfection of the text. On the contrary, the presupposition of traditional rabbinic *midrash* is precisely that the text is divinely given. It is *because* the Torah was given by God to Moses on Mount Sinai that every detail of it is of supreme importance and that endless meanings can be found in it. There's a rabbinic saying about the Torah, "Turn it and turn it again for everything is in it" (M. Avot 5:25). If a letter is repeated where ordinarily it would not be, or if there's a dot over a letter, or if the Torah says one thing in one place and something else in another, according to the rabbis all of these things have religious significance. To generate *midrashim* (pl.) that seem to contradict each other is simply to bear witness to the eternal fruitfulness of the text. We cannot know what the consciousness of the rabbis was in creating *midrash*, but they probably did not see themselves as adding to the text but as discovering and uncovering its original meanings.

In this sense, it seems to me that every textual tradition has *midrash*. I sometimes joke with Catholics who envy Jewish *midrash* that they have lots of *midrash* in their tradition; they just call it doctrine! The perpetual virginity of Mary, for example, is a *midrash*, as is the immaculate conception. I wish I knew the Islamic interpretive tradition well enough to point to some good examples. One that occurs to me is that Muslims consider the son whom Abraham was willing to sacrifice to be Ishmael and not Isaac, even though the son is not named in the Qur'an. That's *midrash*! When you describe Kecia Ali as saying that Muslim scholars have flexibly interpreted Qur'anic principles, even bypassing Qur'anic statements in some cases, she's describing what Jews call *midrash*. There are two types of *midrash*: *halakhic* (legal) and *aggadic* (narrative). The latter is what many people think of when they hear the term *midrash*, but it's *halakhic midrash* that is more binding.

I do have to acknowledge, though, that most Jewish feminists who create new *midrash* do not start from the assumption that the text is from Moses on Sinai. Rather, we share the rabbinic assumption that the Torah is continually generative, that "everything is in it"—including new feminist insights—while bringing a self-consciousness and playfulness to the text that presumably the rabbis did not share (although one has to wonder in the case of some of their more outrageous interpretations). And I can certainly see that this attitude would not be possible for Muslim feminists.

This raises another question for me. One of the things about the Torah that I most value is the fact that the heroes and heroines of the Bible are deeply imperfect and that even God is imperfect and changing. Wrestling with those imperfections generates insights into my own identity and social situation. The Torah often holds up a mirror to destructive dynamics in our own contemporary society—as in the case of Sarah's reenacting her own oppression on the person of Hagar (as I mentioned in my previous letter to you) or of Abraham trying to pass off Sarah as his sister because he was afraid.[9] When I discuss a weekly Torah portion with my Jewish prayer community it is often amazing to me how everything *is* in it, the world in all its complexity. I know that Muslims see the imperfections of biblical figures as distortions that have been corrected by the final revelation to the Prophet Muhammad. I would love to know how someone who lives with a text that's considered perfect, and in which everyone is perfect, understands the ambiguity of the characters in the Hebrew Bible. I also think it would be interesting to discuss the *liturgical* uses of our Scriptures and the ways in which these uses impact women's lives. I'm sorry that these issues, along with others we raised in our letters that we didn't have time to explore fully, will have to await another occasion. I hope it comes soon!

Yours with every hope of continuing the conversation,
Judith

Notes

1. Mary Daly, *Beyond God the Father: Toward a Philosophy of Women's Liberation* (Boston: Beacon Press, 1973), 10. See also Judith Plaskow, "Christian Feminism and Anti-Judaism," *Cross Currents* Vol. 33 (Fall 1978), 306–309; reprinted in *The Coming of Lilith: Essays on Feminism, Judaism, and Sexual Ethics, 1972–2003* (Boston: Beacon Press, 2005), 89–93.
2. "Womanist," a term that comes from the writings of Alice Walker, is the name that many black feminists have taken for themselves.
3. Amina Wadud, *Inside the Gender Jihad: Women's Reform in Islam* (Oxford: Oneworld, 2006), 200.
4. Ibid., 192.
5. Kecia Ali, "Timeless Texts and Modern Morals: Challenges in Islamic Sexual Ethics," *New Directions in Islamic Thought: Exploring Reform and Muslim Tradition*, eds. Kari Vogt, Lena Larsen, and Christian Moe (New York: I.B. Tauris, 2009), 89.
6. Kecia Ali, *Sexual Ethics and Islam: Feminist Reflections on Qur'an, Hadith, and Jurisprudence* (Oxford: Oneworld, 2006), xx–xxi.
7. Plaskow, "Christian Feminism and Anti-Judaism."
8. See Judith Plaskow, "Authority, Resistance, and Transformation: Jewish Feminist Reflections on Good Sex," in *The Coming of Lilith*, 204.
9. Judith Plaskow, "The Wife/Sister Stories: Dilemmas of a Jewish Feminist," in *Speaking of Faith: Global Perspectives on Women, Religion, and Social Change*, eds. Diana Eck and Devaki Jain (Delhi: Kali Press and Philadelphia: New Society Press, 1986), 122–129.

CHAPTER FOURTEEN

Status Quo versus Solution: A New Middle East Playbook

Eboo Patel

The only thing that Israelis and Palestinians seem to agree on is that they are both frustrated with the status quo. American Jews and American Muslims have the chance to chart a different course—if they seize the opportunity. Take the rhetoric surrounding Israel's December 2008 attack on the Gaza Strip as an example. The Council on American Islamic Relations called the Israeli attack on Gaza a "disproportionate and counterproductive...massacre." Its homepage featured a photo of a bombed out building in Gaza with a panicked official ushering civilians to safety. The homepage of the American Jewish Committee (AJC) had a picture of Palestinian militants in ski masks holding guns next to a video of AJC executive director David Harris speaking of the "intolerable situation" Israel faced and how it had "no choice" but to bomb Gaza. The Muslim Public Affairs Council called the Israeli air strikes "brutal" and helped raise money for Palestinian victims. The Union for Reform Judaism called the bombing "necessary" and raised money for Israeli victims.

All pretty predictable, all pretty familiar.

Responding to a crisis in the Middle East is old hat to most American Muslim and American Jewish organizations. All they have to do is call up their standard press releases and fundraising letters, change a few names and dates, and send them off to the media. The playbook was written several decades ago—I think of it as the Status Quo Rules for Middle East Engagement. If you like the status quo, these rules are for you.

Rule No. 1: Use the current crisis to advance your narrative. If you're Jewish, this story involves words such as "security," "terrorism," and "right to exist." If you're Muslim, it includes terms such as "humanitarian crisis," "occupation," and "disproportionate violence."

Rule No. 2: Talk about how bad it is where *your* people live. If you're Jewish, this means highlighting the number of Hamas rockets fired into

Israel and the number of lives lost and disrupted in Jewish Israeli cities such as Sderot. If you're Muslim, it involves talking about the brutal
prison that is Gaza and the disaster that is the West Bank.

Rule No. 3: Blame it on the *other* side. If you're Jewish, this means pointing out the violent and belligerent defiance of Hamas. If you're Muslim,
it means talking about the suffocation of the blockade in Gaza and the
continued Israeli occupation of the West Bank.

Following these rules makes perfect sense for the parties involved
because just about every one of these talking points is true. Hamas *is* violent and belligerent. The blockade and occupation *is* suffocating. For all
too many of its inhabitants, Gaza *is* a prison. Life in Sderot *is* rife with fear.
Suicide bombings in Israel are a reality. Jewish Israelis are perpetually in a
place of worry. Here's the only problem: the Status Quo Rules have not,
and never will, lead anywhere but to the status quo.

On the one hand, who can blame these organizations for hitting repeat?
After all, they have clear and strong loyalties, and large and vocal constituencies. Circling the wagons and ringing the alarm bells has satisfied their
respective communities for as long as anyone can remember. The proof
shows up in their bank accounts during fundraising season. Yet as I was
reading through websites and press releases in 2008 and 2009, I couldn't
help but notice something eerie that Muslim and Jewish organizations
had in common: the mutual sense that the situation was even worse than
before. The Jewish organizations talked about how Hamas rockets could
potentially reach Tel Aviv. The Muslim organizations talked about how
the Israeli Defense Forces had never caused this many Palestinian casu-
alties in such a short amount of time. Both communities said that they
needed to be supported *now more than ever*. Both communities congratu-
lated themselves for contributing to their respective causes.

All of this adds a morbid new twist to the age-old proverb: If you do
what you've always done, you'll get what you've always gotten. The status
quo in the Middle East is unbearable. It should make us all reflect on our
approaches to the conflict between Israelis and Palestinians. But if the
situation is actually deteriorating for everyone (which seems to be the one
thing that Muslims and Jews can currently actually agree on), shouldn't
we tear up the old playbook and try something else? One of my favorite
quotes is Susan Sontag's observation that "Whatever is happening, something else is always going on." And amid a lot of the same old, same old,
there is something distinct taking place that is worth paying attention to.

American Muslim and American Jewish organizations once considered
it a matter of pride to engage in a communications blockade of organizations on "the other side." The basic line I heard from both communities
was, "We can't talk to people we have such fundamental disagreements
with." Subsequently, many interfaith groups broke apart. Friendships
between Muslims and Jews became strained. We reverted back to shouting our own talking points louder and louder. But, slowly, it seemed that
some people realized that increasing the volume on one's own talking

points and trying to drown out the other side is not a strategy for getting to a solution. A senior American Jewish official told me that "Jews and Muslims in America should be modeling positive relationships here, and hoping that pattern offers a way forward over there."

After the 2008 war in Gaza, I exchanged e-mails with senior officials of the Islamic Society of North America (ISNA) and they expressed a similar sentiment. In fact, point five of ISNA's press release on the Gaza situation said the following: "Engage in informed dialogue with other Americans, especially Jewish Americans, so that religious differences do not become a source of civil discord and division..." My guess is that the idea of continuing positive engagement with people holding different opinions than your own is probably gaining ground within Muslim and Jewish organizations, although it is still very much a minority attitude. And so we are looking at a very small step toward a potentially big win. The win is not just a rewriting of the respective playbooks that Muslim and Jewish organizations use when the Middle East conflict heats up. It is the recognition that, if we want to actually solve the conflict, Muslim and Jewish groups should be writing a new playbook together because they are on the same side.

If we are going to move from status quo to solution, we are going to need a whole lot of courage and a different set of rules. Though people are going to have to come up with the courage on their own, let me offer a set of "Solution Rules" for Muslim and Jewish organizations regarding the Middle East.

Rule No. 1: Make your first phone calls to the people who disagree with you on the current situation, but who agree with you on the basic outlines of a long-term solution: two states, with security and dignity for all. That is a Coalition for a Solution, creative and courageous enough to get people's attention. This means, difficult as it may be, resisting the instinct to use the current crisis to find more people who will wave signs for your side, show up at your rallies, or put their names on your petitions. Such logic serves mostly to further prolong the conflict. Instead, use the spotlight on the Middle East to reach out to those on the "other side" who have the courage to play for a long-term solution and say, "Look, the status quo is untenable for everybody. It's time for a different set of rules."

Rule No. 2: Acknowledge the real issues on the "other side." Minnesota U.S. Representative Keith Ellison, the first Muslim in Congress, modeled this in his press release around Gaza when he said that he has been to Sderot and has "seen firsthand both the physical and emotional destruction caused by the [Hamas] rocket attacks." This acknowledgment does not take away from something else that Ellison says, which is that conditions in Gaza are "unliveable." It merely means that Ellison has the eyes and the heart to imagine life on both sides of the fence. In Status Quo Rules, recognizing the challenge in the other community makes you a traitor. In the Solution Rulebook, it makes you a true patriot because it is the fastest way to build trust with the people with whom you have to build peace.

Rule No. 3: Recognize that certain players who claim to be on "your side" are part of the problem. The truth is, you do not want them on your side. They are dangerous and destabilizing to your community. When peace is finally made with the "other side," your first battle is going to be against such internal "allies." Hamas militants are a destructive force to Israelis and a destructive force to Palestinians. Muslims should feel no obligation to defend them. The militant settlers are murderers of Muslim Palestinians and also murderers of Jewish Israelis. No Jews should feel like they have to defend them either.

Rule No. 4: The politics of the Middle East is about where your family is. If your family is in Sderot, it is unbearable. If your family is in Gaza, it is also unbearable. Talking about whether scattered Hamas rockets are the equivalent of precision Israeli air raids, or whether Islamist rhetoric is as bad as Israeli occupation, is logical but irrelevant. Logical because you can write press releases for "your side" using such talking points, irrelevant because it doesn't build a bridge to the "other side," which is the only way to a solution.

The depressing fact of the Middle East conflict is that many Muslims and Jews agree that the Solution Rulebook makes sense to them, but when the crisis escalates and hits the front page the old logic takes over and Muslim and Jewish organizations revert to the Status Quo Rules. The sad truth is that every day is a humanitarian crisis in Gaza and a humiliating subjugation in the West Bank, and every day is a security crisis in Sderot and tightening fear in Israel. All the well-meaning organizations following the Status Quo Rules thinking they are serving their community are really only prolonging the crisis.

But following the Solution rulebook? That is a play that could change the game.

Note

This essay is adapted from columns first posted by the author through the *Washington Post*'s "On Faith" column.

CHAPTER FIFTEEN

Sacred Text Study as Dialogue between Muslims and Jews

Rabbi Reuven Firestone and Hebah H. Farrag

Introduction

In the winter of 2009, two organizations in Los Angeles partnered to establish a novel program using Islamic and Judaic religious texts to foster intergroup dialogue and intentional conversations with the aim of enhancing and bridging relationships between the two communities. The "Muslim-Jewish Text Study Program" was initiated by the Center for Jewish Muslim Engagement,[1] a partnership project of Hebrew Union College,[2] the Omar Ibn Al Khattab Foundation,[3] and the University of Southern California's Center for Religion and Civic Culture.[4] Collaboration on the project was formed from the beginning with NewGround: A Muslim-Jewish Partnership for Change.[5] This essay, which describes our experience with this pilot program, integrates a series of oral and written evaluative instruments with the aim to provide guidance for those who are interested in considering intergroup dialogue through text study. Elsewhere in this essay we provide links to some of the documents involved with this program, including text samples and evaluative instruments.

Sacred Text and Interreligious Dialogue

While textual dialogue has ensued between Muslims and Jews for centuries, it has tended to be polemical in nature.[6] In contrast, contemporary interreligious dialogue is an intentionally constructed framework for the mutual exchange of ideas.[7] Norms for such activities first developed within Christian ecumenical encounters and expanded to Christian-Jewish dialogue in the mid-twentieth century. Modern Muslim-Jewish dialogue is a much more recent phenomenon.

For many, sacred texts are a source of spiritual inspiration and ethical behavior, even representing an integral aspect of personal identity.[8] As sources of spiritual and moral guidance, sacred texts are held up by some nations as the supreme "law of the land" and, in some cases, are used to justify horrendous acts of violence, even genocide. Whatever the orientation, and regardless of the religious tradition or level of ritual observance, many communities exhibit a special sensitivity to messages found in sacred texts. For some even the *notion* of a sacred text enables an opportunity for dialogue. In our experiences, we have observed how text study has the potential to be a potent tool for enhancing interreligious respect and appreciation.[9]

CMJE "Muslim-Jewish Text Study Program"

Islamic and Jewish texts are often manipulated and cited in the media in order to defame Muslims and Jews. Ironically, or perhaps precisely because of these ubiquitous efforts, we have found that joint study of sacred texts between Jews and Muslims can have a profound positive impact on intergroup relationship building. Such a process encourages Muslims and Jews to dialogue deeply and directly through questions and responses that inevitably arise when studying texts within a safe environment where honest and respectful communication is encouraged.

The "Text Study Program" (TSP) was launched in the winter of 2008, immediately after the beginning of the Gaza incursion. As often happens when violence erupts in connection with the Israeli-Palestinian conflict, tensions quickly arose between the Muslim and Jewish communities in the Los Angeles area. Many long-standing partnerships and coalitions between the two communities quickly began to dissolve. As plans to launch TSP predated the new turn of events in the Middle East, planners decided to continue with the program despite increased tensions. The surprisingly positive response to the call for applications served not only to strengthen the organizers' internal resolve to continue with the program, but also illustrated compelling evidence that members of both communities longed for constructive engagement outside of the lens of international politics alone.

TSP was not designed to be a rigorous or academic study of religion but rather to elicit curiosity and inquiry among participants. Two central principles guided us throughout. The first was a strict adherence to absolute parity between Jews and Muslims at all levels, from planning to implementation to evaluation. As such, Muslims and Jews were equally represented among the program's designers, educators, facilitators, and student-participants. Likewise, the venue rotated between area synagogues and mosques. All TSP decisions were made through consensus; no single staff member or student was allowed to dominate. The second principle was that participants were not supplied with any materials that could be construed as "official" or authoritative textual interpretations. In addition, students were not assigned background readings prior to sessions nor were any texts preassigned. This forced participants to read the texts without preparation and to rely on one another to make sense of the material, which, in turn, encouraged students to ask and address questions and to ponder texts carefully and personally.

All of the texts were provided in the original language alongside an English translation without footnotes or comments. The TSP organizers discussed with participants the problems inherent with translations, explaining that pure translation is impossible without some level of interpretation by the translator. Participants were also informed that while the organizers felt that the given translations were reasonable, they were not authoritative, so could be reconsidered or revised. The net result was the creation of an environment that was charged for both inquiry and conversation.

TSP Goals

The primary goal of TSP was to demonstrate how religious texts could become the basis for members of two religious traditions to learn about each other's beliefs while simultaneously developing friendships. As a secondary goal, we hoped this experience would result in participants choosing to engage in activism on behalf of social causes common to both communities. A tertiary goal was to develop curricula and teaching materials that could be used to repeat and perpetuate our success in a variety of different venues (e.g., synagogues and mosques, university campuses, professional organizations, religious schools, etc.).

Deciding upon these goals took some time. In fact, the staff engaged in its own dialogic program in the very process of convening a series of planning sessions for TSP, which were held on a rotating basis at planners' homes and workplaces. The conveners engaged in many discussions over what deliverables might emerge from the pilot program. These included text study curricula, modern informal text commentaries, study guides for self-directed dialogue, reading and discussion methodologies, guides for interreligious engagement through social activism, and more. It became apparent that it was unrealistic to both develop a pilot program and produce an array of deliverables at the same time. It was decided, therefore, to develop the best program possible along with a substantial evaluation component to measure effectiveness from the perspectives of both the organizers and the participants. Each session was carefully planned and evaluated by the entire staff, and through this process the program was adjusted accordingly. (During the pilot period we tested different approaches each session.)

After extensive preparatory discussions the staff decided that there would be no prerequisite for participants to have had prior experience in interfaith work in order to join TSP; they only had to have an earnest interest in interreligious text study and a commitment to loyal attendance and full participation. We subsequently agreed that the pilot program would work on enhancing intergroup relations for lay people rather than training committed activists. We realized that we needed a program that would allow people with various levels of religious belief and observance to interact with one another. Finally, we decided that the core requirements would be an interest in studying sacred texts, a primary sense of religious (as opposed to "ethnic") identity, and an interest in an interfaith program. This idea was clearly attractive, as we were forced to turn away many applicants.

Through these preliminary discussions we decided upon another pedagogical principle: there would be no privileging of any one textual reading or interpretation over another. Session topics would not be announced prior to meetings in order to prevent participants from trying to develop an advantage of expertise ahead of time. This ethic was solidified in our having pairs of Jews and Muslims read texts (i.e., one Jew and one Muslim), a process that allowed participants to experience a variety of ways to understand texts, while simultaneously relating them to their own lives. We hoped that the process of studying texts would also demystify the religious "other" and create a deeper understanding of how meaning is constructed in both religious traditions.

The leadership team considered many areas of interest and concern within and between the two communities. Once we determined general thematic categories, institutional capacity, the availability of team members, and a commitment to a thorough assessment of the pilot program as a prerequisite for creating a lengthier annual program, we planned four sessions to take place once per month for three hours, each of which would include a modest dinner that met kosher, halal, and vegetarian standards. We also rotated session locations in order to expose the group to a variety of Muslim and Jewish prayer spaces.

The four sessions focused on the following topics: (1) prophetic narrative—Moses meets God; (2) the first couple—the story of creation; (3) the other—inclusivity and exclusivity; and (4) law and authority—scripture and tradition. The texts for the first two topics were taken from the Hebrew Bible and the Qur'an, whereas the texts for the latter two topics were taken both from these two scriptures and from the oral tradition of Talmud and Hadith. We also encouraged participants to prepare for sessions by reading general background materials that was prepared for them but, as mentioned earlier, nothing specific to the texts that they were about to study. In addition, each participant was sent a preprogram assessment tool modeled after a template established by NewGround. This was a simple thirty-four-question survey designed separately for Muslims and Jews. The same questionnaires were administered at the conclusion of the entire program to measure attitudinal and perceptual change.[10] Because the program was constructed as a pilot, various assessment mechanisms were built in for evaluation, both during the course of the program and afterward. In the most general terms, success was defined as increased understanding of those from the "other" community and the building of relationships across communal boundaries through learning.

We determined group size based on the notion that a maximum of twenty participants would allow for open conversation. Program managers selected applicants with an eye toward diversity in ethnic and religious orientation and equal gender distribution (more women applied than men). After a rigorous selection review, twenty-two participants were accepted. The pilot class was equally divided between Muslims and Jews and had an equal number of men and women represented in each faith, with both Muslims and Jews having six women and four men joining the program (two accepted students dropped out before the program began). The youngest participant was twenty-two years old and the oldest sixty-two. And a diverse range of professions and ethnicities were represented, from African American to Latino, Japanese American, South Asian, Arab American, Iranian American, and European American. Because the program focused exclusively on Jews and Muslims who represent religious minorities in the United States, students were able to develop a sense of solidarity with one another as similar "others" within a dominant Christian society.

The initial cohort all had a minimal background in "interfaith experience" defined broadly. TSP was advertised as an opportunity for those with previous experience or interest in Jewish-Muslim engagement to enhance their interfaith skills, though participants were encouraged to apply even if they had no previous experience. Participants attained a level of familiarity with and fluency in standard issues affecting Muslim-Jewish relations and gained a remedial knowledge of how to conduct a text study program themselves, as one of the program's goals was to create "ambassadors" to promote Jewish-Muslim dialogue and engagement in other contexts.

Session #1: "Prophetic Narrative—Moses Meets God"

The first session of the series was held at a synagogue amid feelings of anticipation and enthusiasm. Participants received a notebook, pen, nametag, and binder with the session outline, the text for the session, a glossary of Islamic and Judaic terms, and participant biographies and contact information. The evening began with the cofacilitators leading a relationship building ice-breaker where participants were asked to separate into Muslim-Jewish pairs. Each dyad was tasked to share their names and a personal challenge that they had overcome. Thereafter they were asked to introduce their partners to the entire group. This exercise was a comfortable way to begin to assess the group's communication skills, diversity of experiences, educational backgrounds, and levels of religious and ethnic heterogeneity.

Participants were then introduced to the coeducators, who broke the group into new Jewish-Muslim pairs for a text study focusing on the narrative of Moses and the burning bush/tree/fire found in the Qur'an and Hebrew Bible.[11] The study method of pairs was based on the traditional Jewish model of *chevrutah* (or dyadic) study, wherein two individuals read and passionately discuss a text together while simultaneously sharing personal responses and exchanging ideas. This process not only encourages critical thinking but also builds personal relationships; partners form an interactive, creative, teaching, and learning unit.[12] The coeducators functioned as facilitators and catalysts for discussion, and responded to specific textual questions, making sure to deepen the study process while not giving any "official" interpretations. As with all of the sessions, participants were given one set of Jewish texts and one set of Islamic texts to read. Whatever order was used in one session was reversed in the following one.

All four sessions included a short break to allow those who wished to engage in evening prayer (i.e., Islamic *maghrib* or Jewish *ma'ariv* prayers). After the break, participants gathered together for a large group discussion and reflection led by the coeducators that focused on aspects of the readings that stood out during paired study. The session was concluded with a closing exercise, run by the cofacilitators, where participants closed their eyes and reenvisioned the evening, thereafter sharing one word about their experience with the larger group.

Lessons Learned

After the first session we sent participants an evaluation tool designed to measure and assess the lesson's central goals, the overall experience (including venue and refreshments), and performance of the facilitation and education teams. It was administered electronically and distributed via e-mail.[13] The data from the first session paint the following picture: All respondents found the dyadic study enriching. Criticisms were offered about time allotment for the activities and communication between the leadership team and participants, and guiding questions were requested for future text study. It became apparent that the readings were too long, which hindered deep engagement. Study partners tended to spend most of the allotted time on the first set of texts, which represented only one religion, thereby preventing them from giving enough time to the second. Although responses were not all consistent, those that seemed to reflect a general consensus were implemented in the next session. As a result, for example, "time" was called in the midst of the dyadic text study to signal that it was appropriate to shift from one set of texts to the other.

Additionally, because a number of respondents felt that they had difficulty speaking to the larger group, in subsequent sessions two reflection groups were assembled to process the experience of text study, each facilitated by an educator and facilitator (one Jew and one Muslim), after which time the two groups came back together as one large group. Guiding questions for text-study were also developed by the coeducators and implemented at the second session, and thereafter. The issue of having too much text to study was never fully resolved because of differences over whether it should reflect what could be covered in the study session or whether all (or most) relevant texts should be supplied but that the pairs should not be expected to read them all.

The survey also confirmed our expectation that TSP had a significant impact on the participants. The following are a sampling of responses:

> I found it very intriguing to be exposed to such different versions of the seemingly familiar story of Moses and the Burning Bush . . . it was uplifting to be spiritual with people of a different faith.
>
> I was struck by how quickly I felt comfortable. I think that I have begun to develop a level of trust that will serve me well throughout the program and beyond.
>
> Before the session, I thought I was familiar with the story of Moses, and I thought it was mainly about the people of Israel going from slavery to freedom. At the session, however, it was striking to hear the versions of the story of Moses from the Qur'an, which included many familiar details, but had such a different focus.[14]

Session #2: "The First Couple—The Story of Creation"

This session[15] was held at a Muslim facility that serves as both a mosque and Muslim foundation for civic engagement. After handing all participants a sheet on Islamic prayer, the cofacilitators opened the session with an exercise focused on identity and its impact on interpreting the world around us. While participants engaged in the activity, they generally "played it safe" in their responses, demonstrating that they were not yet comfortable enough with the group. A second relationship-building exercise that focused on the different ways in which we construct and articulate identity[16] followed, after which they formed new pairs for text study. Following the paired text study, everyone was divided into two groups to discuss their experiences, at which time, as anticipated, a broader range of participants contributed to the discussion. The entire group was then assembled, wherein spokespeople from each of the two groups presented their findings. This was followed by a coeducator facilitated discussion. The evening ended with a brief exercise led by the cofacilitators.

Topics raised by participants both in pairs and in the larger groups centered on issues related to gender and notions of good and evil. Differences between the two religious traditions began to emerge, which were quite interesting to participants. Thereafter the discussion moved from the different scriptural depictions of the creation narratives to divergences in religious notions and perceptions; as hoped, participants began to articulate disagreements more freely. The interactive exercises prepared participants for discussion in an honest and respectful manner, and participants exhibited an impressive sensitivity to the personal feelings of their partners.

Lessons Learned

According to the survey administered immediately after the second session, all respondents appreciated the adjustment from one to two response groups (i.e., from one large group to two smaller groups), the opportunity to study with new partners, and receiving the Islamic prayer handout. The session also sparked interest in learning about each community's understanding of prayer, the institutional structure of Islam and Judaism in America, the Hebrew and Arabic alphabets, and timelines of the origins, history, events, and important figures relating to each tradition. Sample responses to the session included,

> The whole experience was very enriching.
> It's great to meet other people who are interested in learning and sharing.
> I love reading the texts with partners and learning from the other on a 1:1 basis.
> I am continuing to feel more and more comfortable engaging in this context.

The group expressed some frustration at not having enough time for the paired text study or post–text study larger group discussions.

When asked in the evaluation what participants were taking away from the session, most respondents focused on the differences in perspective and the beauty of discussing such differences in a diverse group. For example,

> Upon reflection, I can see how there are different perspectives on the story of creation and the lessons to be taken from it...I believe that these differences in perspective are shaped by our theological understanding of our respective traditions [and] these understandings shape the way we see the world and the reality of the human condition.

Discussion of difference also prompted thinking about how differences influence behaviors and relationships, such as the following two statements:

> The session made me think about possible differences in our assumptions about the process of text study itself, and that these differences could be between individuals within each religion, as well as between Muslims & Jews more generally.

The session dealt with some very large questions, and I value the rare opportunity to consider them in a diverse, comparative context with others who want to discuss large questions: What is the purpose of human beings in these stories? Is there a moral to the stories? When we tell the stories to our children, what do we want them to take away?

Session #3: "The Other—Inclusivity and Exclusivity"

The third meeting[17] was held in a different synagogue from the first session; the rabbi offered a tour at the end of the evening. Prior to this session, participants were sent the following question in preparation: "When you hear the word 'other,' what people, images and experiences come to mind?" The program team noted that between the first two sessions people did not remember each other's names, partly because of the month-long gap. Recognizing this problem, the cofacilitators started with an exercise in which participants were asked to share their name and the story behind them in Jewish-Muslim pairs. Then they shared their partner's name and story with the larger group. This proved to be effective for remembering names and was a powerful way to share familial, cultural, religious, and ethnic information about the participants.

The second exercise was a short session around the following question: "When have you felt like an 'other?,' " a topic that helped the group focus on identity and belonging. The participants felt safe enough to share difficult personal stories and experiences with one another, many of which touched on issues of race, gender, and religion. It also proved to be an effective segue into the paired text study period. During previous sessions, the coeducators used the time during the relationship-building exercises to review their tasks for text-study and group discussion. But this time, the staff had decided that the coeducators should participate in these exercises. Their participation seemed to improve the subsequent discussions and educator-group interaction.

As in the previous session, after completing the text study two groups were formed for additional discussion, after which time the entire group came together to share insights and engage in a final exercise. In this discussion it became clear that there was significant growth in group cohesion and sharing from the first session until the third session. Participants were then left with two questions through which to contemplate the topic for the coming session: "What is your relationship to religious law?" and "How does religious law affect you?"[18]

Lessons Learned

In an attempt to try out different things, the staff experimented in this session with space by removing the tables (around which the participants had met in previous meetings) and sitting in chairs arranged in a circle. In the post-session survey all participants responded that as a result of the new room set-up they felt closer to the group; as such it was easier to have an open discussion with one another. All participants felt a stronger group bond, but as in previous sessions, participants complained that they did not have enough time for the individual components of the program. The coeducators noted that the relationship-building exercises, which focused on bridging program content from one session to the next, encouraged personal story-telling. But this would not have succeeded as well before the group had begun to coalesce.

Participants expressed the impression that the Jewish texts tended to be more exclusive and the Islamic texts more inclusive. The coeducators responded by leading a discussion in which the form and tenor of sacred texts was contextualized in history. One respondent summarized the conversation as follows:

> I like that we are looking at texts that could potentially be divisive; instead of focusing on common terms we are asking ourselves what is the meaning behind the texts that seem to show exclusivity and even harm to the other? For example, in reading the text, Islam seems more inclusive than Judaism only because the Qur'an includes the Hebrew Bible, Psalms of David and the Gospels as part of earlier revelation. The Hebrew Bible did not have the same history; therefore it seems that Judaism is not as inclusive as Islam, which is not an accurate comparison based on the historic context of the revelations.

Another participant stated, "[W]ho I am, where I come from, my own personal experiences, my culture, my language, all influence how I perceive life. Listening to other people's understanding deepens our own personal understanding. That is the purpose of study and analysis."

The session proved that divisive topics and areas of disagreement could be discussed openly and constructively, leading to conversation and friendly debate.

> I felt that, in this third session, we leaped forward in getting to know each other as individuals and as a group. Perhaps it was part of the natural progression after meeting and talking in the first two sessions; perhaps it was because of the topic or the nature of the discussion itself. In any case, it was a very good feeling.

Session #4: "Law and Authority—Scripture and Tradition"

The fourth and final meeting[19] took place in a new Islamic venue. In the opening exercises prior topics were reviewed through interactive games taken from the "Theater of the Oppressed" curriculum. Immediately afterward, the participants teamed up in Muslim-Jewish pairs and were asked to select index cards with short phrases drawn from previous sessions. They were then asked to prepare silent gestures that represented the phrase on their card. Each pair acted out their phrase before the larger group, which tried to guess the topic. This was an invigorating exercise that produced a high level of energy throughout the evening. Thereafter there was a *chevrutah* text study, except this time participants met in triads rather than dyads. The remainder of the meeting followed the structure of the second and third sessions.

As this was our final session together, we allocated additional time to our group evaluation exercise, which used both verbal and written feedback (proving to be both evaluative and effective in group-building). Participants spontaneously used the session to plan to continue text study beyond the framework of the formal program. The meeting ended with a sense of warm reflection and humor, providing a positive sense of closure and expectation for future collaborations. Two participants were chosen as alumni coordinators for the initial post-program period and two other alumni coordinators were chosen to follow up thereafter.

Lessons Learned

The participants tended to focus in this meeting more on closing the program than on text study, which elicited frustration and criticism from some for lack of adequate time in the various parts of the meetings. As one participant said, "It felt like we were always rushing at each session. I wish we could have done all day sessions on a Saturday, say from 9 to 4. I also wish the sessions were scheduled closer together, say 2 weeks apart." This frustration led to discussions about how to format the program differently for the future. Suggestions included scheduling the meetings more often, reducing the number of participants, and devoting entire sessions to either text study or relationship-building (or alternating between them).

Most importantly, the final session affirmed how the group had become committed to one another; they almost unanimously voiced a desire to continue learning together.

[The text study has] reaffirmed the importance of intra and interfaith engagement and the role of religion in my life.

I enjoy working with and learning from my Jewish brothers and sisters. It amazes me how similar our faiths are, yet I am also comfortable discussing the differences and controversies.

It became clear that the program not only increased participants' interest in intercommunal relations, but also inspired most to recommit themselves to religious learning *within* their own traditions. The diversity among Jewish and Muslim participants encouraged comparison and discussion of difference within and between the two religious traditions. Participants eventually felt comfortable learning from the religious "other" without feeling the need to come to final agreements over the issues.

Post-Program

In the weeks after the program, a closing dinner was organized by the partner organizations, which was opened to the public. The event became an opportunity to publicize the program, garner community support, and model the experience for the larger community. As one participant put it,

> This was not a vaguely conceived, "feel-good" project getting Muslims and Jews together to encourage dialogue or social interaction or the discussion of current affairs although any of those things could happen in the natural course of being together. Our focus from the beginning—our common ground—was our love of text study and our desire to explore our texts together.

Since the close of the program, the group has continued to meet independently to discuss religious topics and continue and deepen friendships. The continued activity has been the most important measure of its success.

Notes

Throughout this study we partnered with Aziza Hasan and Malka Fenyvesi, codirectors of NewGround, in order to plan, implement, collect, and evaluate relevant data.

1. See www.usc.edu/cmje.
2. See www.huc.edu.
3. See omaribnalkhatab.org.
4. See crcc.usc.edu/about.
5. See newgroundproject.weebly.com.
6. See, e.g., Reuven Firestone, *Journeys in Holy Lands* (Albany, NY: SUNY, 1999) and *An Introduction to Islam for Jews* (Philadelphia: Jewish Publication Society, 2008); S. D. Goitein, *Jews and Arabs: Their Contacts through the Ages* (NY: Schocken, 1955); Hartwig Hirschfeld, "Historical and Legendary Controversies between Mohammed and the Rabbis," *Jewish Quarterly Review*, Vol. 10 (1898), 100–116; Moshe Perlmann, "The Medieval Polemics Between Islam and Judaism," in S. D. Goitein, *Religion in a Religious Age* (Cambridge, MA: Ktav, 1974), 103–129; Ibn Qayyim al-Jawziyya, *Hidayat al-hiyara fi ajwiba al-yahud wal-nasara* [Confused Guidance in the Answer of the Jews and the Christians] (Mecca: Nizar Mustafa Al-Baz, n.d.); Shimon ben Zemah Duran, *Sefer Keshet Umagen* [The Book of Bow and Shield] (Jerusalem: Makor, 1970).
7. David M. Freidenreich, "Muslim-Jewish Dialogue," in *The Oxford Encyclopedia of the Islamic World.*, John L. Esposito, ed. (New York: Oxford University Press, 2001)
8. Gordon Mitchell, "Sacred Text as a Platform for Interreligious Dialogue" (2004), 1, found at www.religiouseducation.net/Resources/Proceedings/23Mitchell-Boston.pdf, retrieved December 9, 2009.
9. We are not alone in this observation. Studies in German public schools have shown interreligious text study to be a successful tool to increase understanding among children (ibid.). On the other end of the academic spectrum, a movement in interreligious dialogue called "Scriptural Reasoning" has demonstrated similar results in the higher academy (see www.scripturalreasoning.org.uk/index1.html and www.scripturalreasoning.org/about.php, retrieved December 9, 2009).

10. For samples of pre- and post-change agent questionnaires, see www.usc.edu/schools/college/crcc/engagement/resources/bestpractices.html. One question that enlivened healthy debate within the leadership team was the question of outside observers. On the one hand, we wanted to promote the project and attract supporters and funders. On the other, we were committed to protecting the anonymity, security, and trust of the participants. This remained an issue throughout the pilot study because a number of outside individuals, such as the hosting religious centers and related agencies, were interested. The participants themselves were surveyed, and because some felt a level of discomfort the idea was dropped altogether. (For a summary of participants' responses to the question regarding observation, please see Evaluation Summary #3 found at www.usc.edu/schools/college/crcc/private/cmje/best_practice/ Session_3_eval_summary.pdf.)

11. For the prepared texts, see www.usc.edu/schools/college/crcc/private/cmje/best_practice/ MOSES__THE_ BURNING_BUSH_asad_translation.pdf.

12. Barry Bub et al., "What is Chevrutah?" (found at www.reclaimingjudaism.org/torah/hevruta. htm); see also Rachel Adler, "The Goals of Chevruta: The Juxtaposition of Text and Person," Jewish Funds for Justice, found at www.jewishjustice.org/download/Beit%20Midrash%20I. pdf.

13. For the evaluation used and a summary of the results, see www.usc.edu/schools/college/crcc/ engagement/resources/bestpractices.html.

14. It should be noted that session evaluations had a high enough response rate to be useful (57–70 percent), but the pre- and post-change agent evaluations did not. Although 70 percent of the participants returned preevaluations, only 14 percent of participants returned post-program evaluations. We believe the response rate in general would be improved if evaluations were completed during sessions, data importance was explained more clearly, and responses were posted in a timely manner to the participants.

15. Texts available at www.usc.edu/schools/college/crcc/engagement/resources/bestpractices. html.

16. Exercises available at www.usc.edu/schools/college/crcc/engagement/resources/bestpractices. html.

17. Texts available at www.usc.edu/schools/college/crcc/private/cmje/best_practice/Session_3_ Texts_Combined.pdf.

18. The program team also improved the timing and signaled transitions with the aid of a meditation bell, which brought smiles as it offered a pleasant way to switch activities.

19. Text available at www.usc.edu/schools/college/crcc/engagement/resources/bestpractices. html.

CHAPTER SIXTEEN

American Jews and American Muslims of Love

RABBI MICHAEL LERNER

Two Dominant Worldviews of the "Other"

Jewish-Muslim relations in the United States cannot be separated from the larger struggle between two worldviews that has been taking place in much of the world for the past several thousand years. I refer to the struggle between two fundamentally different conceptions of human life and human nature that has shaped relations between and within the Muslim and Jewish communities, a struggle, indeed, that goes on in almost every other community around the globe.

The first worldview maintains that human beings have been "thrown" into this world as lone individuals, surrounded by others who are fundamentally oriented toward promoting their own well-being, individuals without interest in others except to the extent that such others may help or hinder their own flourishing. These others are usually perceived as selfish, interested in maximizing their own advantage without regard for the consequences for anyone else. Hence they are all too willing to seek domination and control over one another. Moreover, this domination and control is understood to be a necessity of survival, as others are almost certain to dominate and control you if you don't manage to get power over them first. In other words, according to this perspective, the only way to achieve security and safety *for oneself* is to dominate the *other*. Families, communities, and eventually countries seeking to maintain "homeland security" must acquire this power over others and maintain it using whatever forces or other techniques of manipulation and control are available.

The second worldview maintains that, as a matter of fact, human beings don't find themselves all alone, but rather are born into families that potentially provide them with initial experiences of love and security. Mothers, or others who provide maternal functions, give us immediate experiences of care and generosity that are essential to our survival, particularly in the first years of our lives, and they do so without any reasonable expectation of a "significant return on their investment." They give unconditionally. Through this experience, people grow in and toward a very different understanding of human reality, one in which love provides the ultimate foundation for safety and security. Instead of facing the world with the belief that the other is seeking to dominate us, this worldview stresses the possibility of a world based on caring for others, urging us to enact this attitude as a way of generating a reciprocity that frequently provides a more stable path to our own well-being and growth.

As traditional societies giving priority to communities of shared meaning and purpose have receded in the face of oppressive class structures, slavery, feudalism, and, ultimately, the triumph of global capitalism, the struggle between these two worldviews has increasingly become a central aspect of the development of individual consciousness. Most people carry within them both of these worldviews in varying degrees. Which worldview predominates at any given time in any given individual is shaped by childhood experiences, adult experiences, ideological or religious worldviews, and our own assessment of where social energy is moving. When social energy seems to be moving more toward the worldview of domination and fear of the other, the stories we hear—stories that tend to legitimate this perspective—are given greater credence; conversely, when social energy seems to be moving more toward generosity and hope, the stories that give this view credibility become more salient. Correspondingly, philosophers and social theorists, columnists and religious leaders, community activists, poets, writers, media mavens, and practical politicians who represent the worldview in ascendency at any given moment will appear to be more profound and insightful while those committed to the other worldview will seem out of touch or even dangerous.

American Jews and Worldviews of the "Other"

Judaism, Christianity, and Islam were initially sparked by leaders who, like everyone else on the planet, heard God's voice through the framework of their own particular intellectual, religious, psychological, and spiritual inheritances; their holy texts reflect both the worldview of fear and that of hope, the worldview of domination and that of love and generosity. It is no surprise that at different points in the histories of these three religions, one or the other of these worldviews has been in ascendancy within each community, while minorities within each have at one point or another been rejected or marginalized for holding the other worldview.

In contemporary America, Muslims and Jews have both brought with them, from within their own communities, this same struggle. This has impacted how they are seen by other Americans and how they interact with each other. Jews brought with them into America the memories of oppression they experienced in other countries, largely at the hands of a Christianity that consciously fostered anti-Semitic legislation and popular anger leveled at the Jewish people. The discrimination Jews faced in Europe as they sought to enter the economic mainstream, professional life, and academia was encountered again in the United States in the late nineteenth century and in the first forty years of the twentieth century. Yet the experience of oppression would not have been enough to sustain a Jewish attitude of identification with the oppressed had it not been coupled with the parts of their own religious tradition that embedded (even in secular rebels against their Jewish background) a strong tendency to identify with the slaves and the powerless. It was the Jewish tradition itself that created a framework of consciousness—embedded in many aspects of Jewish culture—to incline Jews to identify with the voice of love and generosity toward the oppressed, a hatred of violence, and a passion for peace, social justice, and human rights.

Yet these inclinations were severely weakened in the second half of the twentieth century by the following factors:

1. The Holocaust led many Jews to doubt the existence of a God of love and of a humanity that could be counted on to act in a morally decent way.
2. The Zionist movement insisted that Jews should become "a nation like all nations," encouraging them to rely on the same force and violence that underpins the regimes of most existing states in the world.
3. Threats to the existence of the state of Israel have made many Jews believe that the survival of Israel cannot be left to the goodwill of others. Instead it must depend on its perfection of the same moral indifference that guides the behavior of many other nation states and the fostering within Israel of a culture of "tough Jews," a muscular Judaism that has come to be a major influence in the culture of many American Jews.
4. The Left has not only failed to create an alternative model of states that embody kindness and generosity, but has also embodied a particular form of anti-Semitism that continues to be tolerated in Leftist circles, despite being in sharp contrast with the Left's outspoken campaigns against sexism, racism, homophobia, and in support for immigrants' rights.
5. At the same time that there has been a decline in barriers against Jews entering the economic mainstream, they have had a great deal of success in becoming major players in the banking and investment sectors, in media, law, medicine, Hollywood, government, and education. This has led many Jews to believe that their fulfillment and security can come through "making it" in American society, despite the fact that making it in America, in most cases, requires implicit or explicit adapting to the ethos of materialism and selfishness that is fostered by the dominant capitalist economy, while also supporting America's efforts to provide stability to global capitalism and

the American Empire. This has also led to a strong embrace of the "muscular" liberalism that, while continuing to proclaim loyalty to human rights, justifies and even exalts the use of force and violence as the only "realistic" way to protect "American interests," which this segment of the American Jewish population also believes to be intrinsically tied to the interests of the state of Israel. The more that American Jews become enamored by the values of American society, the more they open themselves up to the worldview of fear of the other and the "common sense" of the Empire: that the only way to achieve security is through domination and power over the other.

In opposition to this trend, there remains a strong countertendency among a growing number of American Jews who seek to retain a commitment to peace, social justice, and the ethos of caring for others that is fostered by the worldview of hope and its accompanying idea that security comes from generosity and love. Among the factors that continue to support this consciousness are the following:

1. The decline of anti-Semitism in much of the Western world.
2. The success of anticolonialist and anti-imperialist movements in the past few decades, including the defeat of the United States in Vietnam.
3. The success of the civil rights, LGBT rights, and women's rights movements, often having a disproportionate amount of their leadership being drawn from Jews with a pro-hope orientation.
4. The emergence of a pro-love and pro-generosity tendency within some branches of Judaism.
5. The decline of economic security in the United States alongside the declining certainty about the ready accessibility of success for those with adequate motivation and talents. This has led some to recognize that their future fate may require identification with the powerless rather than attempts to "make it" with the powerful.
6. A growing alienation, particularly among Jews under the age of forty, toward the organized Jewish community both because of the latter's blind loyalty to the state of Israel and its spiritual vacuity and assimilation into the materialist values of American society. In an effort to replace this alienation younger Jews have gone in two general directions: toward a lessening of their ties to Judaism, even as they unconsciously play out the social justice and caring-for-others values that they inherited from their Jewish families and that stand in stark contrast to the dominant values of American society, or toward attempts to build an alternative Jewish culture unrelated to and not dependent upon support from the organized Jewish community. It is important to underscore that while describing younger Jews who have rejected the institutions of the Jewish world, there are as many who embrace the dominant culture of the American empire, seek

their own economic well-being, reject any of the cultural and religious heritage of Judaism that might have inclined them to identify with the powerless and oppressed, and have no higher vision for themselves than to become as rich, powerful, and "successful" as those they imagine to be benefitting from being either not Jewish or "too Jewish."

For the sake of ease in identification, I'll call the first tendency within the Jewish community "the Jews of Fear," and the second "the Jews of Love." They represent fundamentally different ways of experiencing the world.

American Muslims and Worldviews of the "Other"

It has been my experience that while the specific historical factors differ, the same kind of split that exists among American Jews also exists within the Christian and Muslim communities in the United States, despite the fact that these groups have been shaped by their own unique stages of assimilation to the dominant culture.

In the American Muslim milieu, the fear-based approach is rooted in the long history of worldwide Muslim-Christian struggle, particularly as manifested in the Crusades and the powerful impact of modern global Western colonialism and imperialism, which is often accompanied by a strong "anti-orientalist" worldview that demeans Islam. In the second half of the twentieth century, when this colonial tendency was being defeated in much of the so-called Muslim world, the sudden emergence of the state of Israel, and its alliance with current and former colonial and imperial Western empires, created a flourishing anti-Semitism in many Arab- and Muslim-majority countries that had previously sought accommodation with their own (somewhat oppressed and rights-denied) Jewish minorities. The way that the Jewish state came into existence—simultaneously creating a huge group of Palestinian refugees, most of whom were Muslim; with a comparably large group of Jews from Arab-majority countries fleeing the anger that the creation of Israel had intensified among Muslims and Arabs who had seen Jews advantaged when the French and English colonialists treated them with greater respect than their traditional subordinated roles in Muslim countries had allowed; and then the subsequent colonization of the West Bank by right-wing extremists determined to hold on to this territory as their religious duty and without regard for the suffering they were causing by appropriating Palestinian lands and using violence against Palestinian neighbors—has contributed to the emergence of extremist elements in Muslim-majority countries, though those forces have other more significant reasons for having triumphed in some corners of Islam (not least of which has been the traditional subservience of Jews to Muslims in a *dhimmi* status, and the perceived role of Israel as a frontier of a Western culture and economics bent more on economic exploitation and military domination than on tradition-respecting forms of modernization). Let's call this element of the Muslim community "the Muslims of Fear."

Yet there exists in the Muslim world a far stronger force of "Muslims of Love." These are Muslims who have built their tradition on customs of caring for the stranger, on the experiences of generosity and kindness, and on a long historical period lasting from the eighth to the eighteenth centuries in which most Muslims lived in security and were able to develop a rich culture of social justice, peace, scientific curiosity, and intellectual creativity, along with a deep sense of well-being. Thus, when talking about the relationships between American Jews and American Muslims it is critical to specify which particular group of Jews and which particular group of Muslims we are talking about before the conversation can even begin.

American Jews and American Muslims of Love

My experience is that the Jews of Love and the Muslims of Love are increasingly making efforts toward outreach and building ties with each other; this volume is itself a testimony to these efforts. Yet both of these communities feel disappointed at the results so far. Jews tend to be disappointed that Muslims are unwilling to unequivocally condemn each instance of violence carried out by Muslims or of oppression found in Muslim communities commonly seen in Western media. Muslims often respond to these demands by expressing offense that they are even being asked to be responsible for engaging in this kind of public critique, particularly since the Jews they encounter rarely engage in similar public denunciations of the violence carried out by Jews, such as the day-to-day reality of the Israeli occupation of Gaza and the West Bank. Conversely, Muslims are often disappointed that otherwise sensitive and human-rights-oriented Jews, individuals who express outrage at the behavior of the United States vis-à-vis Guantanamo Bay prisoners or wars perpetrated in Afghanistan and Iraq by the American government, can be so silent about the behavior of Israel toward Palestinian civilians.

These tensions are exacerbated by particular circumstances of the past two decades. For many Jews there is disappointment with what happened when Jews who had played a disproportionate role in supporting the civil rights movement in the first sixty-five years of the twentieth century were unceremoniously booted out of major organizations such as the Student Non-Violent Coordinating Committee (SNCC) and the Conference of Racial Equality (CORE) in 1965–1967, an exclusion that was, in some parts of these organizations, accompanied by anti-Semitic rhetoric that became prevalent in some sections of the black community. Jews of Love were often castigated by Jews of Fear for not having learned the supposed lesson of this experience: Jews can't trust non-Jews, Jews need a country and army of their own, and it is ludicrous to imagine that any attempted alliance with oppressed peoples will increase Jewish security or can be counted on when Jews become subject to global attacks. The internalization of these assaults on Jews of Love has made many of them less willing to take risks in building relations with Muslims of Love. Moreover, attempts to create dialogue and bring Jewish and Muslim communities together to explore mutual interests, fears, and hopes have often had a much more feeble response from Muslim communities than from the Jews of Love.

Conversely, Muslims of Love have been disappointed by the lack of real and sustained support for their efforts to normalize Muslim life in the United States and for the unwillingness of Jews of Love to respond to Israeli attacks on Palestinians as though the life of a Muslim (or Christian) is not as important as the life of a Jew. The pronounced tendency in American Jewish peace organizations such as Americans for Peace Now, J Street, and Brit Tzedek v'Shalom (before it became part of J Street) to frame their critique of Israeli occupation policies solely in terms of the way these policies are destructive of Jewish self-interest, without highlighting the suffering of the Palestinian people, seems to indicate an unwillingness to consider suffering between members of the two communities as having equal importance.

The willingness of many in these Jewish organizations to marginalize or ignore the contributions of other Jewish organizations, such as Tikkun and its interfaith Network of Spiritual Progressives or Jewish Voice for Peace, precisely because these groups insist on highlighting the suffering of Palestinians as a Jewish issue has contributed to a certain wariness among Muslims of Love to trust that a deeper relationship is really possible. Moreover, these Muslims have often been dismayed at the unwillingness of Jews to take seriously how much more difficult it is to get fellow Muslims to trust any Americans (let alone American Jews) at a time in the first two decades of the twenty-first century when Muslims are collectively blamed for the sins of 9/11, continually face harassment and suspicion by much of the law enforcement and transportation security agencies, and often feel themselves to be demeaned in the mass culture of Western societies in general and by Jewish writers from said culture in particular.

American Jews and American Muslims of Fear

Things may be less complicated for the Jews and Muslims of Fear. Each gets a great deal from the other, namely the confirmation of their worst fears, which they can then use as their "proof-texts" when trying to recruit younger Jews or Muslims to their respective causes. They can also count on one another for a steady stream of words and deeds that are demeaning and oppressive, vitriol that makes their ability to critique and marginalize

the Jews and Muslims of Love with whom they have been in fierce struggle even stronger, not to mention their ability to quell the voices within
their own groups with whom the appeal to love and generosity sometimes
resonates.

Jews and Muslims of Fear find themselves in a rather unique position in the United States. They see each other as real enemies, but also
know that the rules of engagement prohibit their battles being fought
on American terrain. So rather than attack one another directly, each
seeks to strengthen its own tendency both within their own communities
and within the communities of their global allies. Jews of Fear present
themselves to America's ruling elites as "hard core realists" who can help
America develop the smartest strategies for repressing Islam all over the
world, as long as they insist that it is only "militant Islam" that they target.
These Jews simultaneously do all they can to manipulate American foreign policy to support the most hardline political elements in Israel, just as
they directly try to support these elements themselves, insisting upon an
ethos in American Jewish schools that repeats a variety of Zionist myths
and falsehoods, without ever teaching younger Jews about the complexities and historical crimes committed in the creation and maintenance of
the Jewish state. Conversely, the Muslims of Fear take similar paths, seeking to recruit younger Muslims for an Islam of Fear to aid the spread
of interpretations of the Qur'an that emphasize the need for wars to be
waged against nonbelievers, and to provide support (usually ideological) for the most extreme versions of Islam that are flourishing in some
Muslim-majority countries. De facto, Jews and Muslims of Fear have a
powerful mutual alliance that supports both sides effectively.

How to Move Jews and Muslims of Love Forward

We Jews and Muslims of Love need to find ways to work together more
effectively. In turn this will require that we include in this common work
Christians, Hindus, Buddhists, Sikhs, Baha'i, and other religious communities, as well as secular humanists. In fact, this is precisely why we at
Tikkun formed the Network of Spiritual Progressives (www.spiritual-
progressives.org). The core of our vision rests on two aspirations. First,
everyone in advanced industrial societies needs to recognize that our
well-being depends on and is intrinsically tied to the well-being of everyone else on earth as well as to the well-being of the planet itself. Second,
the world needs a new "bottom line" so that institutions, social practices,
corporations, government policies, educational systems, legal systems, and
health care systems will be judged efficient, rational, or productive not
only to the extent that we maximize money or power (the old bottom
line), but also to the extent that we contribute to developing our capacities
and willingness to manifest love and generosity, kindness and caring for
others, ethical and ecological sensitivities and behaviors; that we increase

our capacities to treat others as manifestations of the sacred and respond to the universe with awe, wonder, and radical amazement at the grandeur and mystery of All Being. Those reading this essay are invited to join us through our website, www.spiritualprogressives.org.

There is a tendency among some in the larger American society to say that the very existence of the American Jewish and American Muslim communities is the problem, that every time we identify as part of a group we are simultaneously negating all those who are not part of it. Yet the promise of America and what makes me optimistic about our future here is that this "melting pot" (in which differences disappear) has been replaced by a vigorous multiculturalism in which differences are accepted and even validated as an intrinsic part of American life. In this context, our goal should not be a cold tolerance of each other, but rather the building of warm and even loving relationships both on individual and communal levels. I want to meet American Muslims not as people who once were Muslims but now are "true Americans," but rather as fully committed Muslims who maintain that which is most loving and generous in their own tradition while also recognizing me and others like me in the Jewish, Christian, Hindu, Buddhist, Sikh, Baha'i, and other religious communities as genuine allies. Similarly, I am committed to nurturing fellow Jews who can embrace the most loving and generous parts of our own tradition and use it as a bulwark from which we can critique the militarism, racism, and materialism of the global and domestic capitalist marketplace without seeking to validate ourselves in the eyes of the powerful or those indoctrinated by the common sense of a corporate- and empire-friendly media as "realistic" by accommodating to its worst and most destructive aspects. It is from these foundations, and the affirmation of Torah's unequivocal command to "love the stranger" (i.e., the "other"), that I believe real *tikkun*, the healing and transformation of our world, can and will flourish.

Afterword

PETER A. GEFFEN

This volume offers challenge and opportunity. While much of the world continues to convince itself of the futility of dialogue and mutuality, these editors and authors encourage us with their optimism and positive engagement in the critical arena of Jewish-Muslim relations. Advancing mutual understanding and compassion between these two communities is directly linked to achieving peace in the Middle East. And advancing peace in the Middle East may be the single most critical item for the stability of the entire world.

I write after returning from my tenth trip to Morocco, where centuries of positive Muslim-Jewish coexistence offer examples of this challenge. Outside of Taroudant, in southwestern Morocco, there is a small Berber village called Arazane, where little has changed for hundreds, if not thousands, of years. The roads are unpaved. The alleys lead through curved paths to the unknown. The homes are adobe—simple yet formidable.

Raphael David Elmaleh, the last Jewish guide in a Muslim Arab-majority country, tells the story of how several years ago, while traveling through the country seeking whatever remained of abandoned Jewish life in Morocco, he was directed to Arazane. On asking if Jews once lived there he was sent to a village elder named Harim. Upon hearing Raphy's request for the location of the synagogue, this simple Berber man reached into the pocket of his *jalabiyah* (traditional robe) and took out a long wooden key.

"Barukh Habah (*Blessed is the one who comes to visit*)!" he began in Hebrew. "Where have you been? What took you so long? I have been waiting for you to come for 45 years!"

"What?! You've been waiting for ME?!" exclaimed Raphy.

"Yes" responded Harim. "When the Rabbi left he said 'Harim, here is the key to the synagogue. If a Jew ever comes to this village and asks for the synagogue, give him this key.'"

Then Harim chanted "Shma Yisrael," a central Jewish prayer, in Hebrew. Entrusted with the sanctity of this small Jewish house of worship, he protected and preserved what he could for decades.

Stories like this abound throughout Morocco. They are testimony no less significant or determinative than tales of violence and hatred. We continue to ignore them at our own peril. Can we in the United States recreate the gentle, subtle tone of Jews and Berber-Muslims living in mutual respect and tolerance? Can we acknowledge the capacity of people of different religions to become true neighbors and friends? Can we teach our children that Jews and Muslims have historically shared far more than what has separated them? Can we inspire future generations of these communities with optimism?

Reading this book one is also struck by the enormous opportunity presented within this complex international challenge. Of course, we are all prone to skepticism and cynicism when reading the daily press and its reportage on what some portray as an ultimate contest of civilizations. But in this volume we have seen the enormous prospect presented by the same reality. Young and old alike can imagine alternatives and create new settings and institutions to live and act differently. Change is an equally dynamic force of social reality. We all can live our lives in ways that will become effective agencies of change.

Reza Aslan and Aaron Hahn Tapper are both young academics, community educators, and activists whose research and work are prominent examples of charting a new way. Their collection of words can, of course, remain static, yet it contains the seeds of revolutionary change. We the readers will ultimately determine its future. We can only hope that these words become windows allowing in sorely needed fresh air and bright light for a new today and tomorrow.

ACKNOWLEDGMENTS

As this is my first published book, edited or otherwise, I feel it important to briefly mention some of the countless people who have supported me over the years, despite common protocol for a volume of this nature. My first real lessons in writing were at the hands of Elsie Wiedner, z"l , and Laura Novo, academic guidance that continued with Edwin Bryant, Ayman El-Desouky, and David Little at Harvard University, and R. Stephen Humphreys, Mark Juergensmeyer, Roger Friedland, and Richard Hecht at the University of California, Santa Barbara (UCSB). In particular, I am grateful to Stephen for teaching me as much about strengthening my scholarship as how I should carry myself in the field of academia collegially; to Roger for improving my research and modeling the "coteaching" method, which has been central to this project as well as my other professional work; to Mark for taking me under his wing, giving me incredible support both during my time at UCSB and thereafter; and to my primary advisor, Richard, who gave me more support than any other academic mentor during my tenure as a graduate student, helping me secure my current position at the University of San Francisco. It says in M. Avot 1:6, "*asei licha rav*," find yourself a master-teacher. For finding a *rav* in Richard I will forever be grateful. Between Harvard and UCSB I was also privileged enough to be supported by a number of teachers in the CASA program in Cairo, including Jehan, Shereen, Zeinab I., Nevenka, Heba, and Zeinab T.

For generous financial support during my graduate studies I would like to thank Harvard University for the Frederick Sheldon Traveling Fellowship, the Center for Arabic Studies Abroad for an equally important fellowship, the Wexner Foundation for the invaluable fellowship they provided me with for four years and beyond (in particular, thank you Larry, Elka, and Cindy), the Center for Middle East Studies at UCSB for providing me with a Foreign Language Advanced Studies Summer Fellowship, the U.S. Department of Education for providing me with a Fulbright-Hays Doctoral Dissertation Fellowship, and the Department of Religious Studies at UCSB for providing me with the J.R. Rowney Fellowship. For additional assistance during my dissertation research, I am grateful to the more than one hundred Palestinians and Israelis who allowed me to interview them; and thank you to Eliyahu McLean for connecting me to many of these individuals. I'd also like to thank Rabbi Andrew M. Sacks, who provided me with invaluable support during the four years I lived in Jerusalem. During this same time I was also lucky enough to have been given the opportunity to work with Jody Myers at California State University, Northridge, who guided me during an amorphous stage in the dissertation process.

At the University of San Francisco, where I have taught since August 2007, I'd like to thank Provost Jennifer Turpin, and Deans Peter Novak, Michael Block, and Marcelo Campari for their continued support and confidence in my teaching, research, and work with Abraham's Vision and the Center for Transformative Education. I'd also like to thank Vice Provost Gerardo Marin for supporting the many projects USF has integrated into our amazing learning environment. President Stephen Privett has also been central to my positive experiences at USF and has been a great source of inspiration and support. As for my colleagues in the Theology & Religious Studies Department, I cannot say enough about how supportive, dedicated, and compassionate these people are. Thank you to Jorge Aquino, Lilian Dube, Dan Kendall, Mark Miller, Vijaya Nagarajan, John Nelson, and Vincent Pizzuto. In particular, my gratitude goes to Aysha Hidayatullah and Lois Lorentzen (mb), who have become very important to me. Brigid Eckhart and Kristine Massetti have also been incredibly helpful. Thanks also go to my colleagues on the USF Swig Advisory Council: Paula Birnbaum, Amie Espen-Dowling, Elliot Neamen, Rabbi Lawrence Raphael, Esti Skloot, Ruth Starkman, and Stephen Zunes (and Michael, Lois, and Peter). Further, thank you to the hundreds of students I have been privileged enough to learn with over the last few years while at USF, as well as the scores of students, staff, and faculty from universities across the country that permitted me to interview them for my essay in this book.

At Abraham's Vision I, too, have had the opportunity to work with hundreds of amazing students. In addition, I have had the pleasure of working with some of the greatest talents in the conflict transformation world. Aside from a number of important board members, current and past—in particular, Samina Ahmad, Reza Aslan, Danny Fenster, Peter Geffen (special thanks for your mentorship), Ben Korman, Judith Scheuer, Anas Shallal, and Carol Winograd—I have been supported by a number of colleagues, including Gibran Bouayad, Oren Kroll-Zeldin, Megan Martin, and Eitan Trabin. I am also grateful to Reza for supporting Abraham's Vision from its very inception and for suggesting that proceeds from this book go to AV. Working on this project with him has been an extraordinarily positive experience. As for Huda Abu Arqoub, my professional partner and closest of friends, in you I could not have found a more dedicated, personable, intelligent, fun, compassionate, and loving individual. You are the paradigm of professionalism and model how I strive to hold myself personally.

As for other important colleagues and friends, both current and those from "back in the day"—Mons, Al, Cover, Abramson, Deep, Nati, Lucas, Tifel, Eden, Fine, Gib, Gabe, Pam, Webb, Rav Sacks, Spike, Jenn D., Sab, Ari K., Akiba, Caleb, Ghousoon, Jacob B., Schuck, Tali, Marna, Fernbach, Gelb, Debbie S., Kevin E., Elyse, Yedidyah, Dorit, Avi. J., Prags, Gutty, Jeremy A., Amy, Shubbers, Jer, Lora C., Eric B., Lowin, Leesh, Rotey, El, Gregg, Matti, Jill, Nico, Dafna, Rebecca, Ron, Aaron, Rachel, Lauren, Dan G., Kaunfer, Yehuda, Ronit A., Yael, Freed, Fuchs, Pink, Scout, King, Bu, Justin, Natalie, Lital, Margaret, Toby, and Sandy—thank you. Your friendship and support continues to mean the world to me. As for D., A., O., and I., I hope that one day our better selves pick up where we left off. I am also thankful to Lee Bycel for mentorship during the last few years.

In addition to the love of my immediate family—Mom, Dad, Shelly, Stone, Jacob and Jen, Lisi, Becky and Hanan, Debby and Andy, Susan and Michael, Talia, Sam, Elisheva, Nathan, Alice Paul, and Jack Raymond, as well as the Chang Gang (Judith and Karsten, David and Jan, Jan, Joey, and all of the little ones), and Naomi and Dennis, Marc and Sheila, Phyliss and Don, and all of my cousins—I would not have been able to work on this book without the support of my life partner, Laurie. My trips abroad, late-night studying, and early morning writing sessions are only some of the times I was away from my love. Thank you for giving me the support and space to work on this project. And thank you for continuing to be my best friend. Mom, thank you for being the sweet, unconditionally supportive person that you are. Dad, thank you for giving me your best, and for teaching me to strive to do as much as I can in the world for good. Jacob, thank you for being my big brother in every sense (sfg). I look forward to spending time with you, Jen, and our little ones in the years to come, and hope that Alice, J.R., Isaiah, and Delilah continue to grow up together. Shelly, Susan, and Michael, I could not ask for more than your continuing to treat me as your own flesh and blood. For those who have moved onto other realms, thank you Bubbe and Zaydeh for giving me your love, David for teaching me what it means to embrace and live life to its fullest, Grammie for teaching me more than you ever knew, Grampie for modeling the pursuit of knowledge and how to be a *mentsch*, and Isabel for teaching me to face life's challenges with a joke and a smile. May your memories be for a blessing. Finally, as for Isaiah Everett and Delilah Yareyach, to whom I dedicate this book, you are the lights of my life, the joys of the deepest parts of my soul, and the reason I do what I do in the world.

—*Aaron J. Hahn Tapper*

I would like to thank the faculty at the University of California, Santa Barbara, especially my advisor and mentor Mark Juergensmeyer, as well as my colleagues in the Creative Writing Department at the University of California, Riverside. I would also like to acknowledge the support of the board at Abraham's Vision, and the direction of Aaron Hahn Tapper in particular, whose dedication and hard work have led to the enormous success of the organization over the last years. Finally, I wish to thank my partner Jessica Jackley, who has shown me many things but especially this: that one cannot merely talk about changing the world; one must roll up one's sleeves and actually do it.

Finally, we would both like to thank the team from Palgrave Macmillan, including Farideh Koohi-Kamali, Robyn Curtis, Heather Faulls, and Rohini Krishnan, among others. We also want to thank Sara Hughes for compiling the book's index.

—*Reza Aslan*

INDEX

9/11, viii, 2, 11, 40, 46, 47, 67, 72, 76, 77,
   93, 95, 99, 117, 121, 129, 147, 152,
   163, 165, 167, 197
   see also War on Terror

Abdul Rauf, Imam Fiesal, 3
Abou El Fadl, Khaled, 66
Abraham, 18, 39, 42–3, 58, 96, 125, 149–50,
   163, 171, 172
   daughters of, 164
   see also Hagar; Isaac; Ishmael; Jacob; Sarah
Abrahamic, 154–5, 163
   family, 42
   legacy, 150, 151
   relationship, 150
   religions, 58, 163, 165
   tradition, 163
"Abrahamic Ethic," 57–8, 68
Abraham's Vision, x
   see also Aslan, Reza; Hahn Tapper, Aaron
Adam and Eve, 162
   see also Creation Story
Adelson, Sheldon, Jewish Republican
   billionaire, 26–7
Afghanistan, 67, 72, 170, 196
Aish HaTorah (lit. flame of the Torah),
   Jewish missionary group, 23–5
Ali, Kecia, 169, 171
alienation, 43, 75, 194
Alliance schools, 134
Al-Marayati, Salam, executive director
   Muslim Public Affairs Council, 4,
   112
Al-Qaeda, 152
Ameinu, 111
American Academy of Religion (AAR),
   161, 165, 166
American-Arab Anti-Discrimination
   Committee (ADC), 65

American Civil Liberties Union (ACLU),
   95, 99
American Declaration of Independence, 58
American Empire, 194
American government, 26, 64, 67, 72, 77,
   122, 124, 145, 151, 154, 167, 170,
   196
American Israel Public Affairs Committee
   (AIPAC), 27, 67, 79, 109, 110, 111,
   112
"Americanization," 60, 61, 63
American Jewish Committee (AJC), 65, 67,
   68, 74, 149, 173
American Jewish community, *see under*
   Jewish community
American Jewish movements, 63
American Jews, viii, 1–5, 30, 34, 42, 59, 61,
   63, 64–5, 67–9, 71, 74, 75, 77, 78,
   80, 81, 82, 107, 110–11, 112,
   118–19, 124, 129, 131, 146, 149,
   150, 153, 154, 173, 175, 191, 192–7
   see also American Muslims
American Muslim community, *see under*
   Muslim community
American Muslims, 1–5, 34, 42, 57, 59, 61,
   63–4, 65–8, 69, 71–2, 73, 75, 77,
   78–9, 81–2, 97, 99, 101, 107, 112,
   118–19, 122, 124, 128–9, 131, 146,
   148, 149, 150, 152–4, 173, 191,
   195–6, 197, 199
   see also American Jews
American Republican party, 26
American Scholar, The, 101
Americans for Peace Now, 108, 197
anti-Arab, 50, 51
   see also anti-Muslim; anti-orientalist;
   Islamophobia
Anti-Defamation League (ADL), 15, 48–9,
   65, 80–1, 146

anti-Islam, *see* anti-Muslim
anti-Israel, 35, 50, 80, 150
anti-Judaism, 164
   see also anti-Semitism
anti-Muslim, viii, 29, 50–1, 69, 93, 130, 150,
   152
   see also anti-orientalist; Islamophobia
anti-orientalist, 195
   see also anti-Muslim; Islamophobia
anti-Semitism/anti-Semetic, viii, 11, 15–16,
   69, 80, 93, 96, 99–100, 119, 122,
   131, 149–50, 193–6
   see also anti-Judaism
anti-Zionist, 111
apartheid wall, *see* separation barrier
Arab American Institute, 111
Arab Heritage, 48
Arab Women Active in the Arts and the
   Media (AWAAM), 48, 50
Arazane, Morocco, 201–2
Ashkenazi Jews, 61, 75, 77, 133, 140
   see also Sephardic Jews
Aslan, Reza, founding member Abraham's
   Vision, x, 202
assimilation, 1, 23, 59, 60, 63–5, 96, 101,
   133, 134–7, 139, 194–5
Awlaki, Anwar, ix
azan (call to prayer), 94

Bachman, Rabbi Andy, Congregation Beth
   Elohim, 48
Badawi, Professor Jamal, 17–18
Baer, Leah, 136
Baghdad, Iraq, 147
   see also Iraq
Baha'i, 141, 198, 199
barriers, 58, 61
   of mutual suspicion, 118
Barsky, Yehudit, 74
Beerman, Rabbi Leonard, 146–7
Ben-Aharon, Ambassador Yossi, 27
Ben-Ami, Jeremy, executive director J
   Street, 109–10, 112, 152
Ben-David, Lenny, former Israeli deputy
   chief of mission, 27
Berbers, 201–2
Berman, Sara, board chair Hebrew
   Language Academy, 52
Biden, Vice President Joe, 28
Bloomberg, Mayor Michael, 46, 50

boundaries, 40
   communal, 16, 18, 181
   religious, 166
Brandeis University, 97
bridge-building, 12, 14, 45–7, 50–2, 118,
   148, 151, 155, 176
Bridges TV, 3, 11–12, 17
   see also Hassan, Mo; Zubair, Aasiya
Brit Tzedek v'Shalom, 197
Brookings Institution, 154
Brooklyn for Peace, 50
Buddhists, 98, 198, 199
*Building Bridges: Abrahamic Perspectives on the
   World Today*, 12
   see also Bridges TV
Bukhari, Zahid, director of the Muslim
   American Studies Program
   at Prince Alwaleed Bin-Talal
   Center for Muslim-Christian
   Understanding at Georgetown
   University, 75
Bulkin, Elly, 50
Bush, President George W., 27, 73, 154,
   170

campus activism, 24, 71–3, 76–83, 93–5, 96
   see also student groups
capitalism, 192, 193
Carroll, Adem, 50
Carter, President Jimmy, 150
Center for Immigrant Families, 50
Center for Jewish Muslim Engagement,
   177
chevrutah, 182, 187
Chicago's Interfaith Youth Core, 4
Children of Abraham Dialogue Project, 128
Children of Abraham Peace Walk, 46
Christ, Carroll, 160
Christian Children's Fund, 46
Christians/Christianity, 1, 18, 21, 22, 28, 29,
   30, 39, 52, 57, 58, 59, 60, 61, 66, 68,
   95, 97, 98, 100, 117–18, 121, 123,
   129, 130, 133–4, 136, 139, 141, 149,
   150, 155, 160, 161, 162, 163, 164,
   166, 167, 168, 170, 177, 192, 197,
   198, 199
   communities, 46, 47, 195
   feminists, 162, 164–6, 170
   right-wing, 3, 170
   society, 128, 181

Christians United for Israel (CUFI), 28, 29, 109
Christian Zionism, *see under* Zionism
Churches for Middle East Peace, viii
civil liberties, 65, 69, 98, 122, 129, 153, 161
civil rights, 30, 65, 68, 194, 196
Clarion Fund, 23–6
Clinton, President Bill, 154
coalition building, 67, 69
"Code of Ethics," 148
Cohen, Ariel, 27
Cohen, Steven M., 110
collective guilt, 17–18
   see also collective/shared responsibility
collective/shared responsibility, 17–18
   see also collective guilt
College Republicans, 25, 26, 73
colonialism, 195
commonalities, 35, 41
   see also differences
Communities in Support of KGIA (CIS-KGIA), 50–1
Conference of Presidents of Major American Jewish Organizations, 146
Conference of Racial Equality (CORE), 196
Cordoba Initiative, 66, 67
coreligionists, 2, 67, 136, 155, 163
Council on American-Islamic Relations (CAIR), 65, 74, 173
Creation Story, 165, 167, 180, 183–4
   see also Adam and Eve
cross fertilization, 60
Cruise, Tom, see *A Few Good Men*

Dalin, David, 27
Daly, Mary, 164
Darwish, Nonie, 22
defensiveness, 40
dehumanization, 108, 130
Dermer, Ron, 110
dhimmi, 150, 195
dialogue, 4, 30, 36–40, 42, 45, 52, 68, 69, 81, 102, 112, 118, 121–4, 133, 147, 165, 175, 178, 188, 201
   Christian-Jewish, 33, 177
   groups, 3
   intercommunal, 52

interfaith, 33–4, 40, 96, 102, 117, 119, 133–4, 151
intergroup, 4, 177
interreligious, 3, 10, 16, 108, 177
   Jewish-Christian, *see* dialogue, Christian-Jewish
   Jewish-Muslim, 33–4, 37–8, 40, 42, 107, 111–13, 147, 151, 177, 181
   Muslim-Christian, 33, 117
   Muslim-Jewish, *see* Jewish-Muslim
through text study, 177–8
   see also learning through text study
"Dialogue Project," 45–6, 128
differences, 34–5, 38, 41
   see also commonalities
discrimination, 65, 75, 122, 129, 133, 140, 193
domination, 23, 170, 191–2, 194, 196
dorehs, 141
double consciousness, 161–2

Edwards, Rabbi Lisa, 170
El-Amin, Imam Makram, leader of Masjid An Nur, vii
El-Dahry, Mona, 50
Ellison, Congressman Keith, 129, 175
Elmaleh, Raphael David, 201
Endowment for Middle East Truth (EMET), 26–7
engagement, Jewish-Muslim, 37, 41, 94, 100–1, 129, 178, 179, 181–2, 183, 187, 201
Equal Employment Opportunity Commission (EEOC), 51
Ettinger, Yoram, 27
exclusiveness, mentality of, 133, 141, 150, 154
exilic mentality, 134, 142

facilitation, 35, 38, 40–2, 67, 69, 81, 107, 178, 181–3, 185
"Falling in Love with Yiddish," 101
fatwas, 130
fear, 13, 16, 19, 21, 34–6, 37, 41, 95, 110, 118, 122, 137, 149, 155, 159, 167, 174, 176, 192, 194
fear-mongers, 14
Federal Bureau of Investigation (FBI), 146
Feinberg, Rabbi Michael, 49, 50
Feingold, Senator Russell, 152

feminism/feminists, 39, 161–71
  Christian, 162, 164, 165–6, 170
  Jewish, 160, 165–6, 168, 171
  Muslim, 160, 163, 165–6, 167–9, 170, 171
feminist theology, 159, 162, 169
Fetman, Jacob, 24
A Few Good Men, movie, 1, 9
footbaths, 4, 93–5, 99, 102
Foxman, Abe (Abraham), director
      Anti-Defamation League, 15, 49,
      146
Frankel, Rabbi Benjamin, 97
freedom of religion, 128
"Freedom Watch," 27
Friends of KGIA, 47
fundamentalists, 40, 121, 150
funding, 4, 26, 76, 93, 96, 97, 98, 99, 100,
      103, 149

Gabriel, Brigitte, 29–30
Gaffney, Frank, 27
Gaza, viii, 26, 36, 37, 48, 109, 140, 146, 150,
      151–2, 173–6, 178, 196
Geller, Rabbi Laura, 151
generalizations, 31, 38, 40, 162
  see also stereotypes
General Union of Palestinian Students
      (GUPS), 73
genocide, 18, 78, 178
Gephardt, Congressman Richard, 145–6,
      148
Glick, Caroline, 22, 27
global citizenship, 42, 47
God, 14, 17, 28, 29, 39, 40, 42, 58, 61, 80, 96,
      122, 123, 124, 125, 131, 132, 149,
      150, 154, 155, 160, 163, 166, 168,
      169, 171, 172, 180, 181, 192, 193
Goldberg, Jeffrey, 109
Goldstein, Baruch, 18
Goldstone Report, 109
Goodman, Matthew, author of "Falling in
      Love with Yiddish," 101
Goodstein, Laurie, 145
Graham, Franklin, 121
Greater New York Labor-Religion
      Coalition, 49, 50
"Ground Zero," 3
Guantanamo Bay, 9, 196

Ha'aretz, 25, 28
Habonim Dror North America, 111

Hadith, 180
  see also Qur'an
Hagar, 42, 159, 163–5, 166, 172
  see also Abraham; Sarah
Hagee, John, 28
Hahn Tapper, Aaron, founder and
      codirector of Abraham's Vision, x,
      3–4, 202, 204
Hamadan, Iran, 134–5
  see also Tehran, Iran
Hamas, 29, 37, 80, 173–6
hardliners, pro-Israel, 145, 147, 148, 149,
      150
Harman, Congresswoman Jane, 152
Harris, David A., executive director
      American Jewish Committee, 146,
      173
Harris, Rabbi Henry, 24
Harvard University, 93, 95, 96
Hasbara Fellowships, 24
Hashomer Hatzair North America, 111
Hassan, Mo, co-founder Bridges TV, 3,
      11–12
  see also Bridges TV; Zubair, Aasiya
hate, 16, 21, 31
hate speech, 30, 95
Hathout, Dr. Maher, 147–9
headscarf, see *hijab*
Hebrew Bible, viii, 123, 166, 172, 180, 182,
      186
Hebrew Language Academy Charter
      School (HLA), 52
Hebrew Union College, 97, 177
  Jewish Institute of Religion, 97
Herberg, Will, 107–8
Heritage Foundation, 26, 27
hijab, 62, 123
Hikind, Assemblyman Dov, 48
Hillel, 4, 25, 73, 78–81, 93–4, 97–101
Hindus, 198, 199
Hoenlin, Malcolm, leader of the
      Conference of Presidents of Major
      American Jewish Organizations,
      146
"Hollywood Ten," 153
Holocaust, 18, 28, 110, 122, 130–1, 193
holy envy, 42
Honestreporting.com, 24, 25, 26
honor killing, 14
Hoover Institute, 27
Horwitz, Carol, 50

Hossein Nasr, Seyyed, 66
Hughes, Robert, 49
human rights, 13, 30, 52, 193, 194
Hutchens, Reverend James M., 28

iconoclasm, 63
Iden, Ron, 146
identification/identify/identifiers, 10, 21,
    61, 63, 66, 71, 72, 73, 74, 77, 101,
    102, 110–11, 127, 130, 131, 134,
    136, 140, 147, 153, 193, 194, 195,
    199
identity, 5, 36, 42, 55, 59, 61, 63, 66, 68, 69,
    71, 72, 73, 76, 77, 79, 82, 97–8, 99,
    102, 136, 172, 183, 185
  American, 57, 66
  American Islamic, 64
  American Jewish, *see* Jewish identity,
    American
  American Muslim, 59, 64, 101, 147
  communal, 63, 72, 79
  ethnic, 96, 153
  ethno-religious, 134, 140
  group, 93, 97
  Islamic, 57
  Jewish, 66, 78, 97, 102, 136, 140, 153
  Jewish American, 96, 101
  minority, 99
  Muslim, 98, 100, 102
  national, 96, 134, 140
  personal, 178
  religious, 42, 61, 68, 96, 140, 180
ignorance, 121, 122, 131, 162–3, 165,
    167
immigration/immigrants, 1, 2, 46, 57, 60–1,
    64–5, 66–7, 69, 94–6, 102, 128,
    134–5, 142, 164, 193
  American, 57, 59, 61, 63, 65, 66
  Christian, 96
  Jewish, 61, 93–4, 96
  Muslim, 59, 62, 63, 66, 93–6, 99, 127, 140
imperialism, *see* colonialism
insularity, 133, 134, 135, 137, 139, 140, 141,
    142
interfaith, 33, 36, 37, 39, 46, 98, 117, 174,
    180, 181, 187, 197
  collaboration, 100
  dialogue, *see under* dialogue
  learning, 33, 35, 94
  relations, 33, 65, 66
Interfaith Conversations Project, 33, 35

intergroup education, 81
interlocutors, 60, 61, 65
inter-religious dialogue, *see under*
    dialogue
Intifada, 48, 71
Iran, 4, 22, 67, 109, 110, 133–7, 140–2
  modernization of, 135, 137
Iranian hostage crisis, 140
Iranian Jews, 4, 133–6, 139, 140, 142
  see also Iranian Muslims
Iranian Muslims, 4, 133–8, 140
  see also Iranian Jews
Iranian Revolution, 4, 133–5, 141–2
Iraq, 22, 67, 72, 73
  see also Baghdad, Iraq
Isaac, 18, 42–3, 149, 171
  see also Abraham; Ishmael
Ishmael/Ishmail, 42–3, 149, 163, 171
  see also Abraham; Isaac
Islam, 2, 10, 13–15, 17–18, 22–4, 28–30,
    39–40, 46, 47, 58, 59, 60, 62–4, 66,
    68, 93, 95, 96, 99–102, 108, 118,
    121–3, 124, 128, 129–30, 131, 149,
    150, 152, 153, 154, 155, 159, 161,
    162, 163, 164, 165, 167, 168, 184,
    186, 192, 195, 198
  see also "radical Islam"
Islamic Center, 35, 36, 37, 39
Islamic Center of Southern California, 133,
    147
Islamic jurisprudence, 13, 61, 66, 169
Islamic law, 62, 63, 67, 153
Islamic Republic of Iran, 133
Islamic Shura Council of Southern
    California, 151
Islamic Society of North America (ISNA),
    4, 65, 98–9, 117–19, 121, 125,
    127–8, 130–1, 175
Islamic Terror, *see under* terrorism
Islamic University of Minnesota, 97
Islamist, 23, 47, 176
Islamophobia, 15, 16, 30, 119, 146,
    149–50
  see also anti-Muslim
Israel, viii, 1, 21, 22, 23, 24–5, 26, 27–9, 30,
    34, 35, 36, 37, 49, 51, 67, 77, 78, 82,
    107–13, 124, 131, 140, 141, 146–8,
    150, 152–3, 173–4, 176, 183, 193–4,
    195, 196, 198
  Ministry of Foreign Affairs, 24, 27
Israeli Defense Forces (IDF), 27, 174

Israeli-Palestinian conflict/problem, viii, 4, 29, 33–6, 45–6, 48, 51–2, 71–3, 75, 78–9, 81–2, 107, 109, 111–13, 118, 140, 174, 178
  see also two-state solution
Israeli settlement, viii, 109, 111, 112, 150
Israel National News, 29
Israel on Campus Coalition, 22
Israel-Palestine, 1, 52, 67, 149
Israel Project, 109
israiliyyat texts, 167–8, 170

Jacob, 18, 149
  see also Abraham
Jacobs, Rabbi Steve, 149
Jay Phillips Center for Interfaith Learning of St. Thomas University, 33
Jefferson, Thomas, 129
Jerusalem Connection International, 28
Jessup, Nathan, 9–10, 12, 15, 19
  see also *A Few Good Men*
Jesus, 28, 149, 154
"Jesus was a Feminist," 166
Jewish Americans, *see* American Jews
"Jewish anger," 145
Jewish community, 15, 18, 28, 30, 45, 49, 50, 51, 77–8, 79, 97, 111, 112, 118, 128, 129, 131, 139–41, 145–6, 151, 160, 161, 194–5
  American, 57, 59, 61, 65, 68, 69, 75, 77, 82, 97, 107, 111, 113
  Iranian, 134–5, 140–2
  progressive, 48
Jewish Community Centers (JCC), 65–6
Jewish Community Relations Council (JCRC), 46, 47, 50
Jewish Council on Public Affairs, 15
Jewish-Muslim dialogue, *see under* dialogue
Jewishness, 63, 136, 140, 141
"Jewish problem," 96
Jewish settlement, *see* Israeli settlement
Jewish Telegraphic Agency, 152
Jewish Terror, *see under* terrorism
Jewish Theological Seminary, 97
Jewish University Online, 24
Jewish Voice for Peace, 197
Jews for Racial and Economic Justice (JFREJ), 46, 49, 50, 51

Jews of Fear, 195–6, 197–8
  see also Jews of Love; Muslims of Fear; Muslims of Love
Jews of Love, 191, 195–8
  see also Jews of Fear; Muslims of Fear; Muslims of Love
John Allen Buggs Human Relations Award, 147
J Steet, 4, 107–13, 152, 197
Judaism, 2, 10, 17, 18, 23, 40, 58, 59, 60, 66, 122, 123, 149, 160, 161, 164, 167, 170, 184, 186, 192, 193, 194, 195
Judeo-Christian, 68, 97
justice, 13, 30, 35, 37, 46, 50, 51, 53, 68, 123, 154, 155, 168, 169
  social, 38, 50, 51, 58, 69, 108, 193, 194, 196

Kabat, Rebecca, 24
Kaplan, Bob, 47
Kelman, Ari Y., 110
khalifah, 169
Khalil Gibran International Academy (KGIA), 3, 45, 47–52
King, Martin Luther, Jr., 49
King Abdullah II, 110
Klein, Joel, 48, 49
Klein, Morton, leader Zionist Organization of America, 146
knisa, 136
Kurtzer, Ambassador Daniel, 150

learning through text study, 177–8
  see under dialogue
Left, 110–11, 193
Levine, Alan, 51
Levy, Joel, 48
Likud, 26
Lincoln, President Abraham, 122
Lippman, Rabbi Ellen, 46, 49
Los Angeles, 133–5, 139–42, 146–8, 151–2, 177–8
Los Angeles Times, 145, 149
love, 4, 17, 29–30, 58, 61, 117, 119, 122, 123, 136, 171, 188, 191–4, 198, 199

ma'ariv, 182
maghrib, 182
marginality/marginalization, 1, 4, 73, 80, 96, 128, 130, 149, 154, 160, 162, 164, 167, 169–70, 192, 197

Mary, 164, 171
Masjid An Nur, vii
Matalon, Rabbi Roly, 47, 49
Mattson, Dr. Ingrid, president Islamic
    Society of North America, 4, 99,
    118–19
McCain, Senator John, 21–2, 25
McCarthy era, 153
McClure, Jim, 22
media, 1, 10, 12, 25, 40, 48, 51, 65, 68, 72,
    73, 74, 79, 80, 121, 122, 123, 129,
    130, 146, 173, 178, 192, 193, 196,
    199
Megillat Esther, 134
melting pot, 2, 107–8, 123, 199
Meretz USA, 111
Middle East Forum, 22, 74
Middle East Media Research Institute
    (MEMRI), 27
midrash(im), 168, 171
    aggadic (narrative), 171
    halakhic (legal), 171
Mier, Peter, 26
mitzvah, 42
Mohammed Reza Shah, 133, 134, 135
Moore, Demi, see *A Few Good Men*
Moore, Judge Roy, viii
Morgenstern, Ari, 109
Morocco, *see* Arazane, Morocco
Moses, 149, 154, 171, 180, 181–2, 183
Moss, Kary, 95
Mount Sinai, 171
multiculturalism, 199
Muslim American Studies Program
    (MASP), 75
Muslim Americans, *see* American Muslims
Muslim apologetics, 166
Muslim-Christian dialogue, *see under*
    dialogue
Muslim community, 10, 13, 15, 37, 39, 62,
    64, 66, 77, 79–81, 99, 112, 127, 146,
    148–9, 152, 153, 163, 196
    American Muslim community, 11–12,
        14, 59, 64, 65, 68, 69, 73–4, 82, 99,
        127, 128, 129
    Iranian Muslim community, 134–5
Muslim Consultative Network, 50
"Muslim-Jewish Text Study Program," 4,
    177, 178
Muslim Leaders of Tomorrow (MLT), 67–8

Muslim Public Affairs Council (MPAC), 4,
    65, 112, 145, 146, 147, 152, 154
Muslims of Fear, 196, 197–8
    see also Jews of Fear; Jews of Love;
        Muslims of Love
Muslims of Love, 191, 196–8
    see also Jews of Fear; Jews of Love;
        Muslims of Fear
Muslim Student Association (MSA), 76, 78,
    94, 98
Muslim Students Union (MSU), 79, 80
Muslim Women's Legal Defense Fund for
    the Muslim Alliance of Indiana, 112
mutuality, 165, 166, 170, 201

najeeb, 137–9
narrative, 1, 9, 19, 35, 37, 39, 42, 71, 73–4,
    77, 82, 153, 166, 173, 182
    biblical, 164
    creation, 183
    dominant, 73–5, 77–8, 82
    historical, 95
    immigrant, 59
    Israeli, 37
    national, 69
    Palestinian, 37
    prophetic, 180–1
National Commission on Terrorism, 145
National Council of Churches (NCC), 117
National Public Radio (NPR), 25
neoconservative, 21, 26, 27, 47, 167
Nessah Temple, 134, 135
Netanyahu, Benjamin, Israeli Prime
    Minister, 26, 109, 110, 150
Network of Spiritual Progressives, 197, 198
Nevel, Donna, 49, 50
NewGround: A Muslim-Jewish Partnership
    for Change, 150–1, 177, 180
News & Observer, 22
New Testament, 166
New Visions for Public Schools, 47, 49
New York City, 3, 11, 24, 45, 46, 47, 48, 49,
    50, 53, 64, 118, 131
New York City Department of Education
    (DOE), 47
New Yorker, 26
New York Post, 48
New York Sun, 48
New York Times, 21, 26, 30, 47, 145–6
Nicholson, Jack, see *A Few Good Men*

Obama, President Barack, 25, 27–9, 109,
   111, 154
   Senator, 21
"Obsession: Radical Islam's War Against the
   West," 3, 21–31
occupation, Israeli, 146, 150, 152, 173, 174,
   176, 196, 197
occupied Palestinian territories, 1
Omar Ibn Al Khattab Foundation, 177
O'Reilly, Bill, 80
Oren, Ambassador Michael, 79, 110
Osama Bin Laden, ix, 29
"other"/"othering," 2, 11, 13, 30, 35, 37–8,
   40–2, 60, 83, 108, 123, 135, 160,
   162, 164, 165, 167, 180, 181, 185–6,
   188, 191–2, 194, 195, 199
"otherness," 99, 100, 102
"other side," 16, 174–6
"Our Country Deserves Better," 28

Pahlavi regime, 136–7
Palestinian Authority, 26
Palestinian Liberation Organization (PLO),
   22
Palestinians, 1–2, 15, 22, 30, 35, 37, 71–2,
   82, 109, 111–13, 124, 131, 145,
   148–51, 154, 164, 173, 174, 176,
   195–7
Paley, Rabbi Michael, 49
Passover Seder, 39
Paul, 166
peace, 3, 19, 30, 42–3, 46, 53, 68, 69, 108,
   109, 111, 112, 118, 124, 127, 151,
   153, 155, 176, 193, 194, 196, 201
peace-building, 10, 38, 176
peacemaking, 41, 145, 150–2, 154
Peoples of the Book, see *dhimmi*
Peres, President Shimon, 110
Pew Research Center, 64, 74
Pipes, Daniel, ix, 22, 27, 47, 74, 80
pluralism, 2, 31, 38, 39, 65, 66, 111, 123,
   128, 148
Prager, Dennis, viii
prayer, 76, 93, 94–5, 98, 108, 134, 172, 180,
   182, 183, 184, 201
prayer rooms, 4, 98
Prince Alwaleed Bin-Talal Center for
   Muslim-Christian Understanding,
   75
Progressive Jewish Alliance, 150

pro-Israel, 21, 22, 24, 25, 26, 27, 28, 72, 110,
   111, 145, 147, 148, 149, 150, 152,
   154
propaganda, 22, 24, 31, 130, 152
pro-Palestine, 72, 154
protectionism, 19
Purim, 134

Qawwali, 62–3
Qur'an, viii, 39, 58, 101, 102, 121, 128, 129,
   132, 148, 149, 154, 155, 165–71,
   180, 182, 183, 186, 198
Qur'anic exegesis, 167

racism/ist, 50, 51, 52, 193, 199
"radical Islam," 3, 21, 22, 23, 24, 25, 28, 29,
   30, 40
Ramadan, vii, 35, 46, 101
reconciliation, 33, 41, 43
relationship-building, 33, 35, 45, 151,
   178, 181, 182, 183, 185, 186, 187,
   199
Religions for Peace, 117
religious law, 185
Republican Jewish Coalition, 28
Republican Party, 26, 74
Robertson, Pat, 121
Rosh Hashanah, 46, 164
Ross, Gregory, spokesperson Clarion Fund,
   25

sacred texts, 38–9, 178, 180, 186
   see also under individual names
Sarah, 18, 42, 159, 163–4, 166, 172
   see also Abraham; Hagar
Sarmad, Said, 102
Sarna, Jonathan, 107
Schiff, Congressman Adam, 152
Schoenfeld, Gabriel, vii
Schultz, Congresswoman Debbie
   Wasserman, viii
Scriptures, 3, 154, 166, 172, 180
Sderot, 174, 175, 176
seam zone, *see* separation barrier
security fence, *see* separation barrier
self-determination, 167
self-hatred, 13
separation barrier, 1
separation of church and state, 4, 93, 95,
   124, 128, 129

Sephardic Jews, 61
  see also Ashkenazi Jews
September 11, see 9/11
settlement, see Israeli settlement
Shabbat, 39
Shamir, Prime Minister Yitzchak, 27
shared responsibility, see collective/shared
  responsibility
shared values, 1, 10, 67, 69
Shariah Index Project, 67
Sheinbaum, Stanley, 147
Shoebat, Walid, 22, 27, 29
Shore, Rabbi Ephraim, 25
Shore, Rabbi Raphael, 23–6, 28
Sikhs, 198, 199
Silverstein, Richard, 110
Sinai Temple, 97, 133–4, 135
Six Day War, 110
  see also Israeli-Palestinian conflict
social justice, see under justice
Sokatch, Daniel, 146–7
"Solution Rules," 175
Sontag, Susan, 174
St. Paul Interfaith Network (SPIN), 33
Standing With Israel, 28
Stand With Us, 147
status quo, 15, 148, 173–4, 175
Status Quo Rules for Middle East
  Engagement, 173–4, 176
stereotypes/stereotyping, 3, 38, 40, 48, 68,
  80, 108, 122, 145, 152, 161
  see also generalizations
Stern, Sarah, 26
Stop the Madrassa Coalition (STM), 47, 48
student groups, 71, 72, 76, 79, 81, 82, 94,
  95, 99
  see also campus activism
Student Non-Violent Coordinating
  Committee (SNCC), 196
suicide bombing, 80, 118, 121, 130, 174
Sullivan, Andrew, 15
Sultan, Wafa, 149
Swidler, Leonard, 166
Syed, Shakeel, 151

Taglit-Birthright Israel Program, 27, 111
Taliban, 170
Talmud, 180
Tanakh, see Hebrew Bible
Tancredo, Tom, 121

tawhid, 150, 168
Tchen, Tina, director of the Office of
  Public Engagement for the White
  House, 111
Tehran, Iran, 134–6, 138, 141
  see also Hamadan, Iran
Tel Aviv, 174
Temple Emanuel, 151
Temple Israel, vii
Temple Mount, 29
terrorism/terrorists, 1, 22, 25, 28–9, 37, 69,
  80, 108, 118, 121–2, 124, 125, 129,
  130, 145–6, 149, 151, 152, 153, 173
  Islamic, 17–18, 22, 25, 29
  Jewish, 18
text study, 177–85, 187–8
"Text Study Program" (TSP), 4, 177,
  178–81, 183
"Theater of the Oppressed," 186
theologies of revelation, 34, 38
"The Third Jihad," 149
tikkun, 154, 199
Tikkun, 197, 198
tokenization, 162, 170
Torah, 23, 39, 102, 148, 164, 168, 170,
  171–2, 199
two-state solution, viii, 37, 109, 112
  see also Israeli-Palestinian conflict

understanding, 9, 12, 37, 52, 101, 102, 118,
  186
  between Muslims and Jews, 4, 11, 19,
  40, 42, 51, 112, 119, 148, 154, 166,
  180–1
  mutual, 34, 40, 69, 201
Union for Reform Judaism (URJ), 4, 65,
  118–19, 121, 127, 128, 131, 173
Union of Progressive Zionists (UPZ), 111
United Federation of Teachers (UFT), 50,
  51
United States Commission on International
  Religious Freedom, 148
United States Conference of Catholic
  Bishops (USCCB), 117
Unity Program, x
University of California, Berkeley, 110
University of Michigan, Dearborn, 93–5, 99
University of San Francisco, 101
University of Southern California's Center
  for Religion and Civic Culture, 177

"U.S. Jews, Muslims must look forward, not back," 152
USA PATRIOT Act, 152

victimhood, 17, 19, 164
violence, 11, 13, 16, 36, 46, 48, 72, 73, 82, 108, 113, 131, 151, 159, 161, 173, 193, 194, 202
  domestic, 13
  in Israel–Palestine, 71, 72, 82, 140, 195, 196
  and religion, 14, 121, 123, 124, 148, 178

Wadud, Amina, 66, 168–9
Walcott, Deputy Mayor Dennis, 49
Walker, Alice, 164
War on Terror, 2
Washington Post, 27, 146
We Are All Brooklyn (WAAB), 46
Weinberg, Rabbi Noah, 23
Weingarten, Randi, 51
Wellstone, Senator Paul, 152
West Bank, viii, 26, 29, 72, 109, 146, 150, 151, 152, 174, 176, 195, 196
Western Wall, 23
Wiesenfeld, Jeffrey S., 47
Wilshire Boulevard Temple, 147
Wofsy, Ray, 50
Wolf, Dan, 147–8

Wolf, Rabbi Alfred, 147
Women and Religion Section of the American Academy of Religion (AAR), 161
Women Exploring Theology, 160
Women's Islamic Initiative in Spirituality and Equality, 67
Woolsey, R. James, 27
Wurmer, Meyrav, 27
Wyschogrod, Michael, 108

Yeshiva University, 97
Yom Kippur, vii, 46
Youth Bridge, 46

Zakaria, Rafia, 112
Zaytuna College, 97
Zimmerman, Rabbi Marcia, Temple Israel, vii
Zionism/Zionist, 11, 22, 27, 36, 37, 111, 140, 146, 152, 198
  Christian, 28, 29
  movement, 193
Zionist Organization of America (ZOA), 26, 27, 79, 146, 147
Zogby, James, president of the Arab American Institute, 111
Zubair, Aasiya, co-founder Bridges TV, 3, 11–14
  see also Bridges TV; Hassan, Mo